ALSO BY SHERWIN GLUCK

T.R.'s Summer White House, Oyster Bay

PRIVATE
GOOD
LUCK

Private Good Luck

Sherwin Gluck

Tisza Publishing

New York

PUBLISHER'S NOTE

The spelling of place names, family names, and given names varied during the years covered in this memoir. Bodrogmező, Austria-Hungary became Polyán, Czechoslovakia, and now it's Pol'any, Slovakia. Svarc in Hungarian was spelled Schvarc and Schwartz in German. Lajos in Hungarian was spelled Lajosch in German.

Gluck, Sherwin
Private Good Luck / Sherwin Gluck
p. cm.
ISBN 978-0-9672543-0-2 (Perfect Binding)
ISBN 978-0-9672543-1-9 (Hard Cover Binding)

1. Gluck, Irving, 1921-2016.
2. United States. Army. Armored Infantry Regiment, 6th.
3. United States. Army. Military Police Division, 67th.
4. World War, 1939-1945--Regimental Histories--United States.
5. World War, 1939-1945--Campaigns--North Africa.
6. World War, 1939-1945--Campaigns--Italy.
7. World War, 1939-1945--Campaigns--France
8. World War, 1939-1945--Campaigns--Germany
9. World War, 1939-1945--Personal narratives--American.
10. Soldiers--United States--Biography.
11. Jews--Czechoslovakia--History--1921-1938
12. Jews--Czechoslovakia--Personal narratives
13. Jews--Hungary--History--1938-1944
14. Holocaust, Jewish (1939-1945)--Hungary--Personal narratives
15. Jews--United States--History--1938-2016
16. Jews--Israel--History--1948-1952

Printed and bound in the United States of America
Signature Book Printing, www.sbpbooks.com

First Edition
Book Design by Sherwin Gluck

Author's Notes and Acknowledgements

"Private Good Luck" was born from childhood stories that my father told us about his life in the little village of Polyán, Czechoslovakia. Years later, I conducted an extended interview with him to learn his entire story. Its details are supported by photos, a treasured collection of nearly one thousand family letters, official documents (including rare Nazi records), as well as personal memorabilia.

Thankfully my father opened up and shared his story. Without his memories, and his foresight to save and store our family's correspondence, this book wouldn't have been possible. My Aunt Marie began organizing the correspondence into "magnetic" photo albums, giving me the impetus to undo her work, preserve them in acid free sleeves, and discover for myself a nearly forgotten world.

Written in Hungarian or newly learned English (both with a smattering of Yiddish) before, during, and after the War, they provide incredible details from both sides of the Atlantic. It includes letters that my father and his siblings had written before and after coming to America, and letters from the family and neighbors that remained in Europe. Especially poignant in the collection are letters written by little children, my first cousins, who never had a chance to grow old, and from my grandfather, who never had a chance to enjoy his golden years. The V-mail that my father sent home while overseas provided the most accurate way of knowing his whereabouts during the war.

Already in their nineties, my father and aunt together translated the bulk of the letters from Hungarian into English in their head, and then used voice recognition software to input their translations into the computer. Having left their task unfinished, Monika Markacs translated most of the letters that remained. Her herculean effort was invaluable and I gratefully thank her. László Osher also helped with some of the remaining letters as well as the passages that were difficult to make out.

With the collection organized, digitally scanned, and translated, I could recreate a world, and the people in it, 75 years after their destruction. I have tried to do so as faithfully and as accurately as possible, according to the dates, places, and times as recorded in the letters, as remembered by my father, and as confirmed by cross-referencing with the historic record. Now preserved for generations to come, this knowledge of their past will help guide their future.

I want to also thank Stephanie Russell, Peter Newman, and Gina Tong for taking the time to listen, read, edit, and advise (and to Peter for suggesting the title!)

Thanks to my children Naomi, Ayalah, Noa, and Boaz for their patience while I wrote and revised,

Finally, to my wife Hanit, my editor-in-chief. Thank you for your forbearance in reading, re-reading, commenting, correcting, editing, checking, and re-checking. I could not have done this without your help and encouragement!

For the sake of completeness, I also want to recommend the reader to the Yizkor book, "A Short Story of the Jewish Communities of Kralovsky Chlmec Kiralyhelmec and the Bodrog District" by Aaron Ehrman, printed by Friedmann Lipe, Bne-Brak, Israel, 5757-1997. It can be found online at https://www.jewishgen.org/Yizkor/Kralovsky_chlmec/Kralovsky_chlmec.html

I have always been influenced by Benjamin Franklin's advice: Do something worth writing about, or write something worth reading. My father certainly experienced something worth writing about, I hope I have written something worth reading!

To my Father

Chapter 1

די גאלדענא מעדינא

"Die Goldena Medina" - The Golden Country

THE FRANTIC KNOCKING at the door woke me. I should have gotten out of bed to see who was there, but it was warm under the goose feather quilt and the air was cold on my face. I heard the crackle of straw from the mattress across the room and I turned to see my father rising from his bed. He fumbled in the darkness to find his thick, circle-rimmed glasses, then reached for an overcoat to cover his thin frame. "Mr. Gluck, Mr. Gluck! I have a message!" shouted a voice above the howling wind. My sister Marie, who had been sleeping in the other corner of the room, turned in her bed, too. My father lit the wick of an oil lamp, lowered the glass shade into place and walked hurriedly across the cold dirt floor, our eyes following his shadow. As he opened the door, snowflakes began to blow into the room. My father ushered the man in and quickly closed the door behind him. The yellow flame from the lamp illuminated my father's graying beard, but I strained to see the stranger's face. It was no use. He was bundled up against the winter storm. He pulled off his glove, slightly unbuttoned his jacket, and took a small envelope out from an inner pocket.

"Mr. Schwartz sent me with this message," he said, handing it to my father. Putting a few coins in the man's hand my father said, "Thank you, and be careful." With a quick nod the messenger went back out into the snowy night. My father closed the door behind him. We heard a horse whinny as he rode off through the snow. My father set the lamp down onto the old wooden table and sat down.

Only then did he open the envelope. His hands trembled as he silently read the note that was inside.

"What is it, apa[1]?" I asked, now standing next to him. He showed me the message. I immediately recognized the handwriting of our uncle, Márton Schwartz, my mother's brother. "Hermine telephoned. Leave tomorrow." My heart pounded with happiness and excitement. We were leaving Europe!

Without knowing any of the details, the urgent midnight message told us that my sister Hermine had succeeded in getting the passports, visas, and steamship tickets for the four of us. Finally, after struggling for two years, overcoming one obstacle after another, my sisters Marie and Hermine, my brother Herman, and I were going to join our brother Dezső in America.

---

[1] Hungarian for 'father'

Chapter 2

"There are no goodbyes for us.
Wherever you are, you will always be in my heart." - Mahatma Gandhi

IT WAS A RACE AGAINST TIME. It was February 1940, Europe was plunging into war, and we hoped to make it in time to board a ship and escape to safety. Marie and I would travel immediately by train to Budapest to join Hermine and Herman, but we weren't sure from which port we would embark, or on which ship we would sail. We would have to wait until our rendezvous with Hermine to find out. Originally, the plan had been to sail on a Cunard[2] ship from LeHavre or Cherbourg in France, but since England declared war, Cunard was no longer taking passengers on trans-Atlantic voyages.[3] Nazi U-boats were prowling the North Atlantic and had already torpedoed a passenger liner on September 3rd.[4]

Marie and I packed as lightly as possible. Just one trunk. Inside was what few clothes we had, and some dunyha, fine breast feathers from a goose that could be used to make a quilt. To us, they were valuable. We packed nothing else.

I suppose I should have been nervous or afraid, but I wasn't. I was happy to be leaving. Even my father, who must have been heartbroken because five of his six children would be in America, was happy, too. He was worried though. As we packed, he repeatedly warned us: "Do nothing that will arouse

---

[2] Cunard-White Star Limited was a British steamship company that provided trans-Atlantic voyages.

[3] On August 30, Cunard's "Queen Mary" commenced her final commercial voyage from Southampton. Cunard's "Queen Elizabeth" arrived in New York on March 5th, after secretly crossing the Atlantic, for safety away from England.

[4] German submarine U-30 torpedoed and sank the passenger liner "Athenia" 250 miles north of the west coast of Ireland.

suspicion. Behave as you usually do. If a neighbor asks, tell them you're just going to Helmec." Helmec was a city to our south where Uncle Márton lived.

We didn't sleep. Before sunrise we dressed in our regular clothing and my father and I hurriedly said our morning prayers. Marie busied herself by tidying up: the beds needed to be made, the floor swept, the dishes organized. That was Marie. Everything needed to be in its place, and spotless, too! Already 23, she was tall, with warm brown eyes and brown hair. Although thin and pretty, her self confidence suffered because she had poor vision. To compensate, she developed an extraordinary memory and was able to hide the fact that she needed glasses by memorizing her lessons and pretending to be able to see the board in school. As a result, she was shy, quiet, and reserved. She loved to read, especially on Shabbos[5], when there was less housework to do and many of her other activities, like sewing, dressmaking, or crocheting, were forbidden. She was very inquisitive and tried to teach herself everything. When the weather was warm, she would read outside lying on the grass. On cold winter days like this one, she would often read while sitting next to an oil lamp. While my father and I were praying, and after she boiled eggs for our breakfast, Marie put on her winter jacket, and went outside. She trudged through the high drifts of snow that had formed

---

[5] Shabbos (Shabbat, or the Sabbath) is Judaism's day of rest and the seventh day of the week, on which Jews remember that G-d ceased creating the universe after six days and the Exodus of their ancestors from Egyptian slavery. They also look forward to a future time of absolute peace in the world. Jews observe Shabbat by refraining from specific activities considered work and engaging in restful activities to honor the day. Shabbat is observed from eighteen minutes before sunset on Friday evening until the appearance of three stars in the sky on Saturday night. Shabbat is a festive day when Jews exercise their freedom from the regular labors of everyday life. It offers an opportunity to contemplate the spiritual aspects of life and to spend time with family.

during the storm to tell our oldest brother Lajos the news. He lived next to us.

A strong man in the prime of his life, Lajos was 33 and married with four young children. His wife Etelka, née Klein, was pregnant with their fifth. Etelka was especially close to my sisters because she was the only other Jewish woman close to their age in our village, Polyán. Lajos was a farmer through and through. He planted, plowed, and harvested. He raised our animals from birth and trained our horses. He was the family fisherman, too, catching fish each week for the sabbath from the Latorica river that flowed behind our house. As the oldest sibling, he felt responsible for us all. I could only wonder how he felt staying behind. Was he envious? Sad? Happy? He was so busy with his many responsibilities, and exhausted from them, that he rarely shared his thoughts. Marie found Lajos in the barn, pitchfork in hand, spreading clean straw in the horse's stall. The wheel barrow was already full of steaming manure waiting to be taken outside. "Lajos bácsi![6] Hermine telegraphed. Everything is ready. We're leaving right away!" Marie said excitedly. Lajos stopped what he was doing and immediately began to put the harness on the horse.

Traveling after the snow storm would be difficult, and even now there were still flurries, but we had no choice. When Lajos had finished hitching the horse to the wooden sleigh and everything was ready, we hugged Etelka and said our goodbyes. She had woken our nephews and nieces, so that they too could give us one final hug before we left. Bleary eyed, they squeezed us tightly and we gave them each many kisses. The younger children had been told that we were only going to the city. We wanted to spare them a painful, traumatic goodbye.

---

[6] 'Bácsi', literally ' uncle', is a polite form of address in Hungarian for an older man, especially used by children or in case of great age difference, that is meant to show respect or closeness.

My brother Lajos' children.
From Left to Right: Emil (8), Gyula (2), Lenke (6), and Miklós (4).
Polyán, Czechoslovakia, ca.1939

Lajos helped our father climb into the sleigh, with Marie and me following after. We covered ourselves with heavy blankets to keep warm. Lajos took the reins and clucked to signal to the horse to start. We were leaving. After so many setbacks, it was finally happening. I looked back at the house. Etelka and the older children were watching from the window. There was the chicken coop and the barn. I thought of my mother. It had been seven years since her funeral procession had wound through our small town. The sleigh turned onto the snow covered street. My back was turned away from our house and away from the small Jewish cemetery where we buried her. The horse strained to pull us through the snow towards a new life. I refused to allow sadness to temper the joy and excitement that I felt at that moment.

Lajos drove the sleigh a few hundred yards to the house of my Uncle Lázár, our father's oldest brother. He knew we were waiting to hear from Hermine and that we might be leaving at any moment. Our plan was to meet his daughter Bertha at the pier in New York. We stopped, spoke briefly with him, said our goodbyes, and then continued eastward out of Polyán towards the next village, Lelesz, where our maternal grandparents, Samuel and Chaya Schwartz, lived. As the sleigh approached the intersection, we could have continued straight to enter their village to bid them farewell, but we were afraid that someone might see us or question us.

Instead, Lajos steered the sleigh in a wide right-hand turn through the mountainous drifts of snow, heading south for about 10 kilometers. The snow, the wind, and the bitter cold slowed us down. A trip that would have taken less than one hour in good weather had already taken more than two. As we travelled, we broke off pieces of bread from a loaf that Marie had baked the day before.

Finally, we made it to Helmec. Compared to Polyán, our little farming village with just one single street, this was a city!

Its many crisscrossed streets were lined on both sides with stores and multi-storied buildings. Yet, under the white blanket of freshly fallen snow, both streets and stores were empty and still. We made our way to Uncle Márton's house, my mother's youngest brother. He was the one who had sent the message and we knew that he would be expecting us.

Uncle Márton owned a small shoe store in Helmec, but he wasn't just a businessman. He was also a very learned, and pious man; a respected Talmudic scholar in the district. He was dressed smartly as usual, wearing a dark suit with a broad rimmed hat. His beard was much darker than my father's. After all, at 45 he was 20 years younger. "Thank goodness that you received my message!" he said as he ushered us in from the cold. "Hermine telephoned last night. Somehow she did it! Everything is ready."

Uncle Márton turned, faced me, and continued. "The Hungarians issued the passports for the two of you, and on Friday Hermine went to the American embassy and they've issued the visas. On Shabbos she went to the shipping company. Can you believe it? On Shabbos! Never mind that. At first, there was no record of the payment having been made in dollars and, out of exhaustion and despair Hermine said that she started to cry. One of the clerks took notice of her and intervened, 'Oh, no, the money already came through!' Finally, Hermine has all four tickets! We'll need to hurry if you're going to make today's train to Budapest. When you arrive, she'll give you your passports. G-d willing, we'll also secure a sponsor and join you in America soon!" While he was speaking, Uncle Márton telephoned for a special taxi to bring us to the train station in Perbenik. It arrived sooner than we expected, startling us with its horn. Marie and I began hugging and kissing everyone: our Aunt Etelka, Uncle Márton's wife, and those of our younger cousins who were awake: Emil and Magda. We were rushing, but Magda, who had had polio and wore a brace on her right leg, walked gingerly to kiss each of us. She wished us luck with our long trip and we wished her well with the surgery she soon expected to have on her leg. She was so full of hope for our journey, and for hers!

The taxi honked again impatiently. We hugged our brother Lajos. My father hugged us both and kissed us. "Be alert. Whatever happens, remember that you're a family, brothers and sisters. Stay together, look out for one another, and take care of each other...you must promise me that you'll always help one another!" He held us by the arms as we walked outside to the sidewalk. We hugged and kissed him again for the last time. Lajos called out "Work hard and take care of yourselves!" Uncle Márton hurried to the taxi and opened the door for Marie to climb in. My father cried out, "My dearest children, I love you and will never forget you!" Uncle Márton took the seat in the front and I got in the back, next to Marie. The taxi pulled away from the curb, slowly so the wheels wouldn't slip, crunching the snow beneath its tires. In the rearview mirror I could see my father standing next to Lajos. His small figure becoming ever smaller in the distance. I looked back until they disappeared.

The driver struggled to maneuver the taxi through the snow as he drove us the four and a half kilometers to the train station at Perbenik. The ten-minute trip took more than half an hour. Hurriedly, we bought two tickets for the next train to Budapest. As soon as we had paid for them, the old steam locomotive puffed into the station. How could we thank Uncle Márton enough for all his help? There was no time. We hugged him quickly and then Marie climbed the narrow steps of the dilapidated pullman. I followed close behind. Uncle Márton stood alone on the platform like a living statue, tears streaming down his cheeks. He understood that we would never see each other again. It was February 6, 1940.

At the unveiling of my mother's gravestone (Leba bat Yosef Shemaya Ha-Levi.)
Polyán, Czechoslovakia, 1933

From Left to Right: Me, Marie, my father, unknown, and Hermine.
Polyán, Czechoslovakia, 1933

My Uncle Lázár Gluck, in front of his house.
Polyán, Czechoslovakia

My maternal grandmother, Chaya Moskovitz Schwartz
Lelesz, Czechoslovakia

The village of Poľany, Slovakia (Polyán, or Bodrogmező in Hungarian.)
The old, curving path of the Latorica River appears in the bottom of the
photo filled in with land. The river's flow has been redirected. It still joins
with the Ondava River, in Zemplín, gives rise to the Bodrog River, which is
itself a tributary of the Tisza River.

Chapter 3

"All journeys have secret destinations of which the traveller is unaware."
Martin Buber

IT WASN'T OUR FIRST TIME TRAVELING BY TRAIN. We had been to the American consulate in Budapest eight months earlier, to sign and submit documents and to be interviewed for the visa. However, then we traveled with our father, and we were all five of us together. Now, Marie and I were making the long trip alone. I dragged the trunk through the narrow walkway between the worn cloth seats. The tickets allowed us to sit where we chose, and we tried to find a window that was clean enough to see through. There wasn't one. We had to settle for an icy, soot covered window that, as the sun shone on it, had been cleaned by streaks of water from melting snow. I had expected to hear the clickety-clack of the wheels along the track but because of the snow, the train moved silently as it pulled away from the station. "Tickets, all tickets please!" called the conductor. We handed him our tickets. He punched holes in them, gave them back to us, and told us to stay on until Budapest. It was nearly 300 km from Perbenik to Budapest, a journey of several hours.

"Where are you from?" asked a woman sitting across the aisle from Marie. She wasn't surprised when Marie told her our small village's name. Our clothing had already indicated that we were just country farmers. The conversation didn't last long.

Despite being tired, we were excited to be on our way at last and hardly slept as the train traveled steadily westward. We weren't afraid to leave. On the contrary, we were afraid to stay! War had broken out again when Germany invaded Poland on the first day of September, 1939. The Europe we knew was collapsing. Nonetheless, I felt miserable as we left the rest of our family to their uncertain fate. I reflected on the last two years and how much effort it had taken to get to this point. We should have all gone to America with our brother Dezső when he left home in 1938 while Czechoslovakia still existed.

As Nazi Germany grew more powerful, the Czechoslovakian army began drafting young men in preparation for war. Dezső was one of them. He was soon released though, because he suddenly became sick and was unable to move his fingers. Perhaps it was from exposure to the cold or an infection, or both. After he returned home, one of our neighbors, an old woman who knew many natural remedies, went down to the Latorica River, gathered some plants and gave him a home-made ointment. Miraculously, his fingers healed.

At that point, my father decided Dezső should go to America. First and foremost, he wanted to avoid having Dezső drafted again. Secondly, it's what Dezső wanted. He didn't fit in. He didn't want to be a farmer at all. He wanted to run his own business, make his own money, and he wanted to travel, especially to America, even though my father thought that America was for apostates. Dezső had friends who were Zionists[7], and they were trying to convince him to go with them to Palestine.[8] Many young people were making their way there

---

[7] Zionism is the national movement of the Jewish people that supports the re-establishment of a Jewish homeland in the territory defined as the historic Land of Israel (roughly corresponding to Canaan, the Holy Land, or the region called Palestine by the Romans).

[8] With the Balfour Declaration of 1917, Britain expressed support for Zionism and promised to create a Jewish national home in Palestine (what is today both Israel and Jordan) as part of the partition of the Ottoman Empire. The League of Nations approved the British Mandate for Palestine and it covered two administrative areas: The land west of the Jordan River continued to be called Palestine and was intended for the Palestinian Jews and Arabs; and the land east of the Jordan, which from 1922 was a semi-autonomous region under the rule of the Hashemite family from western Saudi Arabia, was called Transjordan,and was intended for the Palestinian Arabs only.

and establishing kibbutzim and moshavim.[9] One of them, 'Kfar Masaryk' established in 1932, was named in honor of the founding father of Czechoslovakia. Although as religious Jews we prayed "Next year in Jerusalem!" life in Palestine would be very difficult, and not at all what Dezső had in mind. Dezső rebelled against our strict religious lifestyle. He wanted to be a modern man. He had driven cars and liked to take pictures, especially of us (despite the religious ban on images!). Our village, even our district, was too small for his personality. Besides, three of my father's brothers had left to live in America, and Dezső wanted to do the same.

Dezső, in a borrowed car, parked in front of our house in Polány, Czechoslovakia

The American quota system limited the number of immigrants from each European country, but the Czechoslovakian quota wasn't close to being full. Our Uncle Jónás, who lived in Columbus, Ohio, and owned real estate, agreed to submit an affidavit of support and Dezső applied for a visa. Ever resourceful, he borrowed money from a non-Jewish lady friend of his, Jana Fabionova, who also happened to be the postmaster in Lelesz. She was a beautiful, young woman about his age, with blonde hair, blue eyes, and long dark eyelashes. She was kind and gentle, and always spoke to

---

[9] A kibbutz is a collective community in Israel that was traditionally based on agriculture. A Moshav is a type of Israeli town or settlement, in particular a type of cooperative agricultural community of individual farms.

us. Even our father spoke openly to her, as though she were his own child. She didn't have a boyfriend even though she knew many people, and joked that she would end up an old maid. Jana was a small town girl who, even if she was aware of her beauty, was a modest, quiet, and very private young woman. Nonetheless, she and Dezső were close friends. She encouraged him to leave the provincial life and go to America to pursue his dreams. Moreover, she reassured him, that despite any difficulties he might face in America, he would overcome them. It would be hard at first to learn English and to find a job, but it would happen. Jana was so confident in Dezső, and perhaps smitten by his charm, that she agreed to loan him money for the trip and he agreed to send her $20 a month to repay the loan once he got settled.

Jana Fabianova, Postmaster
Lelesz, Czechoslovakia

When Germany annexed Austria in March 1938 in what was called the "Anschluss," we were afraid that Dezső's plans would have to be changed. Thankfully, that wasn't necessary and he left for America in April. The whole process to leave Europe took him less than three months.

Dezső, in Király Helmec, Czechoslovakia

My brother Dezső took this picture the day he left for America.
From Left to Right: Me, my cousin Shmuel, and his father, my Uncle Márton Schwartz
Király Helmec, Czechoslovakia, 1938

From Left to Right: Emil's sister Magda, my father, and my brother Herman.
Notice the brace on Magda's right leg.

The international response to the "Anschluss" was so muted that Germany concluded it could act as protector of the ethnic Germans in the Sudetenland of western Czechoslovakia. This was the start of the "Sudeten Crisis."

At first, despite the political situation around us, my father never even considered leaving Europe when Dezső left. We owned land, had a small business, raised animals and grew tobacco. We had grandparents, nephews, nieces, and cousins. Furthermore, and most importantly, we were religious Jews, and my father thought that in America Jews assimilated and lived like the goyim (gentiles). It didn't help that once Dezső left, I began to pester my father to allow me to cut my payois,[10] after all in America, at least how I imagined it to be, young men didn't wear their hair that way. Mine were actually quite short, and usually tucked behind my ears, so my father relented and gave me permission to cut them off entirely. However, he made me promise that I would never forget that I was a Jew.

With each passing day, the news became worse, and my father, despite his earlier misgivings, decided that we should all leave for America. So, as soon as Dezső arrived safely, we began submitting paperwork to get passports from the Czechoslovakian government in Prague. Money for the tickets was still an issue, but at last, my father decided that he would sell some of our farmland to finance them. We also needed Uncle Jónás to sign affidavits of support. My father wrote to him to file the paperwork, but now our uncle was reluctant. The change in attitude was partly because our uncle, having lived in America most of his life, emphasized finances over family. Even though he owned many rental properties, he was worried that our big family would become a financial burden. Dezső pleaded with him to help us, but Dezső himself had

---

[10] Payois, also pronounced pe'ot, peyot, is the Hebrew word for sidelocks or sideburns. They are worn by some men and boys in the Orthodox Jewish community based on an interpretation of the Biblical injunction against shaving the "corners" of one's head. Literally, pe'ah means "corner, side, edge".

become the main reason for our uncle's reluctance. The fact was, our brother hadn't made such a good first impression and Uncle Jónás was old, sickly, and impatient with anyone not willing to do as he was told.

Dezső's first job was working for our cousin Arthur, Uncle Jónás' son. Arthur owned a manufacturing plant that made conveyor belts and stone crushing machines used in coal mines. Dezső worked in the factory as the night watchman. The factory was desolate and isolated, and all he had to defend himself, and to ward off thieves, was a billy club. Moreover, by the time he could get to the phone to call the police, the thieves would be gone. After one incident too many, Dezső felt that without a gun, he couldn't do his job. Since he wasn't a citizen, he couldn't get a gun, and even if he could have, Dezső didn't like the job, or the boss, and he eventually quit. Even though Dezső soon found work in a dog kennel, and sent most of his wages back home to us, he never told Uncle Jónás what he was doing with the money, because he felt it was none of our uncle's business. But this made it appear to our uncle that Dezső wasn't able to save his earnings. Our uncle assumed the worst: that Dezső was mishandling it by womanizing, drinking, or gambling. While it was true that Dezső refused to sit inside studying on his days off, he wasn't misbehaving. He made friends easily, tried to learn English by speaking with them, and like any 28 year old, wanted to spend his weekends with them. After all, he wasn't a hermit.

In addition to our uncle's misconceptions about Dezső's behavior, there were Dezső's actions themselves that only increased our uncle's consternation. Since they had already had their share of disagreements, Dezső decided that if he went to synagogue, he would go to the Russian synagogue instead of the Hungarian one that our uncle attended. Moreover, it didn't help that Dezső made no secret of taking the trolley to get there, even on shabbat. And when he didn't go to synagogue, which was more often than not, Dezső didn't hesitate to take the trolley to the city center three miles away, also on shabbat. Even our grandfather, Joseph Shemaya

Schwartz ha Levi, my mother's father and the respected Hazzan[11] in our synagogue, wrote to Dezső to reprimand him for violating the sabbath and to encourage him to go to synagogue. "There you will learn and achieve better things for yourself and the good G-d will help you in all that you do!" But the plea fell on deaf ears. Dezső also stopped keeping kosher. Although he tried to buy prepared kosher food, he complained that the canned food was tasteless, having been made with coconut milk so that it would be parve (neither meat nor dairy). Besides, it was much more expensive than non-kosher food, and Dezső didn't have money to spare. Uncle Jónás didn't want more family to come if they were going to behave like Dezső. Besides, he also had his wife's family to consider since they wanted to get out of Europe, too.

Uncle Jónás wrote to us saying that he would no longer agree to sponsor anyone. We were shocked! Here he knew us! He had visited us and had stayed with us. My sisters had cooked for him and had fed him! My father spoke to his brother Lázár, and convinced him to write to his daughter Bertha in America to intervene. She pleaded with Dezső to do whatever our Uncle requested and she wrote to our Uncle Jónás to reconsider. Eventually, he did. Even though my father and Uncle Jónás had always been close, he agreed to sponsor only four people from his side of the family.

Unfortunately, Uncle Jónás' heart disease progressed and he grew weaker. His son Arthur, who was also independently wealthy, agreed to sign the affidavits of support in his place. Everyone's fate was weighed. My grandparents were too old to make such a treacherous journey. My father wouldn't leave if he had to leave someone behind. My brother Lajos had young children and wouldn't separate his family. Finally, it was agreed my sisters Hermine and Maria, my brother Herman, and I would emigrate. But it took fifty days or more from the

---

[11] The person chosen to lead the congregation in songful prayer. Those with the best voice and the most knowledge of the prayers serve most often.

time we mailed a letter until we received an answer from America, and all of the back and forth correspondence with Uncle Jónás wasted so much time. However, once the decision was made, our cousin Arthur submitted the affidavit of support, Czechoslovakia issued our passports, and we received our quota number from the American Consul in Prague for a visa. My father hurriedly sold some land so that we would have enough money to purchase four tickets and we started making arrangements with the Cunard Line for passage. Everything was settled. Or so we thought.

On September 30, 1938 Great Britain, unwilling to declare war, agreed that Nazi Germany could annex the Sudetenland. This "Munich Agreement" may have ended the "Sudeten Crisis," but it also unraveled our plans to leave Europe. The agreement included a clause giving Czechoslovakia and Hungary three months to negotiate new borders so that regions of Czechoslovakia where ethnic Hungarians were the majority would be returned to Hungary. Our village, called Polyán in Slovak, but Bodrogmező in Hungarian, had been part of Hungary before World War I. Of its 500 residents, there were only four Jewish families and a few Gypsies that wandered in and out; the rest were ethnic Hungarians.

Gypsy musicians performing, pre-1938

The negotiations were deadlocked, and during these three months, Czechoslovakia, a democratic republic since 1918, crumbled. The Prime Minister of Czechoslovakia resigned, a new government was formed granting significant autonomy to the pro-Nazi government in Slovakia, the region where we lived, and the country was renamed Czecho-Slovakia. We couldn't travel anywhere with our passports since they weren't valid; Czechoslovakia no longer existed. We were in limbo since we didn't know which government would issue passports: the new Czecho-Slovakia or Hungary.

A map of the new Czecho-Slovakia, 1938.
The shaded areas indicate the Sudetenland and the Felvidék territories.
Polyán is located in the southeastern corner, to the south of Uzhorod
https://commons.wikimedia.org/wiki/File:Druhá_Československá_republika_1938.png

Our statelessness didn't last long. On November 2, under the First Vienna Award, Czecho-Slovakia returned the "Felvidék" territories to Hungary. This included our village of Polyán. When Hungarian soldiers marched through it to secure the newly returned territory, our neighbors hung Hungarian flags from their houses to honor the Hungarian soldiers. We hoped that the Hungarians would be less anti-Semitic than the Slovaks, so we put out the Hungarian flag, too. Young rabble-rousers, many of them the children of our neighbors, followed the soldiers and shouted out to us, "Put down that flag, you

Jews! You're not Hungarians!" So much for being less anti-Semitic! With people in the world like this, how could I ever break my promise to my father to remember that I was a Jew?!

With only a few dried, brown leaves remaining on the trees, I was sitting on the branches of an old tree, eating an apple and a loaf of bread for lunch. Suddenly, in the distance, I heard the drumbeat of the town crier, Smoyak Jancsi. He had lost one arm serving in the first World War. Every day he would march through the village banging his drum to announce any news, urgent or otherwise, and to deliver the mail. Ta-ta-dam. Ta-ta-dam. Ta-ta-dam-dam-dam. The drum roll grew louder as he walked closer but his voice was still too faint for me to make out the news. I waited in the tree for him to approach, hoping that I would hear it sooner since I was high above the ground. His message grew louder and louder as he walked closer, and finally I was able to make out the words.

"Hear ye! Hear ye! This message is for everyone! The Hungarian government orders you to immediately bring one horse and one carriage for the army!" Unfortunately for us, along with cows, chickens, ducks, geese, and goats, our family raised horses. My oldest brother Lajos trained them and had, in years past, even sold some to the Czechoslovakian Army.

I jumped down from my perch and ran to find my father. He was already in the barn readying one of our two horses to be hitched to the wagon. "Why, apa? Why are they taking everyone's horses? Can they just make an order like that?"

My father answered, "The day the Hungarians took over was the death of the great democracy that our beloved President Masaryk, of blessed memory, helped to create. The freedom we have enjoyed is no more. We are under martial law now, and the Hungarian government can do whatever it wants. The army is mobilizing and we have no choice but to comply." He continued his work, then turned and led the horse and carriage down the lane and into the main street. I followed him, barely able to contain my anger. Here we were giving our horse, one we had raised since it was born, to help protect the very people who days earlier, had screamed at us to take down our Hungarian flag. We walked together to Uncle Lázár's house. He was my father's oldest brother; my father was the youngest, just like me. Uncle Lázár and many of our neighbors gathered on the street, with their horses and carriages as well. "Don't forget a can for the water!" called out my uncle. My father turned to me, "Ignac, go back to the barn. There is an extra watering can up above in the loft, where we store the Passover dishes. Go quickly!" I hesitated. Then I refused.

"No, apa, I don't want to do it. Let the horse die. The Hungarians don't deserve our animals the way that they treat us!"

My father ignored my insolence and went to the barn himself. I sullenly followed him from a distance, then watched as he climbed the ladder and disappeared into the darkness above. I should never have disobeyed. I watched guiltily as he started to climb down the ladder with the pail in his hand, then to my horror, he lost his footing and slipped down the ladder and landed into the hay below. He walked out of the barn slowly, and without saying a word to me, brought the pail to the carriage and placed it inside. My brother Lajos climbed onto the carriage. He and our other neighbors drove the horses to a central meeting place to register both horse and carriage with the Hungarian army. My father and I walked back to the house. I felt miserably, but didn't apologize.

On November 12, by an act of the Hungarian Parliament, we were officially under the rule of the Hungarian dictator Miklós Horthy. The economy collapsed. At first we had hoped to use our Czechoslovakian passports to travel, but we quickly learned that we had to apply for new ones from Hungary. Despite this, the Americans allowed us to maintain the Czechoslovakian quota number that had already been issued to us. This was our "place in line" to come to America. Had we needed to get a new quota number as Hungarians, we would have been last on line, and there were now thousands of people in that position. For us, it would take time, but we just needed to transfer the paperwork from the American Consul in Prague to the American Consul in Budapest, including the affidavit of support from our cousin Arthur. The six months spent on the emigration process wasn't entirely wasted because we had the Czech quota number, but it felt like we were starting all over again. However, it could have been worse. The Jews that remained under Slovak control began to suffer under the new regime as it passed laws suspending Jewish teachers and confiscating Jewish companies. Those who were poor or foreign-born that lived on the Slovakian side of the new border were ordered to leave their homes and were forced to live in camps on the border. We were lucky for the time being.

Not only did our travel plans with the British shipping company, Cunard, have to be rescheduled, but the chaos also meant that our money, all in Czechoslovakian korona, was now worthless. My father had to find a way to get Hungarian pengos. "Apa, are you certain that Uncle Jónás will refuse to pay for the tickets, too?" I asked.

"You know the story," he told me with a sigh. "After your grandfather Emmanuel died in 1916, my brothers and I inherited his property. Despite their good fortune, my brother Márton's sons, Fred and Samuel of Pennsylvania, and Uncle Henry in New York, forced us to sell the forests and land to pay them their rightful inheritance. By 1931, both Uncle Márton and Uncle Henry were dead, leaving only Uncle Jónás, and it wasn't easy to convince him even to sponsor the four of you, especially after the way he thinks Dezső has been behaving. Look, Uncle Jónás has been in America since 1885. I was only 10 when he left, and even though he's been back to visit us, what the eye doesn't see, the heart forgets. According to Dezső, if we ask Uncle Jónás for money, he won't sign the affidavit because that would prove that we would be a financial burden. Besides, I don't want to ask him if I don't have to. I honestly don't know how he would react. I have heard nothing positive from my brother Henry's wife, may he rest in peace. She simply doesn't have the money. And your Uncle Márton's sons, Fred and Samuel...oye! They are like strangers since your grandfather's estate settlement and never write us. The only

news we hear about them is from Uncle Jónás. Anyway Ignac, it is more important for you to study, especially since your classes have been canceled, and let me worry about getting you to America."

I had no choice but to trust my father. After all, he was a successful farmer and businessman, and in a small town like Polyán, there wasn't a person he didn't know. For years he owned a general store just down the road from our house. In 1928, after it was robbed, he decided to build a new house, and in it a new store, on our property. It was the largest and newest building in the village.

One day, the mayor of our village, Mr. Andras Simon came into the store and my father implemented an idea that he had long considered.

"Mayor Simon, how are you in these changing times?" Despite knowing Mr. Simon for many years, my father was careful to address him properly. Culturally, a person's honorific was paramount. Using the wrong title, or neglecting to use it entirely, would have been taken as an insult.

"Changing indeed! No matter who the government is, the troubles of the mayor remain the same."

"Yes, your honor, I suppose they do." My father refilled his shot glass with Slivovitz, a plum brandy, and continued. "Does your honor still think it's a good idea to have a town hall? Perhaps there, outside of your own home, you will be better able to solve your troubles?"

"No, no, what is the point? The town doesn't have the resources to build a new building and now that the new government is mobilizing, there won't be men available to build one."

"Well, perhaps, your honor, there might be a solution, if you are willing to help an old friend..." My father hesitated, waiting to see the expression on the mayor's face, before continuing. "If you find it acceptable, this house would, in my opinion, make a most inviting town hall." The mayor looked quickly about the store and the rooms behind. "Well," he said,

"it is not my decision alone--the others would have to agree as well."

"Yes, but they will listen to you, and follow your advice."

"It's not entirely up to me, you know..."

"Please, whatever you can do..." My father said.

Over the course of the next week, my father spoke with other influential villagers, and eventually it was agreed that the village would buy our house. Number 35 Polyán would be the new village hall and we would have almost enough money, in Hungarian pengos that could be converted to dollars, to buy four tickets to America. If we could have sold other property for a fair price, we would have. However, we still didn't have enough money for the trip.

The new house, #35, in Polyán, Czechoslovakia.
I am the small boy wearing a hat sitting at the center.

In order to pay the remainder, both Herman and I had to declare our independence from our father. Doing so would release money held in our name. After our grandfather died, money was put in our names and in the names of Lajos' eldest children. Our brother Dezső was appointed guardian for them and my father was still guardian for Herman and me. Since

Dezső was in America, the money held for Lajos' children couldn't be used until they became old enough to declare themselves emancipated. Herman, on the other hand, was already old enough to do so, and in November, I would be too. In July, 1939, with my father's help, Herman was declared a full-fledged adult, with the privilege to lead his affairs and to manage his property independently. We hoped that the monies that were held in his name would be released quickly, and we would just have enough to travel, but they didn't give us a timeline. We simply had to be patient and wait to be notified that it had been released.

At the same time, since Herman was so close to turning twenty-one, we were advised to hire a lawyer to help resolve his Levente[12] Home Guard obligation. Of course, we needed to give him all of Herman's documents. In order for boys older than twelve to emigrate, Herman was twenty and I was seventeen, signed affidavits from the Levente were required giving us permission to leave. As chance would have it, soon after we gave Herman's documents to the lawyer, we were notified by the American Consul that we were to go to the consulate in Budapest at the end of the month for our visa hearing. We had no choice but to appear at the consulate without our passports, and before the lawyer could submit anything on Herman's behalf. With our father, the four of us left our district and travelled by train for the first time. From our correspondence with the consulate, we knew that we could appear at the visa hearing without the passports, but we were

---

[12] **Levente Associations** (Hungarian: *Leventeszervezetek*) were paramilitary youth organizations in Hungary established in 1921 with the declared purpose of physical and health training. In the mid-1930s they became a de facto attempt to circumvent the ban for conscription imposed by the Treaty of Trianon. It eventually became a pre-military organization under the leadership of veterans. By the Act of Defense of 1939, all boys ages 12–21 were required to participate. The *levente* was neither openly fascist nor particularly politicized, although it was not isolated from the political influences of the time. (Wikipedia)

taking a big chance bringing Herman with us. We hoped to resolve everything at once. We were naive.

When we arrived to the consulate, we were told that we couldn't appear without the passports, but eventually after a lengthy explanation, we were brought in to a small room. The consulate personnel interviewed us about everything: our birthplace, our occupation, and our health. We gave them our pictures and each of us signed statements under oath. When it was done, the consulate official approved all of our visas. After such a tortuous process, we were so relieved that Herman, with no documents at all, not even the doctor's certificate, got the visa too. We were advised that when we get home to Polyán, we just had to mail the missing documents to the consulate. All that remained was to get our Hungarian passports, bring them back to the American consulate, have the visas affixed to them, and submit a small fee in US dollars. The catch was that we could get dollars only from America.

Confident, hopeful, and undeterred, we went to the Hungarian Office of Consular Services. Our passports were ready, but like the Americans, the consular officer couldn't release them to us. Since I had already turned seventeen my application needed to be sent to the Defense Ministry for approval, and for Herman we needed to file a formal request that he be released from his military obligation.

The staff at the Hungarian office recommended a local emigration lawyer who might be able to help arrange everything and we went to him hoping for some advice. Without charging us, he told us that we didn't need a lawyer! His advice was to go to the Defense Ministry and simply ask for the status of our case. After looking up our case number, we were told that neither of our passports had arrived to the Defense Ministry yet. However, the officials promised us that as soon as they did, they would arrange everything immediately. They also assured us that Herman and I would be considered as emigrants and we would almost certainly be dismissed from the Home Guard.

We left Budapest without the visas, or the passports, or the military releases, but we did have assurances and we felt accomplished, especially since we had achieved so much without the lawyer. We thought we had settled everything and hoped we would travel in September or October, since that is what they told us at the consulate. Yet we also suspected that some other obstacle would come up again later. Of course, something did, and it wasn't just Germany's invasion of Poland on September 1st!

As soon as we returned home from Budapest, we wrote to our Uncle Jónás that we would need him to send money in dollars to the consulate in order for the visas to be released. We assured him that we had no intention of asking for any more money from him, and promised to pay him back the small amount. No sooner had we sent the letter to Uncle Jónás, we received notification from the consulate that he would have to submit additional paperwork. Since he had also sponsored many people from his wife's family, the American consulate wanted to know exactly who else he had sponsored in the last two years, what countries they were from, and whether or not he really had the resources to care for us all if the need arose. Furthermore, the affidavits he had submitted for us listed Herman twice, and not Hermine. It was a simple typo, Herman vs. Herm-ine, but until he submitted the documents they requested, with the necessary corrections, our visas were suspended.

To our surprise and relief, Uncle Jónás wrote to us in the most loving way, that he would do anything to help, as though we were his own children, all we needed to do was to ask. However, because of our own pride, stubbornness, and independence, we didn't want to ask him for any money unless it was absolutely necessary.

Despite knowing that Uncle Jónás would be there if we really needed him, we were disappointed again because we were notified that the money Herman had hoped to receive by declaring himself emancipated, would not be released until I submitted my request to be emancipated, too. That meant, without asking Uncle Jónás for help, we couldn't even think of leaving until after my birthday in November. We were trapped.

Sure enough, it wasn't until after my birthday that the money was released and we could continue making our plans to emigrate. In December, the American Consulate notified us that our visas had been approved but

"We wish to advise you that the following documents have expired: moral character, current home addresses, doctor's reports. Please mail the new documents so that the visas can be issued."

Even a delay of one day could have derailed everything. Hermine hurried to collect and complete all the paperwork that they requested and she quickly mailed everything back to Budapest. By January 8th the Hungarians issued passports for Herman and me, and the American Consul wrote back to her:

"The money for the visas for you, your sister, and brothers that we requested has been paid to the Cunard organization. Consequently, the chief consul has permitted the visa numbers to be issued. You can obtain the visas after the 25th. In the meantime, we have attached the new affidavits to the existing documents. It was approved after Mr. Arthur Gluck sent the documents."

We thought everything was ready, but we were wrong. We received another letter from Cunard dated January 25th regarding the military certificates for Herman and me. Again, there was a problem:

"We are aware that the American Consul General of Budapest has written to you today regarding the military certificates of Mr's Herman and Ignac Gluck...Please mail to us the certificate of moral character and district certificate for Mr. Ignac Gluck. These documents must be authentic. The moral and district certificates were returned by the American consulate and we need duplicate copies of the certificates mailed directly to us instead. Also we are returning Mr.

Herman Gluck's official moral character certificate and district certificate and are requesting you to obtain duplicate copies and return them to us. We call to your attention that the birthdate for Mr. Herman Gluck is different on the moral character certificate and the district certificate. We are returning Mr. Herman Gluck's birth certificate and we are asking for duplicate copies of the district certificate and the moral character certificate. The birthday must match November 16, 1918.

Most sincerely,
Cunard White Star Limited

The situation had become desperate. Without the requested documents, only my sisters would be issued tickets. There was no time to spare. And so, Hermine and Herman had rushed to Budapest in person to bring the original documents to the American Embassy to get the visas and then finalize the tickets with Cunard.

Zemplén vármegye árvaszékétől.

Szám: 15637 193/ 91

Tárgy: Kiskoru Glück Ignác bodrogmezői

lakos nagykorusítása iránti kérelme.
A válaszirat alapjául szolgáló jelentés, megke-
resés, rendelet stb. száma:
Csatolva:
Határidő:

Véghatározat.

A kérelemnek helyt adunk és az 19 21. évi november hó 14. ik napján
Bodrogmezőn n született kiskoru Glück Ignác bodrogmezői
lakost az 1877. évi XX. tc. 4. §-a értelmében nagykorunak jelentjük ki. Mint teljes korut
ügyei vezetésére és vagyonának önálló kezelésére jogosultnak elösmerjük.

Glück Jeremiás bodrogmezői lakos gyámot, atyát, t. t. gyámot felhivjuk, hogy
nagykoruvá lett gyámoltjának vagyonát annak önálló kezelésére adja át.

Ezzel egyidejüleg megkeressük a királyhelmeci kir. járásbíróságot, mint
tkvi hatóságot, hogy az önjoguvá váltnak kiskorúságát az váltnak a kiskorúságát
a bodrogmezői 415,147,285,502 és 521.
számu tkvi betétben, számu telekjegyzőkönyvben törölni sziveskedjék.

Értesitjük önjoguvá váltat, hogy a számadásokat a gyámhatóságnál megtekintheti, arra
nézve, hogy a gyámot, t. t. gyámot felmenti-e? nyilatkozzék (1877: XX. tc. 132. §); egyéb-
ként jogában áll a számadásokat és okmányait másolatban kivenni (1877: XX. tc. 135. §);
amennyiben pedig a számadások ellen kifogásai vannak, tartozik jelen felhivás kézbesitésé-
től számitandó hat hó lefolyása alatt észrevételeit a gyámhatóságnak bejelenteni (1877: XX.
tc. 135. §). Ha azonban ezen idő alatt a gyámhatóság előtt nem nyilatkoznék, a gyámhatóság erről a gyám részére bizonyitványt állit ki, mely a felmentvény jogerejével bir (1877:
XX. tc. 136. §)

Önjoguvá váltnak gyámpénztárilag kezelt készpénzét kiutaljuk, miért is felhivjuk a sátor-
aljaujhelyi vármegyei számvevőséget, hogy a jelen véghatározathoz mellékelt utalvány alapján
a szükséges intézkedéseket tegye meg, hogy kiskoru Glück Ignác bodrogmezői
lakos javára a közös árvák és
gondnokoltak főkönyv XVII. kötet 131. lapján(ain) kezelt 623 Pengő
80 fillér azaz hatszázhuszonhárom - - - - - - - - - - - - - - - - - Pengő 80 fillér

32. Nagykorusitás
a 4. §. értelmében.

The first page of the Zemplen County Orphanage Certificate of Emancipation, dated
November 21, 1939 declaring me to be an adult.

I thought about all this as our train rumbled through fields and farms. By lunch, we were nearing Budapest. It was a beautiful city during the summer and I wondered what it would be like now, in the middle of a harsh winter. We stopped in a small station. Two businessmen entered the car and sat across from us. They wore wool overcoats and fedora hats, and each carried a briefcase that they quickly stowed on the overhead racks. They removed their hats and sat down to read their newspapers, as nonchalant as we were anxious. Unlike us, they appeared to be seasoned commuters. When the train was delayed for a short time, one of them sensed our discomfort, and said reassuringly,

"Don't worry! We commute to Budapest everyday and this happens all the time!"

Don't worry? We weren't just going to Budapest. We were leaving Europe, and could be detained, or worse, arrested! Thankfully, I kept my thoughts to myself. I merely repeated the word "Everyday?" in utter astonishment and somehow managed to smile politely.

Finally, we arrived in Budapest. We met Hermine and Herman at the apartment building downtown in the 17th district where they had been staying. At 26, Hermine was seven years older than I. She was stunningly beautiful; blonde with blue eyes, a ready smile, and the envy of our district. She excelled in everything, even winning a local math competition. And she was confident in herself and very outgoing. Against our father's wishes she once dressed up in costume as a man for the holiday of Purim,[13] going so far as to draw whiskers on her beautiful face.

---

[13] Purim is a Jewish holiday that commemorates the saving of the Jewish people from an evil decree to kill all the Jews living in the ancient Achaemenid Persian Empire. The story is recorded in the Biblical Book of Esther. It is customary for children (and adults, if they desire) to dress up in costumes on Purim.

Since my mother's illness and death so many years earlier, she cared for us all, and especially for me. She did everything for us as our mother would have done had she been able. Herman, on the other hand, was shy and reserved with deep-set, brown eyes. He had an excellent memory but was self-absorbed, awkward with other people, and more interested in farming than anything else. At home, he mostly kept to himself, grafting tree stems into the stocks of the apple, plum, and pear trees that grew on our farm in an ongoing experiment to create new varieties of fruit. We hugged each other and then, since we hadn't eaten breakfast, went to the restaurant of a nearby hotel.

"May I take your order?" asked the waiter. At home on our farm we usually drank milk and ate bread for breakfast and we saw no reason not to do the same, even in a fancy hotel.

"A pitcher of milk, and a loaf of bread," we ordered. The waiter laughed. What a sight we must have been dressed in our unfashionable clothing ordering milk and bread! He quickly returned with the milk. I drank it, but since it was cold, it didn't taste right. I was used to fresh, *warm* milk. Just thinking about warm milk reminded me of my mother. She often gave me milk just after she finished milking the cow.

"Give me your hand," asked my mother, her voice gentle and soft. I gave it to her gladly. We walked together to the barn. It was early in the morning. The sun had just risen and the bright sunlight colored the walls of the barn with warm golden hues. She led me to the cows. "Stand next to me, and I'll give you a surprise!" She took a wooden stool from the corner and set it down in the hay next to the cow. Hanging by its handle from a peg on the wall was a metal can. She took it and then sat down next to the cow and began to squeeze its utters. With each squeeze, a strong spray of milk squirted into the bucket, making a clanging sound as it hit inside. Steam rose out from the bucket into the cool morning air. In no time the bucket was filled with creamy white milk. She took a small

metal cup, dipped it into the bucket, and brought it close to my mouth for me to drink. The warm milk was delicious and I drank it quickly. Taking a handkerchief out from a pocket inside her dress my mother said, "Come my little boy, let me wipe your milk mustache!" and she did.

My mother, Lena Schwartz Gluck
Polyán, Czechoslovakia

My grandmother Chaia Schwartz, and my mother, sitting in the yard of our house
Polyán, Czechoslovakia

Feeding the chickens! Notice the thatched roof and the wagon wheel on the right.
From Left to Right: Hermine, my mother, Marie, and me sitting.
Polyán, Czechoslovakia

"Ignackám[14]...are you listening?" My sister Hermine's voice jolted me back from my daydream.

"We got to the shipping company just before it closed. It was Shabbos but there was no choice, if we didn't go then we'd miss the ship for sure! She's already left Trieste, you know, which means we'll have to meet her in Naples. And if we had taken the trolley, like I wanted to do, it would have been no problem. They close early, you know, on Shabbos! There was a trolley coming and after I stepped onto it, I called to Herman, 'Come on, get on!' But he wouldn't! 'It's Shabbos!' he yelled. Shabbos! Your stubborn brother! You acted like such a baby, Herman. Really!" Hermine said in a disapproving tone and with a sharp glance at Herman. She drank from her cup and continued. "I didn't want to get separated from him, so I jumped off the moving trolley. Herman made us walk the whole way! I was certain the shipping company's office would be closed, but we made it there just in time. There was a long line in front of us, and as we waited an even longer one formed behind us." She paused for a moment. "We were the last ones they allowed in!"

My head was spinning. Trieste? Naples? My sister read my thoughts from my furrowed brow, and continued.

"Although Cunard is still acting as our agent, we just found out that the company no longer sails across the Atlantic! We had to buy tickets on an Italian ship. Luckily, Cunard transferred the money to the Italia Lines in dollars, but unfortunately they also took a fee from it. I didn't want to ask Uncle Jónás, but there was no choice. If he didn't send the money to make up the difference, it would have been the end with no way out!"

---

[14] "Kém" or "Kám" is a Hungarian suffix added to a name to mean "dear"

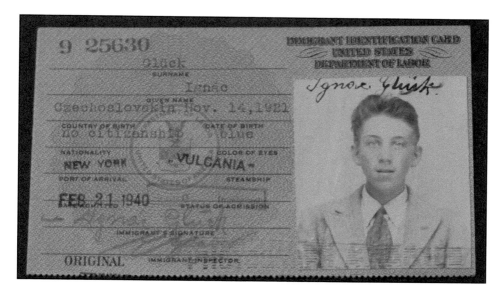

Front and back of my Immigrant Identification Card, issued January 17, 1940
Nationality - "No Citizenship"

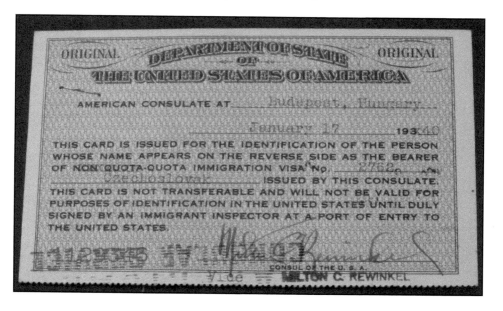

United States of America

County of **Franklin**
State of **Ohio** } s.s. **Affidavit of Support**   Prepaid Ticket No...........

I, ...**Arthur Gluck**.......... residing at ...**178 West Woodruff Avenue**
                    (Name)   (Street Address)
..........**Columbus**..........**Ohio**...... being duly sworn depose and say:
        City   State

1. That I was born a citizen of the United States on:	That I was naturalized a citizen of the United States on:	That I declared my intention of becoming a citizen of the United States on:
...**January 23, 1887**.....In the	Date.............................. In the	Date.............................. In the
Date		
City Of ...**Ashtabula**..........	(City) (County)	(City) (County)
County Of ..**Ashtabula**..........	.... number of my certificate being..............	.... number of my certificate being..............
(State)		(State)
State Of ....**Ohio**	issued by the Court of............	issued by the Court of............

2. That I am...**41**..years of age and have resided in the United States since.......**birth**...........
3. That the undermentioned alien(s) desire(s) to come to the United States because...........
....
                                        (State reasons fully)
4. That the undermentioned alien(s) whose relationship to me is that of wife, husband, mother, father or unmarried children under the age of twenty-one, is (are) in the favored classes under the Immigration law and being an American Citizen I filed Form 633 of the Department of Labor, entitled "Petition for Issuance of Immigration visa" with the Honorable Commissioner General of Immigration in Washington, D. C., under date of ....
OR, that the undermentioned alien(s) whose relationship to me is that of wife, or unmarried child(ren) under the age of twenty-one, is/are entitled to preference under the Immigration Act of 1924 as amended, I having arrived at the port of............................on.............., and having been legally admitted into the United States for permanent residence. I filed form 575 of the Department of Labor, entitled "Declaration Regarding Last Entry Into the United States" with the appropriate immigration officer at the above port, indicating that I arrived via the S.S. "...................."
5. That the financial status of the alien(s) is/are...
....
                            (State whether or not the applicant is dependent on you for support)
6. That alien(s) mentioned herein previously resided in the United States from............................
                                                                                        Date
to..............................., and departed because..
        Date
and did (did not) declare his/her/their intention of becoming an American Citizen(s).
7. That alien(s) mentioned herein are able to read and write the following language or dialect...........
.......**Hungarian, Czechoslovakian, and German**...
....who are exempt by law.
8. That my regular occupation is......**manufacturer**..............**Bonded Scale Company**......
                                                                            (Trade)   (With)
....my average weekly earnings amount to $..**65.00**.
and I possess property to the value of: Real Estate $..............Personal $.**70,000.00**. Yearly Income from Rentals of Real Estate $............, and that the encumbrance on said property, if any, amount to $............
9. That my present dependents consists of..**Flora Gluck-wife-aged 40; Samuel Gluck-son-aged 12;**
..**Jennie Gluck-daughter-aged 8.**...
                                            (Names and Ages)
10. That it is my intention and desire to have my relatives whose names appear below, at present residing at:
..........**Polany, Post Office, Leles, Czechoslovakia**...
                                    Give Complete Address
come and remain with me in the United States until such time as they may become self-supporting.

Name of Alien (s)	Sex	Date of Birth	Country of Birth	Occupation	Relationship to Deponent
Hermin Gluck	female	1914	Czechoslo-vakia	house work	cousin

That I am willing and able to receive, maintain, support and be responsible for the alien(s) mentioned above while they remain in the United States, and hereby assume such obligations, guaranteeing that none of them will at any time become a burden on the United States or on any State, County, City Village or Municipality of the United States; and that any who are under sixteen years of age will be sent to day school at least until they are sixteen years old and will not be put to work unsuited to their years.

That the above mentioned relatives are in good health and physical condition and are mentally sound, to the best of my knowledge and belief.

That I am and always have been a law-abiding resident and have not at any time been threatened with or arrested for any crime or misdemeanor, that I do not belong to nor am I in anywise connected with any group or organization, whose principles are contrary to organized government, nor do the above mentioned relatives, to the best of my knowledge and belief, belong to any such organization, nor have they ever been convicted of any crime involving moral turpitude.

Deponent further States, That this affidavit is made by him for the purpose of inducing the American Consul to issue visas to the above mentioned relatives and the Immigration Authorities to admit said relatives into the United States.

Witness: *(signature) Arthur Gluck*
                                                    (Signature of Deponent)
Name **A. N. Nagel**   Subscribed and sworn to before me, a
Address **477 W. 4 Ave**   Notary Public, in and for said County,
Columbus   this ..**11**..day of..**April**....A.D. 193**8**.
Ohio   *Fiona Baumler*
                                        Fiona Baumler
                                                    Notary Public
                                        My Commission Expires **April 3-1939**

L-8769—ORIGINAL

BONDED SCALE COMPANY

ARTHUR GLUCK, President

M A N U F A C T U R E R S O F

MOTOR TRUCK — MOTOR TRUCK DUMP — TANK — HOPPER — DORMANT WAREHOUSE
MINE TIPPLE — CONTRACTORS — GASTON MOTOR TRUCK SCALES — GASTON SCALES SINCE 1843

COLUMBUS, OHIO
July 12, 1939.

United States Consul
Budapest, Hungary.

Dear Sir:

I am writing you relative to Maria Gluck, female, Hermin
Gluck, female, Herman Gluck, male, and Ignacz Gluck, male,
all residing at Polany, Post Office, Leles, Bodgrogmezo,
Zemplem, Megze, Hungary, formerly of Czechoslavakia. These
are cousins of mine and I have taken care of filling out
the necessary affidavit of support and the verification of
my ability to back up the affidavit by submitting a report
to Dun and Bradstreet and a letter from my banker. I am
under the impression that all details are satisfactory to
the Consul at Prague, and also to your office as you have
these details in connection with an other case, in which
you acknowledged that everything seems to be in order.
This other case is Dr. Pista, (Stephen) Roth, who is a
physician. (File No. 811.11 EVP/ McD)

I received word that the above people are to appear before
you for examination on July 31st, and that you would like
additional affidavits, letters from my banker. These are
enclosed.

I further definitely state herewith that I am prepared to
support these people for all the necessities of life, if
necessary, and guarantee they will not become a public
charge.

I have also asked the Dun & Bradstree, Inc. to send you
by air mail, another statement of my financial conditions.

Very truly yours,

Arthur Gluck

BALANCE INDICATORS . . . . TESTING EQUIPMENT . . . SCALE REBUILDING

Cousin Arthur's letter of credit
July 12, 1939

Opposite Page: Affidavit of Support for Hermine signed by Cousin Arthur, April 21, 1938

The building in Budapest at Sip Utca 17, where we stayed overnight.
Photo taken: July 13, 2018

Inside the courtyard of Sip Utca 17, where we stayed overnight.
Photo taken: July 13, 2018

Chapter 4

"As many languages you know, as many times you are a human being"
- Tomas Garrigue Masaryk

HERMINE HAD HOPED to continue the same day by train to Trieste, Italy to board our ship, the "Vulcania," but because of the many delays, the Vulcania had already sailed from Trieste. Now we had to hurry to meet her in Naples or she would sail again, leaving us stranded. Although desperate to leave, we had no choice but to stay in Budapest and wait; the next available train wouldn't depart for another day. Hermine had already purchased the tickets, so after breakfast, with nothing else to do, we wandered around the city, awed by its size and grandeur. We couldn't help but marvel at the remains of the Great Synagogue a few blocks away on Dohány Street. It had been bombed by pro-Nazi Hungarians a year earlier. Nonetheless, we had never imagined that a synagogue could be so large and ornate. There were two towers capped with domes. The Jewish Stars on them were barely visible as I craned my neck back to see them. There were arched windows that had been filled with stained glass, now broken in shards. Its walls were made with colored bricks in alternating cream and rust colors that created a striking striped pattern. Even in the brickwork there were Jewish stars. The walls towered over the trees that lined the sidewalk and I felt overwhelmed by its sheer size.

We stayed overnight in Budapest. Since we were used to sleeping on mattresses stuffed with straw, the spring mattresses were a novelty. Soft and warm, they beckoned us to sleep late, but we were accustomed to waking early to say our daily prayers. It was February 7th, and our train wouldn't leave until evening. We sat in the train station and waited impatiently as the clock slowly ticked each second.

At 5:15 PM, my sisters Hermine and Marie, my brother Herman and myself finally boarded the train and took our seats. The train's porter took our two trunks to the baggage car. We carried only our passports and train tickets. Hermine had with her everything else: some of the many letters that Dezső had sent home; letters from the American Consulate and Cunard; and most importantly, the tickets for the ship.

"Tickets, all tickets please!" called the conductor.

We handed him our tickets. He casually examined them. "Have your passports ready when we stop at the border. Our border patrol will come aboard and examine them, and then we'll cross into Yugoslavia. There, the Yugoslavian border patrol will do the same." The conductor punched holes in the tickets and returned them to us.

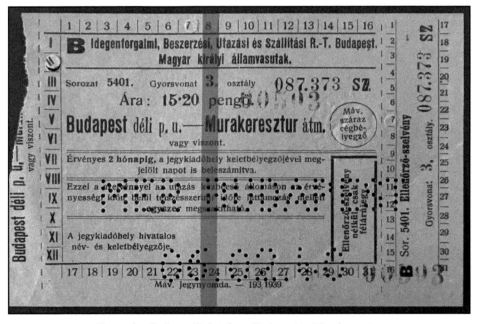

Hungarian Railway Ticket from Budapest to Murakeresztur.
Purchased February 6, 1940

"How long until we change to the Italian train?" asked Hermine.

"About 12 hours, Miss," he replied "Tickets, all tickets!"

It was past 9 P.M. when the train slowed to a stop at Murakereszetúr, a station on Hungary's border with Yugoslavia. The doors of the train opened and the cold night air swept through the car, making us immediately alert. Hungarian border guards boarded the train and walked down the aisles. "Your papers," one ordered. We gave him our passports. They opened them, one at a time, looked at our faces, then looked again at our passports. They studied the visas closely. They looked at us with questioning eyes, and we met their stares with cool indifference. Finally, they stamped our passports and returned them to us. When they'd finished doing the same to all the other passengers, they left the train and it crossed into Yugoslavia. We were relieved, but at the same time we knew, this was only the first of several inspections.

The train steamed on for a short distance, when it stopped again. We had reached Kotoriba, the border station on the Yugoslavian side. In minutes, Yugoslavian border guards stood next to us, their flashlights momentarily blinding us. One of them motioned to our passports and brusquely said, "Pasos." We handed them to him and he examined each one with a flashlight in the dim light. "Destinacija?"

"Rakek," answered Hermine for the four of us. The border crossing with Italy.

"U redo." Very well. He stamped our passports and moved on to examine the next passengers. We sighed silently with relief and waited impatiently for the inspection to end. Again, the train resumed its journey. The gentle swaying of the car lulled us to sleep. We closed our eyes. Hours passed by unnoticed.

The train's whistle blew and we awoke, stiff but rested. It was 5:30 in the morning and the dawn was just breaking over Rakek, Yugoslavia.

"Last stop. Change here for Italy," called the conductor. We went down the mud-encrusted steps of our car and stepped onto the platform. The Italian train that would be our next transport was waiting opposite ours, gleaming in the bright sunlight. Its windows sparkled and its vibrant colors made our Hungarian train look drab and grimy in comparison. We crossed the tracks and waited our turn to show our tickets and passports. The guards examined our papers, and then porters transferred our baggage. When we finally boarded the train, we paused in the doorway, staring in amazement. Everything inside was sleek, modern, and immaculately clean. It really put the Hungarian train to shame.

We took our seats, and without delay were soon leaving the station. The now familiar routine followed. "Bigletti, per favore!" called the conductor. We copied our fellow passengers and took out our tickets. The conductor examined them. "Va bene! Va bene!" He continued, "Al borda, la polizia qua esamineranno i vostri passaporti." The police there will examine your passports at the border.

A short time passed and we stopped again, this time in Postumia, the Italian border crossing. The Italian border guard came aboard. "Passaporti, per piacere." We handed him our passports. Perhaps captivated by Hermine's blonde hair, he only gave them a perfunctory glance.

"La vostre destinazione è Napoli?" he asked flirtatiously. Holding his gaze and smiling widely, Hermine answered, "Igen! Napoli!" I hoped that her affirmation in Hungarian was an appropriate answer to his incomprehensible question. Realizing we didn't understand Italian, he continued speaking directly to Hermine anyway. "Va bene, mia bellissima signorita! Un viaggio piacevole!" All right, my beautiful young

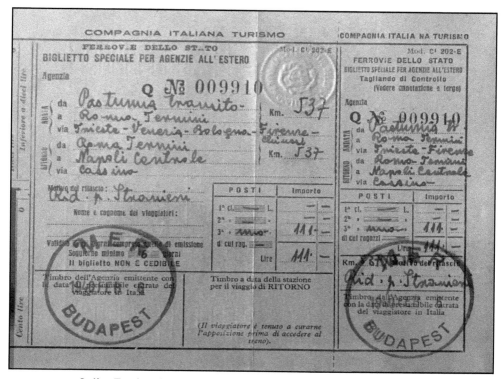

Italian Tourism Company Rail Ticket from Postumia Transito to Napoli
Centrale via Trieste, Venezia, Bologna, Firenze, Roma Termini and Cassino.
Purchased February 6, 1940

My sister Hermine's passport photo.

My brother Herman's passport photo.

lady! Have a pleasant trip! His eyes never left her face as he stamped our passports and returned them. He worked quickly through the car and we were soon on our way to Naples, via Trieste, Rome, and Cassino, a city whose name I had never heard. It took another 12 hours, and many more stations, before we arrived at our final destination. It was 7 PM on February 8th. Exhausted and hungry, we left the train and waited for our trunks to be taken out of the baggage car. When we had everything, we stood on line for one last inspection of our papers before we could continue into Naples and to our hotel. Hermine handed all the passports and papers to the inspection agent. He was tall, with dark eyes and dark hair. His face was emotionless as he thoroughly examined each passport. He paused. We watched nervously as he separated the passports. He stamped Hermine's passport and asked her to pass through the gate. He did the same with Marie's. He handed the other two passports to another guard and gruffly motioned to Herman and me to follow. Hermine stopped us.

"Where are you bringing them? Why are we being separated?" she asked in Hungarian.

"Questi passiporti sono differente!" he replied sharply. "Va! Porti questi uomini essere interrogato!" he commanded to the other guard who immediately took hold of my arm and pulled me aside. Although none of us understood his words, it was clear that Herman and I were to go with him.

"What's happening?!" demanded Hermine. "What's happening?"

The guard ignored her and continued checking the other disembarking passengers. I gave a reassuring glance back at my sisters and then followed Herman and the guard. I wasn't nervous, after all, we had all of our papers in order. They had been examined several times and during the roughest part, that is, passing from Hungary to Yugoslavia, we had had no problem. What was there to be afraid of?

We walked outside the main train station and crossed the road to a dimly lit gray building. On either side of the road was barbed wire. The guard opened the tall wooden door. Herman let me go in first, and followed close behind. There was an armed guard standing at attention on our left, who saluted the border guard that had escorted us.

The room was lit by wall sconces on each side of the vestibule. Hanging from the ceiling was a flag carrying the green, white, and red stripes of Italy. Next to it was the red flag of Nazi Germany with its black swastika emblazoned in a circle of white. In front of us was a long staircase leading upstairs, and to our left and right were large double doors. The border guard led us to the right. He knocked. "Entri!" came a sharp voice from inside. Our escort opened the door, stood at attention and saluted, then said something in Italian. Two questioning voices responded from inside the room. The border guard turned, and motioned for us to enter the room. We hesitated. "Entra, entra" he said. We went in. By the dim light of a single bulb hanging by its wire in the center of the ceiling, we could see an Italian officer sitting behind a large oak desk. Next to him stood a short man, who had in his hand a stenographer's pad. Herman and I stood next to each other, but as I was slightly closer to the desk, the officer sitting behind it addressed his question to me.

"Do you speak German?" I was startled to hear the Italian officer speak German, but was relieved to finally understand what was being spoken. German was so close to Yiddish that I could understand and speak it easily. [15]

---

[15] Yiddish is a language used by Jews from central and eastern Europe and was the lingua franca amongst them before the Holocaust. It was originally a German dialect with words from Hebrew and several modern languages and is today spoken mainly in the US and Israel, but by a significantly smaller percentage of Jews than before the Holocaust.

"Ja!" I quickly replied. Yes!

"Your passports are different than your sisters'. Why?"

"Sir, as you see, we are from the former Czechoslovakia. We had to transfer all our papers from Prague to Budapest...to Hungary. Everything was done so hurriedly, sir."

"Yes, yes, unfortunate situation. But tell me, you are eighteen and your brother is twenty-one. Correct?"

"Yes, sir."

"How is it that you two *men* have been allowed out of Hungary?"

"What do you mean, sir?"

"You should be in the army, protecting your Fatherland! Why aren't you in your own country, in uniform, defending your homes!" Throughout his tirade his voice grew louder until he was shouting at us. I could see the veins on his head and neck bulging as he banged his fist angrily on his desk. "How did you get permission to leave?"

Summoning up all my nerve, I answered him calmly but assertively.

"If the Fuhrer saw fit to give us permission to leave, he must have had his reasons!"

At the mention of the German leader's title, the man behind the desk jumped to his feet, saluted in crisp Nazi fashion, and said, "Heil, Hitler!" He threw our passports onto his desk. They dropped to the floor. "Take them and go!" he commanded. Quickly, we bent down, picked up our passports and left the room. The border guard, looking flabbergasted, brought us back to the terminal, where he gave instructions to allow us to leave the station.

Hermine and Marie were waiting for us outside. Our sisters' wide, warm smiles indicated how relieved they were when they saw Herman and me walk out through the revolving doors. Hermine clasped my hands and entwined her arm through mine so tightly, as though she was afraid we would be separated again if she let go. We waited briefly for a taxi without exchanging a word so as not to draw attention to ourselves. Once inside, my sisters listened as I explained how we were detained and questioned.

"And he let you go, just like that?" asked Marie incredulously.

"Yes!" I answered, as astonished as she that there we were, riding to our hotel, together. We sat quietly for a few moments. Silently, I pondered the fact that minutes earlier one man's capriciousness had made the difference between freedom or detention. One man had the power to shatter all of our hopes. Had he not let us go, all of our hard work would have been in vain.

"I felt so helpless!" Hermine said suddenly. Indeed, until then, Hermine's self-assurance had been a pillar of strength for us all. "What would we have done had you been taken into custody?"

"All that matters is that we're together again!" interjected Marie.

It was a very short drive from the Central Station to our hotel. When we finally checked into the Albergo Iaccheo, we had been traveling for 26 hours and were utterly exhausted. We were supposed to leave Europe in just three days.

Following pages: Signature Pages from my Hungarian passport, and Marie's.

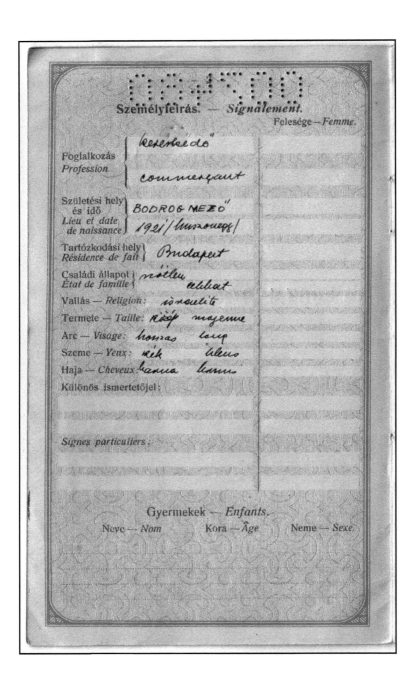

Személyleírás. — *Signalement.*

Felesége—*Femme.*

Foglalkozás
Profession } *kereskedő"*

commerçant

Születési hely
és idő
*Lieu et date
de naissance* } *BODROG MEZŐ"*

1921/huszonegy/

Tartózkodási hely
Résidence de fait } *Budapest*

Családi állapot
État de famille } *nőtlen*
célibat

Vallás — *Religion:* *izraelita*

Termete — *Taille:* *közép* *moyenne*

Arc — *Visage:* *hosszas* *long*

Szeme — *Yeux:* *kék* *bleus*

Haja — *Cheveux* *barna* *brun*

Különös ismertetőjel:

Signes particuliers:

Gyermekek — *Enfants.*

Neve — *Nom*   Kora — *Âge*   Neme — *Sexe.*

Front and Reverse of an advertisement for the hotel, "Albergo Iaccheo"
Naples, Italy 1940

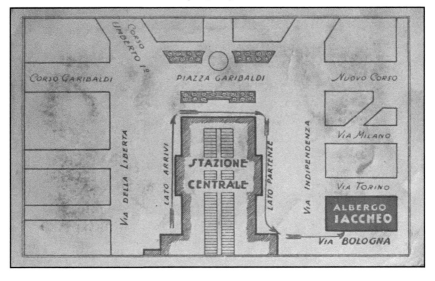

Postcards from Naples. Above, Monte Vesuvius. Below, the port.
Naples, Italy 1940

Chapter 5

"...a mighty woman with a torch, whose flame is the imprisoned lightning, and her name Mother of Exiles." - Emma Lázárus

WHEN WE AWOKE IN THE MORNING, we were stiff from the long journey. After our morning prayers and breakfast in the hotel, we decided that a walk in the brisk morning air would do us all some good. Since we were four youngsters traveling alone, the Italian Lines had assigned a translator, at no charge, to accompany us everywhere. Even though we were dressed in the same clothes that we had worn when we left Polyán, looking no better than many of the street urchins loitering about, he guided us around the streets of Napoli. The cold air didn't keep us from spending the day outside. In the afternoon, we passed a small restaurant, and the aroma of the food beckoned us to enter. Although it wasn't kosher, we remembered our father's instructions: "Do what you have to in order to leave!" We were hungry, so we sat and ate vegetables and pasta. Through the window, we could see Mount Vesuvius, the volcano that had destroyed Pompeii, looming ominously in the distance. We were keenly aware that, unlike the residents of Pompeii, we had been given a chance to escape the wanton destruction now erupting throughout Europe.

It was February 11, 1940. At last, it was time to board our ship, the Vulcania.[16] She was docked in the bustling

---

[16] The Vulcania was built in 1926 for the Italian company, Cosulich Line. In 1932, all the Italian shipping firms were united to form the Italia Flotta Riuniti, although most maintained their separate identities.

harbor in the Bay of Naples. It was by far the largest
vessel that I had ever seen, although my nautical
knowledge was limited, of course, to landlocked
Czechoslovakia. Workers were busy loading the ship as
she lay moored along the docks that ran perpendicular to
Via Cristoforo Colombo. Huge cranes lifted crates
aboard. Gangplanks rose up from the edge of the pier. All
manner of goods were being loaded into the belly of the
ship. Fruits and vegetables, cases of wine, meats, and
baking supplies. My heart raced with excitement. As we
waited to enter the pier, the cold salty air filled our lungs.
The smell of fish and seawater mixed with the gentle
perfumes of the first class passengers walking brusquely
past us. A porter helped us with our trunks. After
immigration officials checked our papers, we climbed the
passenger gangplank and were aboard at last.

SS Vulcania docked in Trieste.
Italian Lines, circa 1940
http://blogs.transparent.com/italian/files/2013/09/Vulcania_Cosulich001Trieste02.jpg

Opposite page: The ticket for passage on the "Vulcania" for Herman and me.
Italia Lines, February 10, 1940

Se il passeggero, per qualsiasi causa riguardante la sua persona, anche se tale causa costituisca caso fortuito o forza maggiore, sbarca durante il viaggio deve pagare il nolo intero.

Italia

N° 30536

135/136

SOCIETÀ ANONIMA DI NAVIGAZIONE
Sede in Genova - Capitale Sociale L. 500.000.000 interamente versato

BIGLIETTO D'IMBARCO IN TERZA CLASSE

sulla Nave di bandiera italiana **VULCANIA**

in partenza da **NAPOLI** il **10 FEB. 1940** Anno XVIII per **NEW-YORK**

toccando di scalo i Porti di **PALERMO - GIBILTERRA LISBONA - AZZORRE**

DURATA DEL VIAGGIO GIORNI **11** (compresa le fermate nei porti di scalo)
La durata del viaggio sarà aumentata di un giorno per ogni scalo eventuale che venisse effettuato

COGNOME E NOME	ETA		POSTI E RAZIONI				Cuccette	
	Anni	Mesi	1	½	¼	0	1	½
1 Gluck Herman			1					
2 " Ignac			1					
3								
4								
5								
Budapest provv. 49138	Totale		2					

Biglietto di Chiamata / Buono di Ritorno N.

Emesso a _____ il _____ Valore

Eccedenza posti N. _____ a L.it. _____ $ 1400

N. _____ posti a L.it. _____ a posto

Tassa d'imbarco

Tassa speciale di passaporto   2

Diritto fisso bagaglio

Tassa portuaria   16

Tassa di sbarco

ITALIA
SOCIETÀ ANONIMA DI NAVIGAZIONE
UFFICIO PASSEGGERI 3ª CLASSE
L'Incaricato

Totale L.it.

Acconto versato L.it.

Da versare a saldo a L.it.

NAPOLI 8 FEB.

A steward led us to our cabins. We passed through
endless hallways lit on either side by polished brass
sconces. Without exchanging words, the steward
demonstrated the call buttons in case we needed
assistance, then left us to ourselves. Hermine and Marie
were in one cabin, Herman and I in another. We shared
our cabin with four other men; Károly Piva, an Italian
candy store owner, Alex Gold from Brooklyn, NY, Imre
Szent from Miskolc, Hungary, which was a town not too
far from our own, and Emil Orosz. Mr. Orosz, an elderly,
heavyset gentleman explained to us in broken Hungarian
that he had made the voyage across the Atlantic several
times. "Don't worry!" he said reassuringly, "there is
nothing to fear from the crossing. Everything will be just
fine!"

The ship's whistle blared, announcing our imminent
departure. We watched through the porthole as the ship
slowly edged away from the pier. We could see hundreds
of people waving to the passengers that lined the decks of
the ship. Having no one to see us off, we stayed inside our
cabins. At last, we were beginning our journey from the
prison that Europe had become to the freedom that
America offered. We were excited to finally be on the
ship, but we couldn't help feel sad that we were leaving
behind our family, our village, and the life that had been
so familiar to us.

That afternoon we had lunch in the dining room. We
ordered from the menu and the waiters catered to our
every need. As we ate, the ship steamed smoothly over the
calm Mediterranean waters. The sun was hanging low on
the horizon when we arrived in Palermo, Sicily and by

late evening, after taking on more passengers, we were sailing to Algiers, North Africa.

When we awoke, the ship was already moored in her berth in Algiers. Additional passengers came aboard and longshoremen loaded on more supplies. In no time, we were sailing again, this time to Gibraltar, the famous Rock turned British fortress. For Britain, the war had started September 3, 1939, two days after the Germans invaded Poland. Already at war, the British ordered every ship passing through the Straits of Gibraltar to stop, unload all her passengers, and undergo a thorough search. The Vulcania was no exception. The ship's whistle sounded and a loud voice came over the intercom speaking Italian.

"All passengers must disembark," Mr. Orosz translated for us. "Let's go, boys!" As if the voice on the other end of the loudspeaker heard our unspoken question, it continued, as did Mr. Orosz's translation.

"The British will check our papers and the ship. We'll be examined by their doctors. We'll be back aboard before you know it! Don't worry, the British won't make troubles for us."

After the last inspection in Naples, how could we not worry?

While British customs officials politely examined our papers and British doctors thoroughly examined us for disease, British soldiers searched the ship for contraband. As promised, after four or five hours, the ship was cleared and we were allowed to go aboard again. For the first time, I felt a profound sense of relief. We had escaped. We were free.

Luggage Tag
"Vulcania" - Italian Lines 1940

INSPECTION CARD. 136
(Immigrants and Steerage Passengers)

Port of departure, NAPLES   Date of departure, 10 FEB. 1940

Name of ship, "VULCANIA"

Name of immigrant,   Gluck Ignac

Last residence,   State

Inspected and passed at	Passed at quarantine, port of U.S	Passed by Immigration Bureau, Port of
	(Date)	(Date)

(The following to be filled in by ship's surgeon or agent prior to or after embarkation)   16

Ship's list or manifest,   No. on ship's list or manifest,

| Berth No. | Steamship inspection | 1st day | 2 | 3 | 4 | 5 | 6 | 7 | 8 | 9 | 10 | 11 | 12 | 13 | 14 | 15 | 16 | To be punched by ship's surgeon at daily inspection. |

Inspection Card
"Vulcania" - Italian Lines 1940

The ship continued along the Iberian coast, stopping in Lisbon, Portugal, and Vigo, Spain before heading out into the Atlantic to The Azores, a group of small islands under Portuguese control. We had enjoyed strolling outside on the deck, despite a light drizzle that eventually forced us inside. I found our little cabin quite calming. I took advantage of the opportunity to speak with Mr. Orosz. Unlike the others in our cabin, he spoke a little bit of Hungarian and English. I was determined to learn whatever English I could from him, and he patiently obliged.

At last, the open Atlantic Ocean lay before us. And yet, even it seemed to conspire against us to hinder our escape to freedom. Over the ship's loudspeaker came an emergency announcement. "They're saying they've received reports that hurricane force winds and heavy weather lies directly ahead," Mr. Orosz told us with a frown. The light drizzle became a torrential downpour. No longer able to breathe the fresh sea air or to take a brisk walk on deck, we tried to make the best of it down below. The waves rose and fell. The ship, which just days before seemed so large to me, was now tossed about like a toy boat in a child's bath. It steamed steadily up the side of a mountain of water, pausing momentarily at the peak, only to plummet down into the next valley. Again, it slowly climbed up another mountain of water only to plummet down. Again and again. Over and over. Waves crashed over the ship's bow and pounded against its side, endlessly rocking it, and its occupants, to and fro. Seasickness became our traveling companion. Like the weather, it was unrelenting. The terrible storm battered the ship and we feared that the crashing water would break not only our bodies and spirits, but the ship, too.

Mr. Orosz tried to calm us. "Don't worry! The ship is a good ship. A strong one! We'll get to America! No doubt about it!" His words may have eased my mind, but not my stomach. Every day and night for the remainder of the voyage, the Vulcania lurched in the storm tossed seas, and I tried, with very little success, to keep down the food that I forced myself to eat. My brother Dezső had advised us, based on his own experience crossing the ocean, not to forego eating, despite whatever anyone told us. He insisted that even if we felt too weak to eat in the dining room, we should request that food be brought to the cabin so that there would be something in our stomachs to bring up when we felt nauseous. Mr. Orosz had a small bottle of Pálinka, a Hungarian brandy, and he was kind enough to share some with us. That helped, too. Despite the weather and the nausea, we remained hopeful that we would eventually arrive safely.

Eleven days after leaving Naples, the Vulcania sailed into New York's harbor and glided silently past the Statue of Liberty. We saw only her silhouette in the evening light. Her outstretched arm, with the torch alit with freedom's flame welcomed us. My heart raced. Our ship slipped into her berth at Pier 92. It was February 21, 1940.

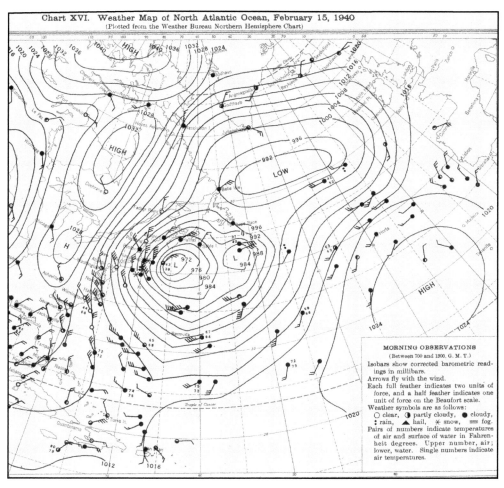

Isobars showing extreme low pressure on North Atlantic, February 15, 1940.
Monthly Weather Review, February 1940
(ftp://ftp.library.noaa.gov/docs.lib/htdocs/rescue/mwr/068/mwr-068-02-c16.pdf)

List ____ 4

LIST OR MANIFEST OF ALIEN PASSENGERS FOR THE UNITED

ALL ALIENS arriving at a port of continental United States from a foreign port or a port of the insular possessions of the United States, and all aliens arriving at a port of said insular possessions from a foreign port, a port of continental United States. This (white) sheet is for the listing of

S. S. " VULCANIA "   Passengers sailing from _____ NAPLES _____ , FEBRUARY 10TH _____ , 19 40

No. on List	Head-Tax Status	Family name	Given name	Age Yrs.	Age Mos.	Sex	Married or single	Calling or occupation	Able to Read	Able to Read what language	Nationality (Country of which citizen or subject)	Race or people	Place of birth Country	Place of birth City or town	Immigration Visa, Passport Visa, or Reentry Permit	Issued Place	Issued Date	Data concerning verification of landings, etc.	Last permanent residence Country	Last permanent residence City or town
18		Speda	Palma	30																
19		Ferrara	Maria	44		f	m	housew.	yes	Italian	yes Italy	Italian	Italy	Napoli	NQIV 445	Naples	Nov 21st 1939		Italy	Triggiano
20	U.S. CIT.	Ferrara	Anna Stella	11		f	s				U.S.A.					A.P. 2505	Naples Feb. 9th 1940			
21		Di Cocco	Domenico	18		m	s	Laborer	yes	Italian	yes Italy	Italian	Italy	Frosinone	NQIV 732	Naples	Jan. 9th 1940		Italy	Fontechiari
22	UNDER 16	Martino Gentile	Florinda	36		f	m	housew.	yes	Italian	yes Italy	Italian	Italy	S.Martino Finita	QIV 2170	Naples	Feb. 9th 1940		Italy	S.Martino di Finita
23		Martino	Amalia	15		f	s	housew.	yes	Italian	yes Italy	Italian	Italy	S.Martino Finita	QIV 2171	Naples	Feb. 9th 1940		Italy	S.Martino di Finita
24		Martino	Paolina	17		f	s	housew.	yes	Italian	yes Italy	Italian	Italy	Casalvieri	QIV 2172	Naples	Feb. 9th 1940		Italy	Casalvieri
25		Silvestri	Domenico	24		m	s	Laborer	yes	Italian	yes Italy	Italian	Italy	Casalvieri	QIV 2605	Naples	Feb. 5th 1940		Italy	Casalvieri
26	EXEMPT	Miceli	Giovanni	39		m	m	Laborer	yes	Italian	yes Italy	Italian	Italy	Locorotondo r.v. 36	QIV 2606	Naples	Feb. 9th 1940		Cuba	Habana
27		Riohli	Alfred	22		m	s	employed	yes	Italian	yes Switzerland	German	Switzerland	Osterfingen	QIV 1196	Naples	Feb. 9th 1940		Switzerland	Osterfingen
28		Giuffrida	Antonino	60		m	m	Laborer	yes	Italian	yes Italy	Italian	Italy	Leonforte	QIV 177	Naples	Feb. 9th 1940		Italy	Leonforte
29		Gluck	Maria	23		f	s	dressmak.	yes	Hungarian	yes Hungary	Hungarian	Hungary	Bodrogenzo	QIV 2760	Budapest	Jan 17th 1940		Hungary	Bodrogenzo
30		Gluck	Ignac	17		m	s	farmhand	yes	Hungarian	yes Hungary	Hungarian	Hungary	Bodrogenzo	QIV 2762	Budapest	Jan 17th 1940		Hungary	Bodrogenzo

Vulcania's manifest - Marie is on line 29, and I'm on line 30

Form 500
U.S. DEPARTMENT OF LABOR
IMMIGRATION AND NATURALIZATION SERVICE

List 5

20   251

LIST OR MANIFEST OF ALIEN PASSENGERS FOR THE UNITED

ALL ALIENS arriving at a port of continental United States from a foreign port or a port of the insular possessions of the United States, and all aliens arriving at a port of said insular possessions from a foreign port, a port of continental United States. This (white) sheet is for the listing of

S.S. "VULCANIA"

Passengers sailing from ____NAPLES____, ____FEBRUARY 10TH____, 1940

No. on List	Head Tax Status	Family name	Given name	Age Yrs.	Age Mos.	Sex	Married or single	Calling or occupation	Able to — Read	Read what language	Write	Nationality	Race or people	Place of birth Country	Place of birth City	Immigration Visa No.	Issued Place	Issued Date	Data	Last residence Country	Last residence City
15		Gluck	Hermina	25	—	f	s	housew.	yes	Hungarian	yes	Hungary	Hebrew	Hungary	Sophia	QIV 2759	Sophia	1939		Hungary	Sophia
16		Gluck	Herman	20		m	m	farmhand	yes	Hungarian	yes	Undefin.	Hebrew	Hungary	Bodrogenso	QIV 2761	Budapest	Jan.17th 1940		Hungary	Bodrogenso
17	DIPLOMAT	Buran	Grasia	26		m	m	servant	yes	Italian	yes	Italy	Italian	Italy	Pocerina	Gov.Of.212	Rome	Jan.30th 1940		Italy	Roma
18	DIPLOMAT	Frare	Alba	31	—	f	s	cook	yes	Italian	yes	Italy	Italian	Italy	Medina di Livenza	Gov.Of.211	Rome	Jan.30th 1940		Italy	Roma
19		Nicholas Vasil	Alexandra	49		f	s	housew.	yes	Greek	yes	Albany	Albanian	Greece	Konitsa	QIV 202	Naples	Feb.8th 1940		Albany	Leskovik
20		Nicholas	Sophia	19		f	s	housew.	yes	Greek	yes	Albany	Albanian	Albany	Leskovik	QIV 204	Naples	Feb.8th 1940		Albany	Leskovik
21		Kondulis Gogol	Alexandra	33		m	m	housew.	yes	illiterate	no	Albany	Albanian	Albany	Bodrista	NQIV 913	Naples	Feb.8th 1940		Albany	Bodrista
22	UNDER 16	Kondulis	Panajot	12		m	s	student	yes	Greek	yes	Albany	Albanian	Kitany	Pepel	NQIV 914	Naples	Feb.8th 1940		Albany	Bodrista
23		Benjamin	Heiumnes	40		m	s	chemist	yes	German	yes	Germany	Germany	Germany	Berlin	Q. 21468	Naples	Feb.1st 1940		Germany	Berlin
24		Arlt von	Ilse	30		f	s	housew.	yes	German	yes	Germany	German	Germany	Wien	QIV 16805	Wien	Jan.22nd 1940		Germany	Wien
25		Ritterman	Leon	43		m	m	tailor	yes	English	yes	Germany	Hebrew	Germany	Wien	Q. 21465	Naples	Feb.1st 1940		Germany	Wien
26		Ritterman	Grete	33		f	m	H.wife	yes	Germany	yes	Germany	Hebrew	Germany	Wien	Q. 21466	Naples	Feb.1st 1940		Germany	Wien
27	UNDER 16	Ritterman	Paul Felix	6		m	s	----		yes	Germany	Hebrew	Germany	Wien	Q. 21467	Naples	Feb.1st 1940		Germany	Wien
28		Bismtock	Chaje	69		f	w	housew.	yes	German	yes	Germany	German	Poland	Arobobljec	QIV 2290	Budapest	Dec.19th 1939		Germany	Wien

Vulcania's manifest – Hermine is on line 15, and Herman on line 16

Chapter 6

"Üsd a vasat, amíg meleg"
Strike while the iron is hot.
-Hungarian proverb

WHILE WE WERE AT SEA, a different storm was brewing back in our small village. High atop the church's steeple, the bell rang out across Polyán. It was midday. My father, Jeremias Gluck made his way cautiously over the snow and ice towards the front door of the church. He had been ordered to appear before Filep Miklós, the headmaster of the Catholic school, and also the local leader of the *Leventeszervezetek,* the paramilitary youth organization. On the front door was a pull cord. Mr. Gluck pulled the cord and the bell attached to it rang out. He waited only a moment before the priest opened it. "Come in, come in out of the cold my old friend," offered the priest. Portly, he was dressed in a long, flowing black robe. A silver chain hung around his neck and on it's end hung a silver cross resting comfortably on his plump stomach. The two men knew each other well; years earlier Mr. Gluck had even bought a coach from the priest. "Headmaster Miklós, please?" inquired Mr. Gluck.

"The headmaster is expecting you in his office." The priest pointed to a door down a dimly lit corridor. Mr. Gluck walked past the candles that burned in front of a statue of Jesus hanging from the cross. Above the statue was the Latin acronym, "INRI." **I**esus **N**azarenus **R**ex **I**udæorum, Jesus the Nazarene, King of the Jews. Of course, because Jews believe that the only king worthy of worship is G-d, Jewish parents taught this ubiquitous acronym differently, so to himself Mr. Gluck whispered, "**I**tt **N**incs **R**endes **I**sten." That is, "There is no proper god here!" He knocked on the door and then entered.

"Mr. Gluck. Thank you for coming." Filep Miklós stood and extended his hand to Jeremias, who shook it, despite the circumstances.

Mr. Miklós was tall and thin, clean shaven, and elegantly dressed. His father had been headmaster before him. Both he and his father knew Jeremias Gluck well. Although Jewish, Jeremias sent his children to the Catholic school, since the teacher there was better than the teacher in the Reformatus school, the only other one in the village. Jeremias would always give the elder Mr. Miklós some tobacco as a gift for the teacher on the holidays or at the year's end, and the younger Mr. Miklós was very fond of Hermine. His stiff military demeanor was just one indication of this status. His adherence to protocol was another.

Filep Miklós sat down without offering Jeremias a chair.

"Do you know why I have summoned you here?"

"No, not exactly."

"Government business."

"Government business?"

"Yes. Your sons, Ignac and Herman did not report this week for their home guard training. Why not?" Boys were required to report once a week for military training in the Home Guard.

"They are gone."

"What do you mean gone? This is a small village in a small district, where could they go?"

"They are in America."

Filep Miklós shot up from his chair and shouted, "What? Impossible! Everybody wants to leave, but it takes years!" The interrogation continued. "Tell me, Mr. Gluck, do you have proof?"

Although he was certain that his children should have arrived that very day, Jeremias Gluck still had not received the telegram that his daughter Hermine had promised to send.

"No, I don't have proof today but give me until tomorrow. I expect to hear from them by then. I will bring you the telegram as soon as I have it. You have my word, Mr. Headmaster."

"Very well, Mr. Gluck. Until tomorrow. Otherwise, you won't like the repercussions..." His voice trailed off, and with a wave of his hand signaled that the interview was over.

Jeremias Gluck returned to the headmasters' office the following day with a telegram from America that his brother-in-law Márton had received and hurriedly brought from Helmec.

"Mr. Headmaster," he said smiling quite happily. "Good afternoon!" He reached into his jacket and carefully removed the telegram from its envelope. "Here, look, they are in America. They arrived yesterday." He handed the telegram to Mr. Miklós. Printed on it in bold letters were the words:

"WE HAVE ALL ARRIVED SAFELY TO UNITED STATES STOP YOUR CHILDREN HERMINE MARIE HERMAN IGNAC STOP"

The fact that Hermine made it a point to include everyone's name on the telegram, even though it was more expensive, saved Jeremias Gluck from more trouble, and both men knew it.

"All four of them! It's unbelievable. I don't know how you did it!" Mr. Miklós exclaimed.

Then he leaned forward in his chair and whispered, so that no one but Mr. Gluck could hear.

"Confidentially, you know, to tell you the truth, I wish that I would be in America, too!"

Delighted that his children had arrived safely, and that he avoided a confrontation with Filip Miklós, Jeremias Gluck returned home to write to his children in America. As he walked on the frozen mud, he kept repeating to himself in astonishment, "Safe in America! America!"

Meanwhile, Márton, who had been waiting for Jeremias to return home, sat at the old wooden table and wrote to his nephews and nieces who had just arrived in America.

1940 February 23rd. Helmec
My Dearest Children - May you live to 120 with G-d's blessings!
We have received your telegram, and the two letters (the one mailed by regular mail, and the one mailed by air). As soon as I received the telegram, I brought it to your father. I also received a card and a letter from the shipping company in Naples in reply to the letter I wrote them. Your telegram from Columbus came in first.
My Dearest Children,
I cannot write down the heartfelt feeling I felt as I remained by myself at the train station. I looked dazedly as the train was leaving. I was there for a longtime and my heart was crying... Will I ever see you again someday? These were my thoughts, and I couldn't walk with them in my mind. I was in such a daze that I didn't even know what people were saying to me. I am sitting alone in your empty house and I miss you as much now

as I did the day you left. I am reminded that my dear sister, your mother, is no longer alive. As I write to you, my heart feels the same as it did when she died. It felt the same way when we said goodbye at the station. Last week, and today your father and I cried together feeling very lonely, but at least today we also cried happy tears because thank G-d you are safe and sound and in a good place. You are not alone because your family is there with you and they have been very good to you! I hope that G-d will give you the very best in everything ...Now I'm going to go to the synagogue for evening prayers...

I've now returned to my own home and I'm continuing this letter there. All day I've been reliving the moment at the station as you were leaving.

Dear Dezső,
You must have been so happy to see your brothers and sisters! I wish I would have been there to see it! Who knows if that will ever happen in this life? If G-d would make peace in this world then perhaps it can... Hermine wrote a letter to you from Budapest.. Did you receive it? I wrote to Bertha asking her to be kind enough to meet the children at the port.

Children,
I thank G-d that you have arrived safely. I was waiting impatiently for your telegram. Please be good to each other and respect one another. Learn English so that you can be a gentleman everywhere. Keep a kosher home, observe Shabbos, and Ignac and Herman - pray as you did at home, because that's all we have. G-d will help us if we just follow our philosophy. That is, get up early in the morning, be smart, and study diligently! This is the most important thing to do in order to survive.

Maintain the greatest respect for your Uncle Jónás. Forgive and ignore any misunderstanding that might arise. Don't forget what he has done for you. The whole district cannot imagine how 4 children were able to get out at once.

Please write me often and I promise to reply. I wish you from my heart the very best to all of you, to your Uncle Jónás, and to his family.

Happy Purim to our Jewish friends.

Uncle Márton Schwartz

Chapter 7

"City of hurried and sparkling waters! city of spires and masts! City nested in bays!" Walt Whitman

IT WAS PAST 11 PM WHEN WE DISEMBARKED from the Vulcania. Our cousin Bertha was supposed to meet us. We worried that we would miss her among the masses of people waiting to greet the arriving passengers. Thankfully, it didn't take us very long to find her. Bertha was almost 20 years older than Hermine, and married. Tall and slender, she was wearing a long fur coat, with red lipstick that matched her pants and high heels. How could we miss her? She looked glamorous, and acted like a movie star. The pants and lipstick suggested something else though, especially in light of our puritanical upbringing. In reality, she was just a seamstress. I had never seen a woman wear pants, and to me she looked ridiculous.

Bertha had been in America since 1915, but somehow she recognized Hermine and Marie immediately. In heavily accented English she quickly hailed a cab. As soon as the driver closed the trunk on our few belongings, we were on our way to Aunt Jenny, the widow of our father's brother Joachim. He had died in 1931 but not before Americanizing his name to Henry. Bertha had lived with our aunt and uncle for several years after she came to America, so it was natural that she would take us to visit as soon as we arrived. I wiped the fog off the taxi's window to observe the cityscape. Despite the late hour, the city pulsed with activity. People, cars, and trucks moved through the city streets as though it were daytime. Horns honked, sirens blared. Outlined by the lights shining from their windows, I was able to make out the varied forms of the buildings from a distance. Driving past them, and craning my neck to see, I could make out lights ascending high into the sky.

I had dreamt of America ever since Uncle Jónás visited us in Europe when I was little. I truly believed that the sidewalks would be paved with gold. Stepping out of the cab in front of my aunt's house in Rosedale, Queens, I was disappointed to find that they weren't.

Bertha escorted us inside where our Aunt was waiting. "Dragaaim!" Dear ones! She hugged each of us. "Come in, come in! Welcome, welcome to America!" Aunt Jenny, born in Pennsylvania, was in her sixties, with gray and thinning hair. She spoke a hodgepodge of Yiddish and German, and a smattering of Hungarian learned, I suppose, from her parents and our uncle. Regardless of the language she used, her words were infused with a heavy American accent. She greeted us as though she had known us all her life.

We walked into the main room from the foyer. Beautiful paintings adorned the walls and the sweet smell of fresh flowers wafted through the air. The floors had Oriental rugs upon them and hanging along the walls, from ceiling to floor, were long, elaborately embroidered draperies. To one side, there was a staircase leading up to a balcony that overlooked the entire room. Along one wall was a great wooden cabinet with glass doors and antique brass mullions. Inside was a varied collection of silver Judaica that included a Hannukah menorah, a kiddish cup for the Sabbath, a laver for ceremonial hand washing, and a large Passover plate, along with other fancy serving dishes. On a round marble table in the corner was an electric lamp with a broad silk shade, tassels dangling about its edge. A display of ceramic knickknacks and family photographs, including one of our uncle, were arranged neatly around the lamp.

"Children, I have hundreds of questions to ask...you must tell me everything, but first go upstairs and bathe yourselves. You are filthy." We had showered on the Vulcania and were not in the habit of bathing daily. After all, bathing at home was not easy, as our village didn't have running water! However, we were too tired to feel embarrassed or to argue, and we dutifully followed her pantomimed instructions. Aunt Jenny pressed a button on the wall, turning on lights that illuminated a sink, a sliding glass door opposite it, and at the far end of the bathroom, a toilet. She pushed open the sliding glass door to reveal a bathtub, and turned the knobs that protruded from the wall to demonstrate how we were to operate the shower. We bathed, each in our turn, and dressed in the same clothing that we had just removed.

Our aunt had food ready for us to eat, but, true to her earlier statement, she did have hundreds of questions to ask us. "How is your father? Your brother? His children? Your grandparents? How was the growing season? Was the winter cold? How many animals were born? Is the government taxing you as much? Did the tobacco grow well? Who tends the animals? Who does the cooking?"

While politely answering her questions, we ate slowly as the food quickly cooled. Disregarding our readily apparent exhaustion, her incessant questioning continued until 4 o'clock in the morning. I kept asking myself irritably, "Doesn't she realize how tired we are?" However, Aunt Jenny knew that our time together was limited. Finally, she excused us and allowed us to retire. "Enough for tonight, go to bed," she said, and without any hesitation or argument, we did as she bade.

Aunt Jenny was an early riser and she expected us to be up early too. After she woke us, we dressed, said our morning prayers, and went downstairs for breakfast. Aunt Jenny, Bertha, and her husband Maurice Weingarten were waiting for us. Bertha, and Mannie as she called him, had been married for many years, but they didn't have any children. Mannie made his living manufacturing and selling fur coats. He was short, clean shaven, and a little bit chubby. He wore a suit, with a white shirt and tie, no hat and no tzizit (the fringes on the small prayer shawl worn by observant Jewish men under their shirts). Clearly, he was not religious. He was a quiet man and left it to Bertha to monopolize the conversation.

"This morning we received a telegram from your brother Dezső and a special delivery, too. He has purchased train tickets for you." Bertha handed us the tickets. "You will leave for Ohio in the evening. Your brother and Uncle Jónás are expecting you." Bertha excitedly added, "But before you leave, you have to see New York! One day is not nearly enough, but we'll squeeze in what we can!"

Quickly finishing our breakfast, we hurried out to Mannie's car for a whirlwind tour of Manhattan. If I thought the city was bustling at night, I was mistaken. During the daytime, it seemed as if all of mankind had converged onto one small island, each individual joining his fellow in a throng, crowding the sidewalk like an army of ants. Never before had I seen such a congregation of humanity in one area. Here were Chinese, Negroes, and Jews, rich and poor, businessmen and beggers, all mixing together as though the messiah had come while we were asleep and had proclaimed peace throughout all the land.

As we drove alongside the soaring buildings, their spires vanished into the blue sky. As amazing as the skyscrapers were, they all paled in comparison with the Statue of Liberty. The day before, from the deck of the Vulcania, the darkness of the evening concealed her beautiful face, the flowing robes, and her outstretched arm which bore her shining beacon. Now, her torch glistened in the golden light of the setting sun. Her gift, freedom to those yearning to be free, imprinted itself upon our souls on this, our first full day in America. I was in love with Lady Liberty and in love with America. It was February 22, George Washington's birthday.

Evening came quickly as Bertha and Mannie whisked us all about Manhattan. Our last stop that day was Pennsylvania Station, where we were to meet the train that would take us west to Ohio. The four of us entered the cavernous station, while Mannie stayed at the wheel and Bertha searched for someone to help us with the trunks. There were no guards inside, nor any passport control to pass through. Hanging from the arched ceiling that towered above were ornate chandeliers. Around us, masses of people were walking to and fro, each rushing to their destination. We found our track. Bertha seized the arm of a pullman porter and put him to our service. He quickly loaded our trunks from the car outside and accompanied us to the waiting train.

We hugged and said our goodbyes. Then, as an afterthought, Bertha reached into her purse. "Here, you might need this" and she handed each of us a one dollar bill. This, combined with a dime that Mr. Kis, a neighbor in Czechoslovakia had given me to use "when you get to America," was all the money I had.

Chapter 8

WE FOUND OUR COACH AND SETTLED DOWN in seats that faced each other for the overnight trip to Union Station in Columbus, Ohio. The train's bell rang out rhythmically, its pleasant clang echoing through the car's open door. As the train began to move, small signal lights passed outside the window and I realized that I was facing the rear of the train. The train accelerated and my ears started to pressurize. Swallowing relieved the pressure. Suddenly, with a great whoosh, the train exited the underground tunnel. I swallowed again. The train raced along the tracks, faster and faster. The city's bright lights grew fainter as the train sped westward. I strained to see the Statue of Liberty's lighted torch, uncertain if I actually saw it, but convincing myself that I had. I leaned my head against the window and felt ready to sleep. As my eyes began to shut, the conductor came through the car to check our tickets. Silently, he took the tickets from Hermine's hand, punched a hole in them, and attached them to the top of her seat. That was all. There was no questioning, no demands to show identification documents. He moved on, quietly marking everyone's ticket, and leaving us to our thoughts and dreams. The dull, repetitive clickety clack of the train's wheels lulled me into a deep sleep. I dreamt of my parents and of the last time I saw my mother alive. I was only 11.

"Apa, how long will you be gone with Mother?"

"Only a few days..."

"But I want to come too!"

"No, Ignac. The trip is too long, your mother is not well, and the doctor's office is no place for you. Be a good boy and don't argue." *My father finished tying the knot in his tie. It was crooked. I didn't insist further. I had learned my lesson when my mother first started getting sick. I was three or four years old and I pleaded and cried hysterically that they take me with*

them to the doctor. They finally agreed. My brother Lajos brought out a wooden basket with a rope attached to it and placed the basket behind the carriage. I was so happy when I climbed into that basket and the horse began to pull both the carriage and the basket with me inside it. My joy turned to unbridled disappointment when Lajos let go of the rope and the basket slid to a halt. I could only stand in the middle of the road, warm tears streaming down my face, as the wagon became smaller and smaller in the distance. Mrs. Gerenyi, our neighbor from across the street, came out to comfort me. Now, almost eleven, I acquiesced to stay home.

My mother, usually a strong woman, was very weak now. She wore a solid gray dress, with a collar at the neck that was buttoned closed, and her hair was tucked neatly under her sheitel, a wig worn by married religious women to cover their hair. She slipped her stockinged feet into her plain black shoes and, being an avid reader, tucked a newspaper under her arm.

My father walked across the dirt floor, still adjusting his tie. He took his vest off the back of a chair and, after putting it on, he reached for his jacket and hat. My father's beard had already begun to turn gray but because of his slight frame, he still seemed young. His bright blue eyes always twinkled beneath the oval-rimmed frame of his glasses. Taking his pocket watch out from his vest, he turned to my mother. "Lena, it's time. Let's go."

My father held my mother's elbow and helped her out of the front door to the waiting carriage. The sweet smell of blossoming flowers from the front garden filled the warm summer air. I stood in the doorway, my head leaning on the doorjamb. I watched as my father helped my mother climb into the carriage. He followed in after her. The horse whinnied as Lajos raised the reins. The black, covered carriage gently rolled forward. They were going to a doctor in Sátoraljaújhely, just across the border in Hungary. They had already seen a specialist in Budapest and at that time they were told that my mother would need surgery to remove the growth. My parents hesitated to agree to the surgery because they were afraid my mother wouldn't survive. Now, as her condition worsened, they reconsidered their earlier decision.

The doctor was expecting them. It was not the first time that he had examined Lena Gluck because she had been ill for so long. After his cursory examination, he gravely said, "I'm sorry, but there is nothing that can be done now. The growth is larger than it was before. Its location makes removing it impossible. If you had come back sooner, perhaps. I'm sorry."

Lena and Jeremias held hands in the taxi as it slowly made its way back to the border. The heat of the summer's day was magnified inside the dark car and the two were exhausted from the long journey and the devastating news. Lena felt faint.

"Driver, turn around! Go back to the hospital!" Jeremias cried out. The driver raced back to the hospital. After examining his patient again, the doctor spoke to Jeremias, privately.

"I'm not even certain that she will be able to survive the trip back."

"There must be something that you can do so she can at least make it home alive. Our children are anxiously awaiting our return!"

"Perhaps there is...but my help will be expensive."

"Yes, yes whatever you ask."

"I will order a car and travel with you. I will give her an injection of medication so that she can rest on the journey. Heaven forbid, in the worst case we will tell the border patrol that she is sleeping, otherwise, you will not be allowed to cross back into Czechoslovakia. That must be our plan." The doctor hurried out with Jeremias and Lena. He carried with him his black medical bag.

The car that the doctor had ordered quickly arrived. The doctor climbed in with my father and mother. The journey to the border was only a few minutes. As the car approached the border, Jeremias turned to his wife. Her eyes were closed, as if asleep and her head cocked to one side, resting on the window.

"Lena?" he questioned. There was no response. He gently stroked his wife's face. Again, there was no response. The

doctor took her pulse. There was none. They were at the border.

"Passports!" asked the border patrol.

My father handed the border patrol the passport for himself and my mother. The doctor did the same.

"Please wake your wife for identification!" ordered the border patrol.

"I am her doctor, from Sátoraljaújhely. Mrs. Gluck is my patient. She is resting." He tapped his hand on his medical bag.

"Very well. You may continue. Good afternoon!" The car crossed the border and my father returned home to Polyán with my mother's body.

We buried her the same day, August 2, 1932. The entire town of Lelesz, came to the funeral. Of course, Uncle Márton was there, too. We walked from the house to the cemetery, a distance of about two miles. My brother Dezső was one of the pallbearers. He carried the coffin on his shoulder. When anyone tried to take his place, he steadfastly refused.

My mother, sitting with some of her flowers.

"Pittsburgh, Pittsburgh next." I shifted in my seat. Opening my eyes momentarily, I saw only darkness outside the train. I closed them again. The train's bell rang out. The cold air rushed into the coach as a few passengers gathered their belongings and stepped out of the train. Others quickly took their places. The doors closed, the conductor silently made his rounds, and the train rolled onward towards Columbus. I glanced at my watch. It was 2:30 AM. I rested my head again against the cold window.

"Good morning! Columbus, next stop. All passengers! This is the train to Columbus, Ohio. Columbus next!" I turned in my seat, not yet ready to allow my nostalgia to fade away so quickly. The conductor opened the door between the cars. The chilly winter air blew in and filled the car. I shivered. The chill reminded me of how I felt during an illness I had as a child. I allowed the memory of my father to linger. I drifted off to sleep again.

My father pulled the covers up over my shoulders. I still had a low fever, but was beginning to feel stronger. It had already been three weeks since the doctor ordered me quarantined by myself in the new house. Nobody lived there yet. My mother was to stay in the old house anyway. She was too weak. My father didn't want to risk spreading the infection to her or to the people that worked for us. The symptoms were unmistakable. Chicken Pox. My father was the only person the doctor permitted to see me. Each day, when he brought me food, he would also sit with me for a little while. After I ate what little I could hold down, I often drifted to sleep while he sat beside me rubbing my back and humming softly. Days had passed in this way, and weeks too.

After four lonely, solitary weeks, the doctor permitted me to return to my bed in the old house. A large truck stopped in front of the house as soon as I left. My father had hired men to fumigate the house and burn the clothing I had worn while sick. I watched them work from the window.

Herman tapped my shoulder, startling me. The train had stopped. I looked out of the window only to confirm what I suspected. Union Station, Columbus, Ohio. The four of us, Hermine, Marie, Herman, and I stepped down from the coach. A black man dressed sharply in a porter's uniform stood before us. He wore a red cap. "This way for yo' baggage, ma'am!" he said to Hermine. He found our bags in no time, put them on a dolly, and led us up a long flight of stairs into the main arrivals room of the station. The stairs were white marble, grayed and worn in the centers with the passage of time and thousands of feet.

As we stepped off the last steps that had led us up from the platforms below, there was on either side of us a low knee-wall, also from marble. On the other side of each knee-wall were large, ornately carved, wooden benches. At the end of the knee-wall, stood Dezső our brother, scanning the crowd of people that had already exited. As soon as our eyes met, his voice boomed out above the din, "Szervusz! Szervusz! Ignac!" Welcome! Welcome!

If Bertha had looked like a movie star in New York, Dezső could have easily passed for her leading man. He was tall and although slender, his face was rounder than mine. His bright blue eyes twinkled with excitement and his smile accentuated his deep dimples and the unmistakable cleft in his chin. He wore a dark gray suit, a silk tie, wing tipped shoes, and a hat. Dezső was not the oldest sibling, but his personality and charisma demanded your attention and respect. His way was right, and if you disagreed, you were both wrong and disrespectful. He quickly stepped away from Uncle Jónás and Cousin Arthur, his arms outstretched, ready to embrace each of us. His hug expressed what words could not: love, anxiety, relief, home. He made such a scene that I'm sure passers-by must have looked on and understood that we really had arrived from half a world away! We respectfully greeted our elderly Uncle and cousin, who, although overjoyed at our arrival, could in no way match the reception that Dezső had just given us.

Together we travelled to 110 West Park Avenue, a small two-story building owned by Uncle Jónás. On the first floor was Kroger's Grocery Store. Arthur led us up to the second floor where there was a furnished apartment with rooms in the front and back, a salon, a bathroom, and a kitchen. These plainly furnished rooms would be where we'd live temporarily, until we could find something larger. Hermine and Marie placed their jackets in the front room. Herman and I would share the rear one.

Uncle Jónás made it a point to explain that he would help us until we found jobs. Opening bank accounts for us, he emphasized that once we started making money, we were to put some aside in the bank. He insisted that although it might seem like we didn't have enough money, we must learn to save anyway. Even if it was just a deposit of $0.50 each time, it would accumulate and grow. This was how we'd learn to manage our money. He made sure we all understood his next point. "Save your earnings, because when you need money, no one will give it to you!" We learned that lesson very quickly. He instructed us to write down all of our expenses and he let us know that we were also to pay him $8 a month rent for our apartment.

Combined with pangs of hunger, my curiosity got the best of me. I excused myself and went downstairs to Kroger's. I had in my pocket the American dime that my neighbor Mr. Kis had given me in Czechoslovakia. "Was it real?" I wondered to myself. I brought a loaf of bread to the counter and handed the dime to the clerk. He took it, placed it in the cash register, and handed me two pennies change!

Dezső in America, circa 1940

Opposite page: Uncle Jónás (Julius) standing outside on the porch.

Chapter 9

ON OUR SECOND DAY IN OHIO, Arthur was excited to show Columbus to Herman and me. He tried to give us a grand tour, but it was all such a blur as there was so much to take in. However, Arthur stopped the car in front of Lázárus' Department Store.[17] "This man Lázárus came to America with nothing," he told us. "He started selling on the street from a pushcart and look, look at what he has accomplished!" In front of us stood a huge building that took up an entire city block. "Don't be discouraged! At first it will be difficult for you, but here in America, you can also succeed!"

F & R Lázárus and Company, Downtown Columbus, Ohio

---

[17] Simon Lazarus (1808–1877) opened a one-room men's clothing store in downtown Columbus in 1851. By 1870, the family business expanded to include ready-made men's civilian clothing and eventually a complete line of merchandise. It was one of the four founding members of Federated Department Stores in 1929.

Arthur knew this first-hand. His father, Uncle Jónás, was a successful real estate entrepreneur, and he himself was a successful industrialist. He owned a factory that manufactured heavy equipment for the coal mining industry. His factory produced all the tools needed to bring the coal from the mine to the point of sale: crushers, scales, conveyor belts, and more. He set the highest standards for himself and would arrive at work at five a.m. every morning. He lived only a few blocks away from Ohio State University, his alma mater, and because of his position in the business society of Columbus, he associated with many professors at the university, particularly in the Department of Philosophy, from which he had received his degree.

In order to succeed myself, however, I needed to do something, and quickly. We all did. After all, our uncle wanted his rent and we needed to buy food. With his help, we looked for employment where we could speak Yiddish. Uncle Jónás brought a nice woman over to meet Hermine. She was a working mother, and she needed help around her home. Our Uncle reassured her that Hermine was responsible and had experience. They agreed to give it a try and Hermine started to work as a nanny taking care of her children and cleaning her house.

Since Marie still felt weak from the journey, our Uncle thought that she needed different work. Marie knew how to make dresses, after all she made her own clothing in Europe, so he found her a job in a dry cleaners doing alterations. She took a bus to work five days a week, nine hours a day, but the work was easy and she enjoyed it even though the owners spoke to her only in English. Luckily, she knew how to sew and was a quick learner. Herman went to work in a machine shop in Arthur's factory.

As for me, my Uncle found a job cleaning newspaper debris from the floor at a newspaper factory. My employment there

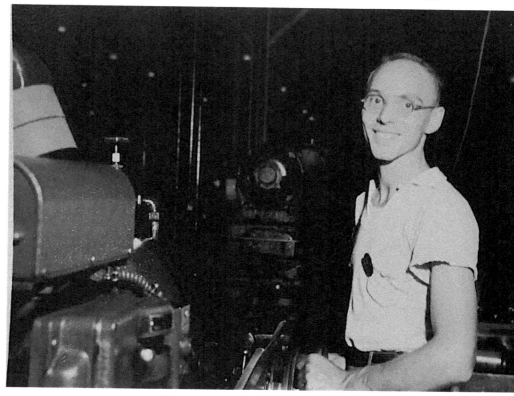

Herman at work in the machine shop.

lasted just one day. When I arrived to his house at the end of that first day, my Uncle saw that I was covered from head to toe with dust and said, "Ignac, this job is not for you. We'll have to find another one!" It wasn't long after that he did, this time at the Frey-Yankin Paint Company. Old Mr. Yankin himself met me that first evening. I arrived at five p.m., and he showed me around the huge factory building and the paint store next door. Speaking in Yiddish, he explained that I was to be the night watchman. My duties also were to clean up the offices and load the boilers with coal, as necessary. He gave me a telephone number that I was to call if anything should happen, and then he left.

Well, later that evening a truck drove into the driveway. The driver stepped out of the cab, approached the main door, and knocked. I went over to the door to see who it was, but I didn't want to open it since nobody had told me to expect a delivery. Moreover, I didn't understand a word that the driver was shouting to me through the glass. I motioned to him that I would make a telephone call. I went over to the desk and dialed the number that Mr. Yankin had given me. "Mr. Yankin?"

"Yes, this is his son" replied the voice at the other end.

"This is Ignac, the night watchman. There is a man here that wants to come in, but I don't understand anything else that he's saying."

"Yes, yes. We are expecting a delivery. Let him in and bring him to the telephone. If it isn't our deliveryman, then I'll call the police!" So I went over and opened the door. I waved the man into the office and gave him the telephone. After a moment, he handed the phone back to me and Mr. Yankin's son explained that everything was okay. The man finished his delivery, and I went back to my cleaning. I didn't leave until 8:30 the next morning.

To make life a little easier, my uncle bought me a bicycle. One of the police stations sold bicycles that were unclaimed after they had been stolen and subsequently recovered. It cost just a couple of dollars. You get what you pay for though, because it was old, rusty, and the chain often fell off. As soon as Dezső saw it, he insisted that I buy a new bicycle and I did, on credit. I quickly learned the correct hand signals and from then on, I used the new bicycle every day to commute back and forth through the heavy traffic to my job at Fry-Yankin. I never told my Uncle about the new bicycle, though. He was a frugal man and would have been upset to learn that not only was the old bicycle that he had bought sitting unused, but that I spent money I didn't have to buy a new one. Earning only 15 cents an hour, it took me seven months to pay off the bicycle.

On my prize winning bicycle decorated with paper flowers hand made by Marie.
Columbus, Ohio

Chapter 10

"There is no such thing as a hyphenated American who is a good American. The only man who is a good American is the man who is an American and nothing else." - Theodore Roosevelt

As soon as we arrived in Columbus we knew we had to learn English quickly. There was a Jewish organization nearby that offered night classes, and we registered and went to study. For me, I couldn't learn English quickly enough. One morning, I went to the grocery store to buy some bread, butter, and milk. With my limited knowledge of English, I had to point to what I wanted to buy. It was easy to get the bread since it was there on the counter. However, when it came time to buy the butter and milk, I was stumped. When the clerk asked "What else?" I was so focused on *how* to pronounce them, that the words I had been practicing a moment earlier just vanished. I walked away from the counter as though I knew exactly what I else I needed to buy, but since I didn't know where the milk and butter were kept, I decided to pick random items up, look at them, and try to decipher their contents. The other customers made me feel self-conscious, so I figured I would wait until they all just left. Finally, I'd waited so long that I just didn't care anymore, and approached the clerk, using my hands in a kind of sign language. With one finger representing a knife, I spread imaginary butter on the outstretched palm of my other hand, hoping he'd understand I wanted butter; he brought me jelly instead. I took it from him just to be polite. For milk, I pretended to pour into an imaginary glass. It didn't work. I began speaking to him in different languages, hoping he would understand one of them. This didn't work either, because he became angry. Perhaps he thought I was cursing him. Finally after drawing a picture of a cow, I got a tin of canned milk. I probably should have mooed at him instead.

AND SPEAKING OF refugees, Mrs. Levinger, I had the pleasure the other day of talking to two of them that managed to get out of Czechoslovakia after its capitulation to Germany.

They were Herman and Mary Gluck and they both live at 175½ W. Second-av with a brother, Irving, 18, and a sister, Hermine, 27, who left with them.

The Glucks have only been here a few months but already they can talk English well enough to make you understand and they can grasp what you say.

It is hard to get a story from them but it seems that with money they obtained from their 65-year-old father they managed to go over the border into Italy and take a boat from there for this country.

Herman is working for a scales manufactuirng company and taking care of his sister, Mary. A brother, David, was already here and it was a happy reunion for the little family.

Can you imagine, Mrs. Levinger, what America means to these refugees from Hitler's hate? We ought to be happy to live in a land which can receive these unfortunate people with open arms and say to them: "Here you are in a free country. Remain in peace."

An article about us in the local newspaper, "The Columbus Citizen," 1940

Another funny thing happened when I tried my luck eating in a restaurant. When I walked in, I sat at an empty table in the corner. The waiter came over and asked me something that I didn't understand but presumed it to be a question. I took my chances and answered "Yes." He brought a menu. I looked at it as if I knew how to read it. I spent a good half hour "reading" it for practice, much to the consternation of the waiter. Finally, I said the word five, pointing to the item number on the menu. Again, he asked me something, which again I didn't understand, and I answered "Yes." This time I wasn't so lucky because he brought me five hamburgers. Not wanting to offend anyone, I ate them all. People stared as though they had never seen someone eat a hamburger before.

After I finished, I went over to the cashier to pay. I knew from the menu that item number five cost twenty-five cents, so I gave him a quarter. The cashier then started speaking to me. I nodded as though I understood every word, but I didn't. His temper rose, and he pointed to item number five on the menu. I nodded in agreement, "Yes." However, he wasn't satisfied. He then pulled out a pencil and wrote out one - twenty five cents, two- twenty five cents, etc. Then I understood what he was talking about. I took out five dollars and paid him. He said, "thank you." Not knowing the expression, "You're welcome," I also said, "Thank you," as I carefully counted my change.

I wanted to learn how to speak English as well as an American and the night classes lasted only a short time. So by September, I decided to register at Everett Junior High School even though I had already finished high school in Czechoslovakia. My uncle introduced me to Mrs. Higgins, the English teacher.

"What is his educational background?" she asked. He turned to me and asked in Hungarian, for he himself did not know the answer. Before I began to answer him, the earliest memories of my education flashed before me in my mind's eye. Our daily routine was etched into my soul.

"Ignac bácsi, it's time to get up," my father would say softly. I'd open my eyes and sit up slightly in bed, the straw underneath the canvas covering crinkling beneath my shifting body. In winter, the cold chill would come through the straw from the dirt floor, even though there was a sheet over the canvas. I'd begin to recite in Hebrew: "Modeh ani lifanecha melech chai v'kayam shehechezarta bi nishmahsi b'chemlah, rabah emunasecha" which meant "I thank you, living and eternal King, for You have mercifully restored my soul within me; Your faithfulness is great." I continued: "Rayshees chamah yeeras adonay sayhel tov l-hol oysayhem t-heelaso omedes l-ad." That is, "The beginning of wisdom is the fear of G-d - all who fulfill his commandments gain good understanding; His praise is everlasting."

The last embers would still burn a dull red inside the cast iron stove that stood on the left side of our front door. At night we often sat in front of the stove to watch the flames dance in the darkness before going to bed. What little heat the stove provided during the night did nothing to remove the chill from the room in the morning. The beds were on the other side of the door, filling the right side of the room. My bed was in front of the window that faced the street. I'd stand at the side of my bed and take off my gatkes, the long johns that I had slept in, pull on my worn pants, and put on my shirt over my tzitztis, the ritual prayer shawl, tucking its fringes into my pants. After, I'd pull my sweater over my head and then finally, put on a suit jacket. While I slept, I kept my yarmulke on my head. Once dressed, I'd look around nervously, checking to see if the melamed, our teacher from the city of Munkacs, was ready to begin the morning prayers. He usually wasn't. I'd grab the bucket I had used as my toilet during the night and quickly bring it outside. I'd walk out the front door, turn right, walk past the cellar where we stored all of our produce, and continue straight to the end of the house. There, behind the horses' stables, was a pile of straw, which was where we dumped the horse manure and dirty straw from the barn. I dumped the bucket there as well.

On one side of the straw pile, was the outhouse. It was a mud brick building with a toilet inside. The hole beneath the toilet needed to be cleaned out at least once a year. It was freezing inside and everyone did their business quickly, using corn husks or newspapers as our toilet paper. I'd run back into the house and wash my hands in a portable basin. In it was water that my sisters had drawn from the well earlier that morning. As I poured the water over one hand and then the other, I'd say the blessing for washing the hands. Then I'd brush my teeth with my fingers, back and forth, using a homemade toothpaste concoction.

My sisters, my brothers Lajos, Dezső, and Herman, as well as our parents shared the great room with me, but it wasn't just our bedroom; it was also our kitchen. Lajos would have already left to care for the animals and then to fish in the Latorica River, and Dezső, who had no interest in farming whatsoever, would be out selling household items of some kind or another door to door in neighboring villages. My sisters Hermine and Marie would be busy preparing breakfast: fresh milk from our cows, eggs from our chickens, slices of bread cut from huge loaves baked with their own hands made from wheat grown in our own fields, baciturk, a homegrown squash, and homemade cheese and butter. Girls were not required to daven, or pray, like the boys. Herman and I would hurry to the other side of the room to wait for the teacher. He slept in a small room off of the kitchen. He was hired by the three Jewish families in the town to teach the boys.

Tall and thin, he dressed entirely in a dark black suit, making him appear even thinner. Unshaven but not with a thick beard, he'd come out into the kitchen, still adjusting his black hat upon his head. Immediately, Herman and I would stand respectfully as he approached the table. He'd motion to us to sit. We would. Then, he'd begin the morning prayer by saying one phrase, baruch ata adonay, G-d, you are the source of all *blessing, and then pointed his finger at me to continue reading. I would. Then he'd point to Herman. "Translate into Yiddish!" he'd order. Herman found it easier to remember the meaning of the Hebrew words by translating them into Hungarian. He had written his translations into the prayer book above the words that he didn't understand, which angered the teacher. He'd make Herman put his fingers together, all pointing straight up, and then he'd take a ruler and whack the tips of Herman's fingers. Herman would silence any cry and translate, as best as he could, into Yiddish.*

All this happened unbeknownst to my father. He'd stand off in the corner, a short distance from us, entirely engrossed in his morning prayers. He'd cover his head with a large tallis. Protruding from under his tallis, would be the leather box of the head tefillin, sitting on his forehead. The box of the arm tefillin couldn't be seen since it faced his heart, but the seven wrappings of the black leather strap around his left forearm were visible. The strap continued around his hand three more times, and then finally ended around his middle finger. The leather boxes of the tefillin contained excerpts from the Torah commanding a Jew to teach his children.

When we had finished reciting and translating the morning prayers, we'd hurry to eat our breakfast. We sat around a large and very old wooden table that was so old it probably belonged to my grandmother. Once we had finished, Herman and I would gather our school books, remove our yarmulkes and start for the front door.

"Wait!" Hermine would call. "Don't forget the rest of your breakfast!" She'd give each of us two hot potatoes, one for each hand, to keep us warm while we walked to school. We would eat them only after we arrived. She and Marie would hurriedly put their coats on and gather their books as well. After all, they had to go to school, too! And then we'd all walk together to the Catholic school.

This would happen daily. I was six years old. Herman was nine.

The Catholic school consisted of one large room with children assigned to classes from kindergarten to eighth grade. Our teacher was Filip Miklós. His father had also been a teacher there. Once when I was very small, even before I was old enough to attend school, my sisters took me with them to visit their classroom. The elder Mr. Miklós picked me up and put me on top of the credenza. He knew our family and liked us well enough. His son Filip went away to college and upon graduating, he returned to our village and replaced his father as the teacher.

All of the children would enter the classroom at the same time. In the front of the classroom was a wooden cross. Affixed to it was a man, their god, and below it the letters INRE. I took my seat in the third row. I was in first grade. Again, there were morning prayers to be said, but we Jews did not participate. "Put your hands flat upon your desks!" motioned our teacher to us. We did as we were told. Meanwhile, the other children put the palms of their hands together, their fingers pointing upwards to heaven. They began to recite the Lord's Prayer, in Hungarian. "Ishten ag zegbe..." Our Father, who art in heaven, Hallowed be thy Name... When they had finished their prayer, they would have a short lesson and discussion about Catholicism and then everybody went about their own work, whether reading or writing, history or math, each class with its own assignment. In this way, only one class would talk with the teacher at any given time.

The punishment for talking out of turn was the same as Herman had received at home for writing in the prayerbook. Fingers up, and a good hard whack on the tips of the fingers with a flat board. It was very painful. Herman liked to talk with his friends and got punished often, so I quickly learned the consequences of speaking out of turn! Upon graduating from first grade we recited this poem:

"My teacher loves me because I answer the question only if I am asked."

The Catholic School. Marie is seated 2nd row, 3rd from left. Herman is standing, 3rd row 2nd from left. Hermine is seated 3rd row, 5th from right. Next to her is Filip Miklós, our teacher and Home Guard Commander.

Although my sisters went to the Catholic school until the eighth grade, I went only through first grade. At its conclusion, Herman and I were transferred to the Reformatus school. Apparently, the Catholic school needed the space for other students. The Reformatus school was very different from the Catholic school. The Church's sanctuary and its single classroom were very simple and plain. Their walls were not adorned with pictures of their saints and most importantly, there was no crucifix to be found anywhere. Its similarity to the synagogue made it completely inoffensive to us. We felt so comfortable there that we would even attend lectures by guest speakers inside the sanctuary with the rest of the community.

Our teacher, Mr. Kövendi, was heavy set and very strict. His punishment for talking out of turn was, like at the Catholic school, a whack on the fingertips with a flat board. However, he also had a switch, a small bendable twig that he would use to flog anyone for this reason or that. He would hit children over the head, the back, the arms, anyplace, like a crazy man. Poor Herman and his friends would get beaten for talking. Herman hated him, but nothing could be done because it was common for a teacher to behave that way, and everyone just accepted it. Despite this, he liked me and our family very much.

When I was 9 years old, my brother Dezső was in business selling stove heaters (one of many businesses that he would try!) The stove heater was just a simple metal plate. It could be heated in the stove while the wood was burning, and after the fire died out, it would stay in the stove to keep it warm longer. Dezső suggested I show one to the teacher. He liked it so much, and perhaps because his daughter liked me quite a bit too, he bought it from me. I liked his daughter, but she was a little older than I, and she wasn't Jewish, so there was nothing more to it.

On the right side of the classroom, by the doorway, were maps of the world hanging upon the wall. One lesson that we reviewed often was history. "Look at Czechoslovakia on the map, children." He pointed with his fat finger. "Do you see this area?" he said, gesturing to a point outside the borders that he had just outlined. "This land is considered to be part of Hungary and this, over here, is considered to part of Romania." He paused briefly, then added ominously, "Don't be fooled, these lands, including our own village, all used to be part of Hungary, and one day they will be again."

We would walk home at noon for lunch and then return to school from 1 pm until it ended at 5 pm. After the school day ended at the Reformatus school, we would go home and eat something, usually potato soup and bread, or noodles and lekvar (prune butter) and then we would go to study with the melamed until late in the evening. Herman and I and the two Lefkovics boys, our neighbors, would meet either in our house or theirs. It all depended on which family was hosting the melamed. Our families took turns. The Lefkovics family lived about a dozen houses down the road on the way to Lelesz. Since it was already evening, we would study by candlelight or by oil lamp. We interpreted every week's Torah portion from Hebrew into Yiddish and Hungarian. On the side of the book was Rashi's commentary. We had to translate and interpret that as well, in order to understand what we were reading in the Torah portion. We all sat together as we studied. We did this every day, except Shabbos, of course, and Thursday, which was examination day. When we finished the lessons, we would walk home in the darkness and go to bed.

When I was about 12 years old, my father sent me to the public high school in Lelesz. Herman, already 14, had no interest in continuing school so he stayed at home to help out on the farm. He liked being outdoors and preferred the life of a farmer. Since I was the youngest, my father felt that I must get as much education as possible. My maternal grandparents, Joseph and Chaya Schwartz, lived in Lelesz and I went to live with them in their small house. When I was little I would ride my bicycle and bring them tobacco, potatoes, squash, nuts, and corn from our farm. Sometimes my father would sit on the handlebars while I peddled to visit them! I slept on a small sofa in the kitchen/living room/bedroom. They had an outhouse in the yard and located some distance down a hill was a well. The water needed to be pumped by hand and carried back to the house. During the day I went to the high school and afterwards, in the afternoons, to the heder, the Hebrew school that was held in a private home with a private tutor. My grandmother saw to it that I ate well. My favorite was her cornbread, but whatever she made was always delicious. My grandfather saw to it that I studied. During the holidays, I went with them to the synagogue. They were very strict about observing Jewish law. My grandmother's sister was even married to a rabbi in Munkacs. The whole family from Polyán would come to Lelesz for the holidays. The synagogue was quite large with more than 500 people attending holiday services. My grandfather was the hazzan, the respected prayer leader. Their home was mine until the school year ended and only then did I return home to Polyán. I lived with them for four years.

During the fourth and last year, the teachers encouraged us to continue studying at the Polgári in Király Helmec. The Polgári was a school in between high school and college. I, and many others, decided to go. However, in order to be accepted to the Polgári, I needed to actually live in Helmec. Thankfully, my brother Lajos' wife Etelka came from Helmec, and her family still lived there. At first I stayed in the Klein household and became better acquainted with Etelka's brother Ignac, and her sisters Manci and Rozsi. However, my brother Dezső soon rented a storefront in Helmec and opened a small store selling items for the home, and I went to stay with him. In the front of the store he displayed the items for sale in large cabinets, and in the back of the store, behind a curtain draped from one wall to the other, was a narrow bed that we shared. In order to have what to eat, and to not be an imposition upon my brother, I also went to study at the Yeshiva. The large Jewish population of Helmec opened their homes to us and provided meals for two or three students at a time.

Each day I would go to the Yeshiva and study until late in the evening. The Yeshiva was located in a large, two story building and there were at least 30 students that studied there. Every Thursday we were tested. My Uncle Márton was the "observer." He was, in my opinion, a brilliant man. His job was to make sure that the teachers were doing their job. He could quote whole sections of the Talmud from memory. He would ask each of us students to read from the Gemara (rabbinic commentaries on Jewish law) and translate, sentence by sentence, into Yiddish. Afterwards, he would ask questions to see if we understood what we had read. We knew there would be trouble if we didn't know our lessons. He would remind us to use high caliber language at all times and not to debase ourselves by speaking poorly like a peasant. "Only through language can you impress others that you have been properly educated."

Although I was hardly home, Dezső and I were very close. We spoke often at night and from him I learned the rudiments of business, or at least how he understood them.

"Ignac," he would say, "I need you to go to our Cousin Klein, he is expecting you. He will give you 50 kronin. As soon as you have it, bring it to Uncle Márton. I promised to pay him today for a loan I borrowed from him last week." That was Dezső, always borrowing so that he could pay off another debt.

A postcard advertising Dezső's home furnishing business.

Dezső standing outside his store in Helmec. I'm standing in the background.

*In the Polgári we studied everything, but I was most
interested in botany. Studying farming came easily to me, and I
had a beautiful, young teacher that first year, who explained
things so clearly. When to plant, how to plant, how to
recognize and identify good plants and bad. However, she
became ill and was replaced by another teacher that I did not
like as much. I suppose I had a crush on that first teacher
because botany became less interesting after she left. Although
she eventually returned, she was different, changed by her
illness perhaps. By the end of the year, I was glad to get out of
school.*

*As soon as the Hungarians returned in 1938 the government
changed and the Polgári was closed. I was forced to return
home to Polyán. However, I was still eager to continue my
education, so I made arrangements to meet with Mr. Kövendi,
my former teacher at the Reformatus school. Since I was now
"educated," he was very happy to meet with me and talk just
to pass the time.*

My daydream abruptly ended when my Uncle Jónás cleared
his throat and coughed on purpose. Somehow, I regained my
composure. Even though my uncle had just asked me how far I
had gotten in school, I must have stood there for a long
moment before answering. Finally, I explained to him that I
had finished high school and would have continued my studies
at the Polgári if not for the territorial dispute between
Hungary, Czechoslovakia, and Germany. He explained this to
Mrs. Higgins and she accepted me into her class in Everett
Junior High School in Columbus. I eagerly registered with my
new American name, Irving. Someone told me that I needed a
more American sounding name, so I searched for one that
began with the same letter as Ignac. Isaac, the English form of
my Hebrew name, would have worked, but it sounded too
Jewish.

Despite my new English name, I was still the only foreign
student in the class, and the only one that had to register as an

'alien.' Yet, I participated as best I could and whenever I understood the question, I answered it. Mrs. Higgins quickly realized my aptitude since, apart from my limited English and poor grades, I knew more than the other students in her class. I continued studying at Everett until the spring of 1941 and progressed quickly with my English.

My report card from Everett Junior High School

After two terms, Mrs. Higgins suggested that I register at the Ohio State University to learn English, and I did. The University gave me permission to attend workshops in the speech pathology and language department. Apparently there were so few foreigners registered at the University that I was a novelty of sorts. The language professionals and their students had new, modern equipment in the laboratory so that I could listen, using headphones, to their voices and learn how to enunciate the different sounds of the English language. They helped me tremendously, working tirelessly with me, even whispering the strange sounds of English in my ears so that I could repeat them and pronounce words properly. I made a commitment to myself then and there that I would speak English better than a native born American. One of the students, a young woman that tutored there, enjoyed helping me learn to speak better. "Irving," she told me, "you must practice reading out loud using texts that have the most beautiful language. Do you know the Lord's Prayer?" I did...in Hungarian, though! She read it for me in English:

Our Father, who art in heaven,
Hallowed be thy Name.
Thy kingdom come.
Thy will be done,
On earth as it is in heaven.
Give us this day our daily bread.
And forgive us our trespasses,
As we forgive those who trespass against us.
And lead us not into temptation,
But deliver us from evil.
For thine is the kingdom,
and the power, and the glory,
for ever and ever.
Amen.

I repeated the words slowly after her, mentally translating the English into Hungarian, as my tongue twisted to form the difficult sounds. As hard as I tried some words simply couldn't come out right. Hungarian has no equivalent sound for 'w' or 'v' and I constantly confused the two. For me, it was always, 'vatermelon', 'wanilla' and 'Thy vill be done!'

TRIPLICATE
(To be given to declarant)

No. **5812**

UNITED STATES OF AMERICA

DECLARATION OF INTENTION

(Invalid for all purposes seven years after the date hereof)

United States of America
Southern District of Ohio
ss:

In the United States District
Southern District of Ohio Court
of Held at Columbus, Ohio

I, **Irving Gluck**
now residing at **110 W. Park Ave., Columbus, Franklin, Ohio**
occupation **Factory hand**, aged **18** years, do declare on oath that my personal description is:
Sex **male**, color **white**, complexion **fair**, color of eyes **blue**
color of hair **sandy**, height **6** feet **—** inches; weight **152** pounds; visible distinctive marks
None.
race **Hebrew**; nationality **Czechoslovakia (now Hungary)**
I was born in **Bodrogmezo, Hungary** on **November 14,1921**
I am **not** married. The name of my wife or husband is
we were married on , at , she or he was
born at , on , entered the United States
at , on , for permanent residence therein, and now
resides at . I have **no** children, and the name, date and place of birth,
and place of residence of each of said children are as follows:

I have **not** heretofore made a declaration of intention: Number , or
at
my last foreign residence was **Bodrogmezo, Hungary**
I emigrated to the United States of America from **Naples, Italy**
my lawful entry for permanent residence in the United States was at **New York, N.Y.**
under the name of **Ignac Gluck**, on **Feb. 21,1940**
on the vessel **" Vulcania "**

I will, before being admitted to citizenship, renounce forever all allegiance and fidelity to any foreign prince, potentate, state,
or sovereignty, and particularly, by name, to the prince, potentate, state, or sovereignty of which I may be at the time of admission a citizen or subject; I am not an anarchist; I am not a polygamist nor a believer in the practice of polygamy; and it is my intention in good faith to become a citizen of the United States of America and to reside permanently therein; and I certify that the photograph affixed to the duplicate and triplicate hereof is a likeness of me.

I swear (affirm) that the statements I have made and the intentions I have expressed in this declaration of intention subscribed by me are true to the best of my knowledge and belief: So help me God.

Irving Gluck

Subscribed and sworn to before me in the form of oath shown above in the
office of the Clerk of said Court, at **Columbus, Ohio**
this **26th** day of **September**, anno Domini, 19 **40** Certification No. **9-25630** from the Commissioner of Immigration and Naturalization
showing the lawful entry of the declarant for permanent residence on the date
stated above, has been received by me. The photograph affixed to the duplicate
and triplicate hereof is a likeness of the declarant.

Harry F.Rabe
U. S.District Court.
By *Parker*, Deputy Clerk.

[SEAL]

Form 2209—L-A
U. S. DEPARTMENT OF LABOR
IMMIGRATION AND NATURALIZATION SERVICE

Nº 262302

Irving Gluck

My application for American citizenship, September 29, 1940

3500 Aliens Here To Be Registered

Begin Tomorrow; Hits All 14 or Older

The estimated 3500 aliens living in Columbus will participate in the nation-wide registration of all aliens, through local post offices,

Irving Gluck, 19, of 175½ Second-av, is shown above filling out his specimen form for registration at the South Side Settlement House where naturalization classes are held.

An article in 'The Columbus Citizen' that shows me filling out paperwork for the Alien Registration Act of 1940

Form AR-3   Registration Number   **1740240**

ALIEN REGISTRATION RECEIPT CARD

Irving Gluck
175½ W. 2nd Ave.
Columbus, Ohio

KEEP THIS CARD. Keep a record of the number.

UNITED STATES DEPARTMENT OF JUSTICE
IMMIGRATION AND NATURALIZATION SERVICE
ALIEN REGISTRATION DIVISION
WASHINGTON, D. C.

To the Registrant:

Your registration under the Alien Registration Act, 1940, has been received and given the number shown above your name. This card is your receipt, and is evidence only of such registration. In writing to the Department of Justice about yourself, always give the number on this card.

GPO

Director of Registration

Complying with the Alien Registration Act of 1940

Chapter 11

NOW THAT I WAS STUDYING at Ohio State during the daytime, there was no way that I could work at Frey-Yankin's at night. I didn't want to burn the candle at both ends, and I knew that it would be impossible because I would be too tired. They agreed that it would be best for me to work part-time there during the daytime. So instead of working as night watchman, I learned how to use a duplicating machine to make labels for the different varieties of paint cans. My wages increased from 15 cents an hour to thirty cents, the minimum wage, but still, I earned a mere $15 per week. My brothers and sisters, being older, were unable to take advantage of the educational opportunity that had been afforded me. They continued to work full time.

When Dezső first came to America, he lived and worked in a kennel raising and training dogs until the kennel burned down. Dezső was lucky to have survived the fire. He even managed to save the photos and letters that we had sent from Europe, and a tiny bag of sand from our mother's grave that he had brought with him. At the same time, he worked for our Cousin Arthur as a night watchman at his company, Bonded Scale and Machine. Later, he found work with Amster-Kirtz, a wholesale tobacco company, and he was working there when we arrived to America.

Hermine left her job as a nanny and for a short time joined Marie as a seamstress before going to work as a salesgirl in Lázárus' Department store. Marie continued working as a seamstress, and took other jobs as a cashier. Although she worked diligently, she often felt ill due to the trauma of leaving our family behind. Herman, like Dezső before him, had started working for Arthur's company. However, he left Bonded Scale for a different reason. While Herman did the work that was assigned to him, he also noticed that many of the workers stole not only time, but also material, from the company. Out of loyalty, he told Arthur about this, but Arthur was unwilling to believe him. Instead, he confronted the individual Herman had accused of stealing, who naturally denied any wrongdoing, remained on the job, and made Herman's life miserable. Herman had no choice but to leave Arthur's factory and find work elsewhere as a machinist.

With our meager salaries combined, we were able to send money home to our father. However, we did it in a rather convoluted way. First, Hermine, with the help of our Cousin Bertha, made connections with a wealthy Hungarian living in New York named Israel Zsupnik, and he agreed to help us. We would send money directly to him and he, after receiving it, would contact his family in Hungary and instruct them to give the equivalent amount to our father. That was the only way that we were able to send money home. At first, we could manage to send only ten dollars at a time. Our father would receive 240 pengos, but it was never enough. Each letter we received from our family in 1940 told of their deteriorating situation and how hard life was becoming for them: the winter frost destroyed the wheat leaving mostly weeds; Emil, my brother's oldest child had outgrown his clothes and with no money to buy new ones they altered pants from my father to fit him; the Latorica river that flowed in our backyard flooded over its backs and destroyed our fields and the crops that had been planted; they had to borrow potatoes from the neighbors; there was no firewood, and even bread was scarce. At least the hens and ducks were laying eggs nicely. They had 11 little ducks and 47 chickens, with 3 of 19 hens incubating eggs. Our nephew Emil wrote, "We have eggs, thank G-d. We will give some to our Grandfather too for Passover and beet soup [cibere]. We just don't have milk, because the calf drinks it. We must eat the calf for Passover."

We yearned to send them everything they needed, but we simply didn't have it. Not only did we have to buy food for ourselves, but we also had to pay rent to our Uncle Jónás. Sometimes we sent home packages, and sometimes we sent just one dollar.

Our brother Lajos was conscripted into the Hungarian army soon after we left and he rarely came home. Despite the hardship this created for our father and sister-in-law, since Lajos managed the day to day operation of our farm, his wife Etelka managed to put a positive spin on his absence: "If you could only see him, how good he looks! He's changed for the better. He's surrounded by big shots and all kinds of honorable people, and he eats kosher food. I send a package from home to him and money. What stress it gives me, but I must!"

The synagogue in Lelesz where my grandfather prayed was closed down because the back corner had collapsed. Even though they brought in columns to support the roof, the doctor and the notary condemned the building. Eventually, the same "building department" ordered that the synagogue be taken down because it was too dangerous, so during Passover they had to pray in a private home.

My sisters ate up the news that Etelka wrote about our nephews and nieces: Emil, Lenke, Mityu, Gyula (Gyuszi), and Zoltan, whom we had never met since he was born just a month after we arrived to America.

"The children, thank G-d are in good health. Little Zoltan is like Gyuszi, only he has blue eyes. He is cute. He is already laughing. Your father chose his name. He should just have good luck. He is such a precious, nice, good child. He is very cute, he listens nicely and his dark blue eyes are often like the nicest violet. Gyuszi is full of mischief and his black eyes light up so sweetly under his golden blonde hair! There is no match, not to his beauty nor to his intelligence. Now he is home with me, because the others go to the "heider" [school], but he is so wonderful I could eat him up! Mityu is the best child. He would also like to write to you. Gyuszi and Mityu are like twins. They are big and they wear the same overalls. They are nice together like that, only they make too much noise for their Grandfather's ears. Lenke is writing and reading beautifully and she has two nice braided ponytails, which take a long time to wash, and an even longer time to dry! Emil will write the news next time because he was sleepy at night, and in the morning he was in a hurry to go to school. Thank G-d, they are all more wonderful everyday."

Eventually, the children were no longer allowed to study Hebrew and the "heider" and the yeshiva in Helmec were closed. Jewish stores were required to be open on Shabbos. This had an extraordinary impact on a town like Lelesz, where my grandparents lived. Except for four stores owned by Christians, the rest were owned by Jews, and they would never have considered being open on Shabbos!

Etelka summed up the situation: "We are struggling to be ok somehow, but I wish we would struggle for a good reason and they would leave us in peace. But when will we be able to live in peace? The bad news we hear about the Jews all the time makes us nervous. I don't know how it is going to end. You are indebted to our dear G-d, because he helped you get out."

Jews were no longer allowed to be in business without a Christian partner, and our farm was no exception. The Szabo's, a family who years earlier had wanted to buy some of our land, were appointed administrator of our fields. Not only did they believe that they were now getting the land they would have had to pay for for free, but they also thought, incorrectly, that they were entitled to half of the harvest. Julia Szabo knew us very well, and was even friendly to our family before we left. However, now she thought that she could shout at, frighten, and intimidate my father because he was just a Jew with no rights. Unbowed, my father hired a lawyer, who also needed a Christian partner in order to practice law, to defend him in court. Incredibly, the judge ruled in my father's favor: just because they were appointed administrators, the Szabo's had no right to take the harvest.

And 1941's harvest was indeed bountiful despite the previous summer's flooding: 12 wagons of carrots, 15 wagons of potatoes, and a sea of sunflowers, poppies, and hay. Our father even sowed 14 bushels of wheat, which was incredibly optimistic. Alone, he plowed the field with his own strength since both Lajos and the horses had been taken into the army. Somehow my father took care of everything despite having little formal education. The first letter he wrote to us after we arrived to America was signed as follows: "My dearest children, please take care of each other. Everyone will be okay. Don't worry about me, G-d will help us. My best wishes to all of you and many kisses to you all, individually, every one of you, your loving father who never forgets you not even for a moment. When I see your clothing I think that you are still here with me, but I cannot speak with you. With all my love, again, forever, your father. Jeremias Gluck." My father was 66 years old.

My father, Jeremias Gluck
Polyán, Czechoslovakia

Chapter 12

I GOT ALONG QUITE WELL with my employers, the Yankin family, especially since I spoke with them in Yiddish. Consequently, they invited me to join them at their synagogue, an Orthodox congregation, many times larger than our small synagogue in Lelesz. So, on Saturday mornings I rode my bicycle, weaving in and out of traffic from our apartment to their synagogue on Washington Street. It took at least a half hour to get there. However, because riding a bicycle on Shabbos was prohibited by Jewish law, I would get off my bicycle a few blocks before the synagogue, lock it to a pole, and walk the rest of the way. After the first day when the Yankin family introduced me to many of the 100 or more congregants, I felt right at home. I spoke Yiddish and so did many of them, and I was often called up to the Torah for an aliyah. Of course, this was an honor and each time I was given one, I was reminded of my own bar mitzvah. Back in Polyán, we didn't even have a minyan, a quorum of ten men over the age of thirteen. We had to pay someone to come just to be the tenth. That is, until I turned thirteen. The day of my bar mitzvah, I became the tenth. There wasn't a big celebration, just a small glass of wine and some pastries at the kiddush, but it was enough. I never forgot how important it was for our small community to have a minyan.

Obviously, as a young bachelor in Columbus, there were families in the congregation who were interested in introducing me to their daughters. One in particular, was an older gentleman who, unbeknownst to me at the time, was the wealthy owner of a junkyard. He was an ardent Zionist and spoke often about Palestine. However, because of his deteriorating health, he was even more interested in seeing his daughter married. She too must have thought highly of me since I was soon invited to their home for dinner. The table was set so elegantly that they were clearly interested in impressing me. However, I was not established in any way yet and was in no way ready to be married.

Yet, our situation as a whole was improving. We moved to a new, larger apartment at 175½ Second Avenue, in a building also owned by our Uncle Jónás. He and Aunt Helen would come to have dinner with us on Sunday evenings. Sometimes, even Dezső grudgingly joined us. Our uncle came to check on us and to inquire what news, if any, we had received from Europe. Tragically, although not entirely unexpected, he died of a heart attack on April 1, 1941.

Julius Gluck

Stricken with a heart attack at his home yesterday afternoon, Julius Gluck, 72, 110 West Park Ave., was dead on the arrival of the inhalator squad. He was born in Polony, Hungary, and had lived in Columbus for the last 24 years.

Surviving Mr. Gluck are his wife, Mrs. Helen Gluck; a son, Arthur Gluck of Columbus; a daughter, Mrs. Elsie Schallheim of Cleveland; two brothers in Hungary and three grandchildren.

Rabbi Nathan Zelzier and Cantor Leo Halpern will officiate at funeral services which will be held at 10 a. m. today at the Snider funeral home. The body will be taken to Glenville Cemetery, Cleveland, where a brief service will be held at the grave.

Uncle Julius' death notice in the local paper, April 1941.

In Judaism, one is not invited to a funeral, but our cousins neglected to tell us the details of the ceremony or the burial, so we didn't attend. Shortly after his father died, Arthur decided to raise our rent. We began to resent paying our cousin because not only had we already paid back the money his father had sent to help us travel, it allowed him to have power over us. Like our uncle before him, he felt that we owed him an accounting of our expenses. Asserting our independence, we decided to move to a property that he didn't own. While riding my bicycle, I noticed a "For Rent" sign at 50 Linwood Avenue. I didn't hesitate to look at the apartment myself and when I did, I decided right then and there to rent it, and the four of us moved there. Arthur didn't let us take any of the furniture, so we had to buy new beds and a sofa. However, now I was able to walk to the closest synagogue, Bet Knesset Tiferet Yisroel, that was just at the end of the block.

After Shabbos services, I would return home, where my sister Marie would be busy setting out food. Hermine would often stay at her job even on the weekend so most of the shopping, cooking, cleaning, and laundry fell on Marie. She washed the clothing and sheets in the bathtub and cooked delicious foods from scratch, just like at home in Europe. She even managed to find the time to bake danishes filled with cheese and poppies (kifli), and cookies (pogacha), too!

By mid-1941, not only did Aunt Helen stop coming every week, but we received what would be the last letter from Europe with the tragic news that our father's oldest brother, Uncle Lázár, had died. After that, we no longer received letters from our family and those we sent them were returned to us as "undeliverable." However, we were still able to send money through Mr. Zsupnik, but because of inflation we had to send thirty dollars in order for our father to receive the same 240 pengos. Soon after, even this became impossible.

Envelope of letter sent to my father returned and marked
"Return to Sender Service Suspended." November 6, 1941

Europe was engulfed in war. While we struggled to make a
living, learn English, and become acclimated to our adopted
country, the Nazi regime and its Axis allies had invaded
Denmark, Norway, France, Belgium, Luxembourg, the
Netherlands, Egypt, Greece, Romania, Yugoslavia, and the
Soviet Union. The Battle of Britain had begun. We always
assumed that the lack of news signaled nothing other than the
difficulty of communicating during wartime. It was on one
such Sunday, December 7, 1941, that I was lying in bed
listening to the radio. Suddenly, the announcer came on the
air:

"The Japanese have attacked Pearl Harbor Hawaii by air,
President Roosevelt has just announced. The attack also was
made on all military and naval activities on the principal island
of Oahu."

The following day, everybody sat and listened to President
Roosevelt address the nation: "Yesterday, December 7th, 1941
-- a date which will live in infamy -- the United States of

America was suddenly and deliberately attacked by naval and air forces of the Empire of Japan."

Herman and I registered with the military draft in 1942, but with the exception of that, life continued on as usual until the beginning of 1943. I waited impatiently to receive my induction notice. I wanted nothing more than to fight the Germans! There were already newspaper articles reporting that the Nazis were systematically killing Jews, and I wanted to save my family. However, Herman received his induction notice first. He went for his medical exam and the doctor found him fit to serve in the Army. However, during basic training, Herman developed a nervous stomach condition that the doctors couldn't cure. It earned him an early discharge. On March 16, 1943, I reported to Goodhill Street in Columbus for my medical examination.

I stood in line with hundreds of other young men and waited my turn to be examined by the doctor. I was 21, healthy and strong, and was classified as 1A, fit for military duty. I was given a crew cut, a uniform, a tanach (the Jewish bible) and a siddur (the Jewish prayerbook). I would keep my promise to my father to remember I was a Jew, however maintaining Judaism would undoubtedly become more challenging.

I had one week to get my affairs in order. I said my farewells, and promised my sisters and brothers that I would write often. My sisters felt miserably, and were very apprehensive about the future. They hoped that I would be stationed in America and stay out of danger. I had called Columbus, Ohio home for three years and three weeks. Even though I felt like an American, I couldn't officially call myself one yet, since I still hadn't received my citizenship.

From Left to Right: Hermine, Me, and Marie dressed in our finest for a
visit to the Columbus Botanical Gardens. circa 1940-42.

Hermine, standing, and Marie in 50 Linwood Ave.
The photos on the mantle are of Uncle Julius and Cousin Arthur. July 1944.

Chapter 13

"What is the use of living, if it be not to strive for noble causes and to make this muddled world a better place for those who will live in it after we are gone?" - Winston Churchill

THE SKY WAS BEGINNING TO BRIGHTEN as the train that would take me to basic training pulled slowly out of the station. It was March 23, 1943. I had climbed aboard taking my shaving kit and the bible and prayerbook. The carloads of fellow recruits didn't know where we were going or what awaited us, but I for one, was excited and ready for anything.

Although three years had passed since I had left my village of Polyán by train, I was immediately brought back to that moment. As then, I was leaving my family again. We said our tearful goodbyes, and now I sat, surrounded by my new family, a band of brothers whose bonds were just being forged. I was amazed that many of the boys on the train, none of whom were Jewish, were interested to see the books that the Army had issued to me. A few decided to request the same books for themselves.

Each of us, dressed for the first time in our uniforms, peered excitedly out of the windows as the train left Columbus and hurtled toward the unknown wilderness. The boys who were more familiar with the country tried to guess what our final destination would be from the mountains, forests, rivers, and the train's direction. We passed through several small towns that reminded me of Polyán. Here and there people waved to us. I sat, like the others, staring out into the beautiful, unmarred, natural wonderland through which our train passed. We knew that we were heading south, but that was all.

My first week in the Army
Camp Wolters, Texas, March 1943

Cover of the "Abridged Prayer Book for Jews in the Army and Navy of the United States."
The Jewish Publication Society of America. 5678 - 1917

As the hours passed, the cold weather mellowed. The panes of glass on the windows grew warm to the touch as the sun began to shine brightly in the sky overhead. I was amazed because at this time of year, the fields of Czechoslovakia would still be covered in deep snow! We passed houses built upon stilts and passed through sandy desert areas. As the train pulled into a station in Arkansas, I thought to myself, 'This is the place that I would like to settle...sunny, warm, and beautiful.' We were there for only a few hours. Well-wishers from the town came up to the train to say hello, shake our hands through the windows, and to give us food and snacks. The hours passed like minutes and just as quickly as we had arrived, we were underway. As the train's whistle rang out again, the crowd cheered and waved us off.

As we continued further South, oil wells dotted the landscape, tirelessly pumping out barrel after barrel. There were also tall chimneys with smoke billowing from them as they refined the oil into gasoline. It was extraordinary! After a journey of nearly two days, we arrived late in the evening to Fort Worth, Texas. Dingy old school buses were waiting for us at the station. We climbed aboard and were driven another hour to Camp Wolters. Upon arriving, we were assigned to our barracks in groups of thirty. The barracks were plain buildings with just the basic necessities: two neat rows of 15 beds and at the far end were toilets and showers. In all, there were 20,000 recruits in Camp Wolters.

Tired as I was, I sat down and quickly wrote a postcard to my family. "I have arrived to Camp Wolters, Texas. All is well! I will write you all about it tomorrow." The sound of taps rang out in the darkness. I tucked the postcard away to mail when I could, undressed, climbed into my cot, and allowed sleep to quickly overtake my weary mind.

No sooner had my head hit the pillow, or so it seemed, the same bugle I heard before I went to sleep sounded again, only this time it played the harried sound of reveille. It was 5 AM. Even before our feet had touched the floor, the sergeant opened the door, turned on the lights, and made sure that every man was up.

"Ok, boys, you have five minutes before inspection. In these five minutes, I expect you to dress, shine your shoes, and make your beds, wrinkle free! Be sure to pick up all your cigarette butts, too. From this moment on, you are soldiers in the Army of these United States. I am your sergeant and your lives are mine. Whatever I say, you do. Is that clear?"

"Yes, sir!" we answered in unison.

"Good. Four minutes 25 seconds. Fall out!"

In five minutes, the 30 men in my barracks had lined up outside and stood at attention in the dry, hot Texan breeze. Sometimes, the breeze would kick up sand and blow it around us. The sunrise was incredibly beautiful, beyond words. The commanding officer explained to us the current political situation in the world. Their job was to train us not just for combat, but to follow orders. Every aspect of our lives was in their hands. If we didn't follow orders, our punishment was kitchen patrol, KP duty. That is, peeling potatoes. Our beds had to be perfect, our shoes had to be shined, and our faces shaved. We had our heads shaved...again. Now, I was almost bald! This was day one of 12 weeks of basic training. From then on, I made sure that my bed was always neat. Sometimes other boys would sit on it as we talked. It bothered me because the crisp sheets would get wrinkled and the tight corners would loosen. I would never say anything, but as soon as they would get up, I'd made my bed wrinkle-free again. I didn't want KP duty!

The drill sergeants were very strict and pushed us to our limits physically and mentally. After all, we had to learn the skills they were teaching us as though we were actually in combat. Our lives depended on it. I took each day of training as both a challenge and as an opportunity to learn what I would later need to survive. The day started at 5AM and lasted until 5PM or later. We went on morning runs, that is 4 minute runs with 6 minutes of rest, repeat. Over and over. Then we went on four mile hikes carrying 60 pounds of equipment.

We ate breakfast by 7:20, and afterwards, sat in the shade next to the buildings for educational classes. We were lectured on different types of weapons and how they worked, and after the lecture, had to practice what was taught. We learned and practiced disassembling our weapons so often that eventually, I could do it in complete darkness. We were told to assemble them in 8-10 seconds, but usually, it took us 15-20 seconds or even longer. However, we had no choice but to keep trying until we succeeded. We also had to clean our rifles so that not even a single speck of dust could be found on them. My rifle was often the best of the 60 men.

Nearing the end of the second week, my commanding officer called me into his office. There was nobody else present. He looked up from his desk.

"Private Gluck. You're from Europe, aren't you, son?" he said.

"Yes, sir."

"I'm giving you the option to fight your own people or to fight the Japs. Where do you want to go?"

"Europe, sir! Definitely Europe." I replied without any hesitation.

"Now why the hell do you want to fight your own people?" he asked, leaning back in his chair. He was about to put his feet on his desk, when I answered him.

"Sir, my people, my family, are being killed in Europe. I want to go there to fight for their freedom, sir."

Instead of raising his feet to the desktop, he pulled himself in close to the desk. "That's the right attitude, son! It'll definitely help you get your citizenship sooner!" He reached for his pen and continued, "Do you want to go as an infantryman or as a medic?"

I had been conflicted about this decision ever since I was inducted in Columbus and had discussed my options with Hermine before I left home. I signed up for the infantry as my first choice, but I also put my name on a list to be considered for officer training, and another to learn to be a medic. I was willing to do anything for America. Now I had to make a choice. Although a medic would be able to save lives rather than take them, I decided that the infantry would be safer since when they were doing their job, they not only carried a weapon, but they used it, too. He signed my orders. I was going to Europe as an infantryman.

After eight weeks of training I had learned eight different weapons. Though I understood each one very well, it was hard to remember their individual names. Eventually I was issued an M1 carbine, a lightweight rifle. We learned to shoot both at targets on the ground and in the trees. Our instructors tested our marksmanship with both rifles and machine guns. From a distance of about 200 meters, we were given 60 seconds to fire 20 rounds at a paper page marked with circles. Five points for the center, then 4, 3, and 2. I received 90 points. That is, 18 of my 20 shots hit the center of the target. I was awarded a 'sharpshooter' marksmanship qualification badge for the M1 rifle and a 'marksman' marksmanship qualification badge for the 0.30 caliber machine gun.

We also learned to crawl on the ground while bullets from said machine guns flew over our heads (an activity affectionately called "the bottom of hell"), to throw grenades, and even how to kill another man with our bare hands. We exercised. Daily. Exercise included a basic morning fitness routine, walking, and running while carrying our 60-pound packs up and down mountains and through the harshest terrain during the hottest hours. Luckily, I enjoyed the dry, desert heat, drank plenty of water, and took my salt tablets as directed. Even so, everyone, including me, became tired and weak when we were ordered to put on our gas masks while we were climbing mountains.

Our activities weren't limited to the heat of the day. In the cold night air, we often had combat exercises. We were divided into two groups: one 'enemy', the other, 'friendly'. We had to go out on patrol and engage the other group. One night, I was captured by the 'enemy'. All I could do was think about how I might escape. Other nights, I had guard duty all through the night. Most of the time we were active for 20 hours and slept just four. There was hardly a moment to breathe between this, cleaning our weapons, clothes, and barracks, and answering letters.

People were friendly to me and some were as curious about my accent as I was about theirs. Occasionally I would go on the same bumpy school bus back to the neighboring town of Mineral Wells on an eight-hour pass to mail letters or make phone calls. The local people spoke English so slowly compared to Ohioans that I was sure that I would learn English very well from speaking with them. However, since the prices were high, and there were long lines in the stores because of the many soldiers, it often didn't pay to go there. I would need to wait hours just to have a picture taken or to make an audio recording to send home.

A postcard sent to my family.
Camp Wolters, Texas

On Friday nights or Saturday mornings I often went to synagogue services on the base, and I tried to lay tefillin during the week as often as I could. Another man from Cincinnati conducted the services. I celebrated the first night of Passover by taking an hour and a half bus ride to a seder in Fort Worth, which was about 50 miles away, with about 200 other Jewish soldiers. We had to leave by 5PM and return by midnight. The Rabbi didn't read much from the hagadah (the story of the Jewish liberation from slavery in Egypt), just a few words here and there. It was nothing like our seder in Polyán. Like the Hungarian poet Sandor Petöfi wrote, "black bread at home is better than white bread abroad!" I returned to the base the same evening. For the second night, I stayed on the base for the seder. They served gefilte fish, chicken soup, roast chicken, potato kugel, cooked vegetables, salad, and sherbert. This was a real treat for me. Since they usually served bacon, which I wouldn't touch because I still tried to keep "kosher," I usually just ate bread with butter, some fruit, milk or coffee, or cereal. On the last day of Passover, I stayed on the base and davened Yizkor for my mother, the memorial prayer said at the conclusion of the major Jewish holidays. Even though the United Jewish Appeal sent a package containing matzos, nuts, salami, cookies, and honey, I still needed to eat whatever there was. Violating the laws of the Passover had to be permitted under the circumstances. This took some getting used to considering my strictly observant upbringing.

At home in Europe, we observed the Jewish dietary laws meticulously. A shochet, the ritual slaughterer, would come once a week to slaughter an animal, usually a duck or a chicken for Shabbos or a goose for the holidays. Unlike our non-Jewish neighbors, we never slaughtered our own animals. That was the shochets's job. He was a very religious man, educated in the Jewish laws of animal slaughter, so we were certain that the laws were being followed. Without the shochet, we wouldn't have eaten meat. Since Jews are forbidden from eating blood, my sisters soaked the meat in water and salted it, too, in order to remove any trace of it. To our disgust, our non-Jewish neighbors cooked their food, usually pig or rabbit, in the blood from the animals they slaughtered. Now, in Texas, I made sure that whatever food I did eat, even though it wasn't kosher, was at least from a kosher animal, like chicken or cow.

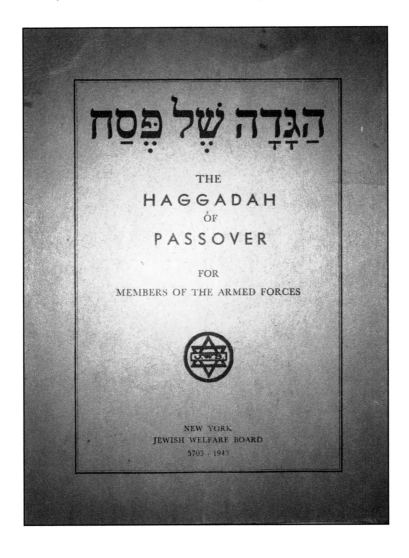

There was a recreation room, but it was rare that I sat there. Sometimes they played movies for the soldiers, and I tried to watch them in order to practice my English. Some movies taught the history of the German regime and explained how they came to power. There were also ping pong tables, a radio, and a desk to write letters. I often wrote home, but not while sitting there. It was usually so noisy that I could hardly think to collect my thoughts and put them down on paper. I listened to the radio once or twice a week, but couldn't read the newspaper as often as I was accustomed to for want of time. It was still a struggle to read quickly in English, so I got most of my news from daily briefings read to us by the officers.

At the end of the first week of July, I received my reward for completing 12 weeks of basic training: a furlough to Columbus to visit my family. To me, there was nothing better than being at home and eating stuffed cabbage! Unfortunately, it was only for a few days and I was once again on a train heading back to Mineral Wells, Texas. The train stopped in St. Louis, Missouri for about an hour and I thought I'd have a chance to get something to eat. However, the line was too long and I just went back to the train. It turned out to be a good thing since I was able to secure a seat, while those that came later had to stand. At the next station, I was able to get a pie to eat, but at double the price of one in Columbus! The warm afternoon heat felt good when the train arrived to the station in Texas, and I didn't mind the bus ride back to Camp Wolters, at least I knew what to expect. It wouldn't stay that way for much longer.

Oil Gushers in Oklahoma

4A-H321

Above and below are postcards that I sent home from Camp Wolters, Texas.
I marked the postcard above in ink to show the barracks in which I was stationed.

CAMP WOLTERS CHAPEL BULLETIN

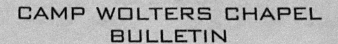

MAJOR GENERAL BRUCE MAGRUDER, COMMANDING
INFANTRY REPLACEMENT TRAINING CENTER

COLONEL EARL C. FLEGEL
CAMP COMMANDER

LIEUT. COL. PETER C. SCHRODER
CAMP CHAPLAIN

Camp Wolters, Texas

"I was glad when they said unto me:
Let us go into the House of the Lord."

Jewish Services were held Friday and Tuesday evenings at 8:30 P.M., and Sunday mornings at 10:00 A.M. Samuel D. Hurwitz, Chaplain

Boxing Finals Next Week--See Story, Page 7...

THE
CAMP WOLTERS
LONG HORN
PUBLISHED FOR SOLDIERS BY SOLDIERS

EVERY TWO WEEKS   CAMP WOLTERS, TEXAS, THURSDAY, MAY 13, 1943.   VOL. 2. NO. 21

BACKGROUND FOR BATTLE!

Upper left: Wolters soldiers scramble up a barrier in Hell's Bottom's new obstacle course. Center left: Taking barbed wire entanglements on the fly in the landing trainer program. Lower left: FALL OUT, ONE! Here are machine gunners in the making. Upper right: Crossing a stream under real, live fire—another phase of Hell's Bottom. Lower right: Action like this featured the 55th Battalion's prelude to the camp boxing tourney. (SIGNAL CORPS PHOTOS.)

Chapter 14

IT WAS THE LAST WEEK OF JULY, 1943. I was on a train heading East with no idea of our final destination. It turned out to be Camp Shenango, a Replacement Depot in Greenville, Pennsylvania. We were to be here until we received our next assignment. Perhaps we would be deployed overseas, but we weren't told. I understood quickly that this camp was different than the one in Texas. We were trained to be prepared to leave at anytime. The first day, after unpacking, we were ordered to pack again and get ready to leave. Then we were told to unpack and check to see that we had everything. The whole procedure took about three hours from start to finish.

On the fourth day, we had a contest to see which of the six barracks would be the cleanest. The winner would get a free day: no exercise, no duties. I suggested to our Corporal that we should line up in height order. I thought that this would make us look even neater. When everything was ready and it was time to be inspected by the Captain, the Corporal assigned me to be leader of the barrack. When the Captain arrived, I stood straight and answered directly, "Yes, sir!" to any defect that he pointed out. There were only three: a shoe wasn't polished, there were cigarette ashes on the floor, and a matchstick was on the window sill. He overlooked them all because I answered him the way I had been taught in Camp Wolters: standing at attention and with a sharp "Yes, sir!" My barracks won their freedom for the day.

Although the barracks we stayed in were similar to the ones in Texas, the buildings were much more crowded and the soldiers around us were all strangers. They had all come from different bases around the country and were waiting to be transported overseas. I hated every minute I spent there. There were more thieves in the barracks than you could imagine. Most of the boys sat around playing cards until dawn because there was nothing else to do. If they won, they walked away with as much as $400 or $500. Unbelievable, but true. If they lost, and someone always did, they stole money from the rest of us until they were caught. We were packed so closely together that theft was inevitable. Someone was robbed every day, me included. I had only 20 or 30 dollars at the time, and I kept it in a money belt around my waist. One night, while I was sleeping in my bunk, I felt something pulling at my waist, but exhaustion clouded my mind, and I didn't wake up. The next morning, the money belt was gone, along with all the money that I had. I called my sisters, asking them to telegraph some money to me, even though I did not know when, or if, I would need it, and they did so right away. It was the same amount from my salary that I had sent from Camp Wolters to help them.

When we weren't exercising in the 99 degree heat, we were guarding prisoners, that is, soldiers who had tried to escape from the army or who had simply disobeyed orders. Five of us would accompany 16 of them from a large jail to a smaller one. There were a lot of prisoners because this camp was very close to where they lived, and they had tried to go home without permission. They thought they would get only 30 to 60 days, which was nothing, but they also thought they wouldn't be sent overseas.

I was very close to Youngstown, PA, a little over an hour away, and I considered going to visit my cousins, the children of my father's brother Martin. The trouble was that I had no idea when I would get new orders and every day some groups of men were leaving.

Sure enough, as we had been warned, news that we would be leaving came suddenly. I had been in Greenville for about three weeks. It was a lazy day, at least compared to what we had done in Texas. We went out early in the morning for an eight-mile march. It was nice and cool, and I didn't get tired at all. How easy it was to get accustomed to this kind of exertion! Before noon there was a movie, and after that some of the boys played a game of baseball. Since I didn't know how to play, I went into the nearby woods to lay down and rest. By the time I woke up, most of the soldiers were back at the camp. When I returned, there was just enough time for me to wash up and change for retreat, which happened every evening at 5:15. The flag was taken down and the trumpet sounded. After that we went into the mess hall to eat. However, on this particular day, before we went to eat an order came in that nobody should leave the area until further notice. I knew that if we were ordered to pack our barracks bag, we could be next. It was just a matter of days or even hours. The whistle blew. There was an announcement. It wasn't my group. Not yet. But strong rumors indicated we would be sent soon.

I packed up whatever I really didn't need, shoes and whatnot that I couldn't take with me, and sent them home. I wrote my family that from this point I would not be able to write freely. The letters would be censored. Also, I added that I didn't have permission to write in Hungarian any more, only in English. I explained that as soon as I knew our destination I would tell them, but in code: if to Europe I'd write that I was going to visit our father; if to Africa, I'd write about Szatmar, the region south of us in Yugoslavia that our cousins lived in; if to England, that I am close to our father; and if to Austria then I would write about the yellow paper.[18] I hoped my family would

---

[18] "Yellow paper" may be a reference to "yellow journalism," that is, journalism or a newspaper that distorts the news by exaggerations, scandal-mongering, or sensationalism, and generally presents the news in an unprofessional or unethical manner.

understand this. It was all I could do to let them know where I was. I asked them not to share this letter with anyone else.

On August 21, 1943, I was standing on the deck of a ship called the SS Monterey, staring longingly at Lady Liberty, hoping to see her again. I was crossing the Atlantic, going back to Europe, eager to serve my adopted country and save my people.

There were 6,855 soldiers aboard. Its peacetime capacity was just 701 passengers and 360 crew members.[19] Packed like sardines, with four or five soldiers in bunks one upon the other, there was plenty of time to talk or read. Some became seasick. Many of the soldiers openly said that they weren't going to come back anyway so they might as well do whatever they wanted to do. Gambling was a favorite activity for many of them, but one that I wanted no part of.

Every fiber of my being was against this negative fatalism. I felt none of us should think that way, never mind speak it. I wanted to maintain a positive attitude. I will return, I told myself. I will survive. My family is depending on it. I tried to preach this philosophy to my fellow soldiers. "Think that you will come back! G-d will protect us!" Although this was unrealistic as surely many of us would not return, I preferred the dream to the reality. It is a kind of optimism that could be found in no other people but my own, people who have suffered for two millennia while maintaining their hope for a better world and a better future despite their present conditions. "Yea, though I walk in the valley, in the shadow of death, I shall not want for G-d is with me!" I lost no friends in talking to them this way, but found few allies. I became known affectionately as "the preacher man."

---

[19] https://en.m.wikipedia.org/wiki/SS_Monterey

SS Monterey
http://www.shipspotting.com/gallery/photo.php?lid=1443723

Chapter 15

"Per me si va nella città dolente, per me si va nell'eterne dolore."
Through me you go to the grief wracked city;
Through me you go to everlasting pain;
Inferno (Canto III), Dante Alighieri

ON SEPTEMBER 2ND, after 12 days at sea we landed at night in Oran, North Africa. Jeeps took us to a replacement depot located in Canastel, about 2 kilometers northeast of Oran. The camp was on the edge of a large, tall mountain, and a multitude of military tents capable of holding a dozen men each were spread out over the plateau. Immediately I was assigned to a tent. I was glad to be on land again, so I slept soundly. At daybreak, I awoke to the din of men and machinery moving methodically about. I didn't know it, but the invasion of Italy had begun.

Inasmuch as I was not yet an American citizen, and I couldn't become one until a Federal Judge arrived from the United States to administer the oath of citizenship, I wasn't permitted to be sent into combat. Those that came with me were soon shipped out to fight as part of the invasion of Italy at Salerno on September 9th. Hundreds and hundreds of more men eager for combat came and went while I processed their paperwork. That was one of my assignments. I was called in to an office to register all newcomers. My duty was to write in all the information about them: when they arrived, where they're going, had they been paid and how much, as well as their personal information. I met many people this way. I could only surmise their fate since the war continued raging on and many more of them than I can remember were sent into the combat zone.

September came and went and with it the Jewish New Year ushered in what I hoped would be a new beginning. As the huge fireball that was the setting sun hung in the far away horizon, I hurried to have dinner with a Jewish family in Oran. The local Jewish families had extended invitations to the Jewish soldiers to share a meal for the New Year. I needed special permission to travel to #10 Rue de Paris and thoroughly enjoyed my evening so much that I nearly forgot where I was and what was happening to the men that I was processing. The head of the house, Monsieur Raymonde El-Kaim, was a Jewish Frenchman who was able to speak Yiddish and owned a manufacturing company in Oran. He had a very beautiful daughter to whom I was very attracted. At some point that first evening, I excused myself to use the toilet. I followed my host's instructions to the room, but found nothing but a hole in the floor. I suppose I spent too much time looking for the toilet because his daughter came to show me that the hole in the floor was indeed the toilet. She explained this using broken English, a lady-like uplift of her dress, and sign language. I had no idea how I was supposed to use this and maintain my dignity, so I waited to relieve myself at the camp's latrine.

I enjoyed meeting Mademoiselle El-Kaim, and speaking with her as she tried to improve her English. Unfortunately, our relationship didn't progress very far, but it wasn't because of the language barrier. Her mother, who I'm sure had her daughter's best interests at heart, adhered to local custom and accompanied us wherever we went. That certainly put a damper on things! It also didn't help that some areas of the city were still off-limits and I needed a special permit from the commander and a Rabbi each time I wanted to re-enter the part of Oran in which they lived.

We were allowed to go into many other areas of the city without any permit and I did so every week. I ate near the Red Cross and occasionally saw a movie. Sometimes they brought cakes and ice cream. That was a pleasant surprise since it was such a novelty! Eventually, the Red Cross opened in the camp and gave us coffee for free. I was also able to take pictures of myself there so that I could send them home.

I wrote a letter to my family almost every day that I was in North Africa. Most letters began, "My dearest brothers and sisters..." and closed "With kisses from your little brother Irving." I apologized for the monotony of my letters, for the similarity of my questions and of my answers. Nothing new had happened, but I just wanted my family back home to know that I was alive and well. In the moment I didn't recognize the beneficence of the banality of my existence. It took at least 18 days for their letters to reach me so the news from home was new to me alone. In that time, I often had to wait for answers to questions or read questions that I had answered in a previous letter that my family had not yet received. Although I had received permission to continue writing my letters in Hungarian, I usually wrote in English. Hermine also wrote to me in English for practice, but Marie wrote in Hungarian. It didn't matter since they could write about anything they wanted, while my letters always had to pass through the base censor.

I asked about their health, they about mine. I expressed my longing to be with them, for their food (especially cabbage and cookies), and for their conversation. They told me of their jobs and of the neighbors or of my co-workers. I told them of the letters that I received from Bertha, who didn't realize I had already left for the war zone and thought that I was still in the USA, and Cousin Arthur, who wrote me infrequently. I thanked G-d that I was well and I fervently prayed that the war would soon be over. They worried about my weight, since I lost my baby fat but gained muscle, and they asked for pictures so that they could see me. I asked for theirs. I asked for care packages of chocolates and candy. The censors required me to request each item I wanted and if I didn't request it, they couldn't send it in their package. I sent almost all of my pay home, everything I could buy was overpriced anyway. I gave hints to my exact location and where I might be heading. They guessed where I was and hoped that I was safe. I put my trust in the Almighty that I would be. I heard each of their voices in the words they wrote, and I reread their letters over and over so that I could feel that I was closer to them. I did this especially when I didn't receive mail. Somehow we were able to keep in touch. Dezső, now calling himself by his Hebrew name, David, suddenly moved to California. I didn't know why he had moved, but I sent a letter asking them to tell me all about it. I received an answer the following month. Columbus had grown too small for him, so he went looking for better jobs, and more opportunities. Waiting for their replies and their care packages was extraordinarily difficult. Sometimes I received dozens of letters at once. Although it was the greatest pleasure to get mail from home, I joked that I'd need to hire a secretary to answer them all!

I met many soldiers who were unable to write well, and they often asked me to write to their families or girlfriends for them. I did this quite often to keep myself busy, pass the time, and improve my English.

When the sun shone less brightly, the mountain top encampment at Canastel was shrouded in fog. One morning, a plane misjudged its altitude entirely and crashed into the side of the mountain, rocking the ground mightily and waking me from my cot. Although I looked forward to moving out to combat as so many of my friends had done already, I hadn't expected the war zone to come to me. Until that moment, it hadn't dawned on me that GI's sent out from a replacement depot meant they were replacing those that had been killed. I also realized that I would remain safe in the rear area until I received my citizenship. I began to hope and pray that the war would soon end.

I had been in Oran since August. It was now November. The Battle for Salerno was long over and the Allied forces had taken Naples in the beginning of October. The nights were cold and I missed the dry heat of the Texas desert. Some of the boys in my tent thought it would be a good idea to light a fire inside to stay warm. They forgot that where there's fire, there's also smoke. The tent filled up quickly with it and instinctively I even put on my gas mask to help me breathe as we put out the fire. After that, we all decided it would be better to enjoy the brisk night air. Then the rains began. Even if we wanted to stay warm by a fire, how could we burn wet wood? It didn't matter anyway. Finally, a United States Federal Judge arrived to administer the oath of citizenship.[20]

I became a naturalized American citizen on November 18, 1943 with about a dozen other soldiers in a small tent in our camp. We raised our right hands and repeated:

> "I will bear arms on behalf of the United States
> when required by law. I take this obligation freely
> without any mental reservation or purpose of
> evasion; so help me G-d."

How many new citizens could swear such an oath knowing that their allegiance would so soon be tested. If ever I needed G-d's help, this would be the time. I soon received orders to sail to Naples. It was to be my second journey to this city. I was a replacement.

---

[20] US government officials performed 13,587 overseas naturalizations from 1942-1945.
https://www.uscis.gov/history-and-genealogy/our-history/agency-history/military-naturalization-during-wwii

See also:
https://www.uscis.gov/sites/default/files/USCIS/
History%20and%20Genealogy/Our%20History/INS%20History/
WWII/INSMRev1944.2.pdf

My little black book, 1943-1944. Actual size.

Chapter 16

SOME PEOPLE CARRY LITTLE BLACK BOOKS to record names, addresses, telephone numbers. Mine had all that information of course, but I also marked out important dates on the tiny calendar that was on the front page. Each date that I blackened was significant. I had marked the date that I reported to the Army in Ohio, March 16, 1943, the dates I arrived in Texas (March 29), in Pennsylvania (July 21), New York (August 20), and also when I arrived to Africa.

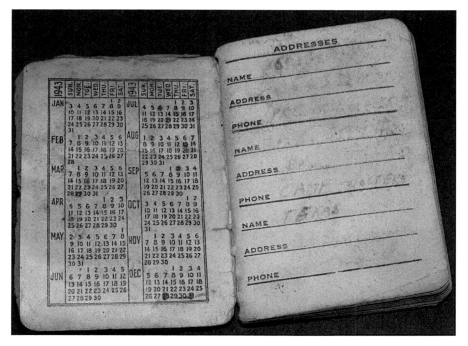

I also marked December 28th, 1943, because it was late in the evening of that day, after the Army's usual hurry up and wait, that we boarded a British ship bound for Naples. It was cramped. Soldiers stood and sat anywhere that there was space. We waited patiently for the ship to leave the harbor. We waited patiently for the ship to enter the open sea. We waited patiently for food that never came. Everyone's patience had grown thin and incessant hunger pangs did nothing to calm the rising discontent. We were hungry. Eventually, someone's patience wore out, and in no time, a group made its way to the storeroom and broke open the locks. There wasn't much there, just some bread, but at least it was something. Loaves were passed out. I broke off a piece and ate slowly, trying to make the ill-begotten dinner last. Besides the music that played constantly in the background there was not much else to do, and nothing more to eat.

On December 31st, our troopship sailed into the darkened harbor of Naples. We had eaten nothing for the last 24 hours. Alongside the pier lay a capsized, burned-out wreck of a ship. We glided in next to it. At first, it looked like it could have been the Vulcania, the ship that had taken me from this port just three years earlier. It wasn't.[21] However, it did hinder our ability to disembark from our own ship. In order to do so, we climbed down cargo nets that were thrown over the side of our ship and lay on the side of the capsized one. From there we crossed boards to the pier of a port buzzing with activity.

It was eerily similar to the last time I'd been in Naples, but this time rather than crowds calling out "Bon Voyage" in celebration, there was the constant din of all manner of military vehicles, supplies, and men moving about. The hum of aircraft engines passed overhead and in the distance, the reverberating echoes of artillery fire. The air was colder than nighttime in Oran. I saw my breath as I blew into my hands to warm them. Again, hurry up and wait.

---

[21] The Vulcania was requisitioned by the Italian government in 1941 to carry troops to North Africa. In October 1943 she became a US troopship (keeping her original name) and on March 29, 1946 was chartered to American Export Line. She was returned to the Italia Line in November 1946.

Somewhere north of Naples.

We ate C rations that had been handed out, our first meal in more than a day. Trucks arrived and brought us to bivouac in a small town outside of Naples. There was a PX, an Army retail store, that sold newspapers, writing paper, pens, pencils, cigarettes, and chocolate, among other things. I went inside to buy some chocolate. When I came out, I noticed children running and laughing. I later learned that many of them had been displaced from their villages and their lives turned upside down, but they laughed and played chase as though the war were a thousand miles away, rather than just miles. A small barefoot boy of five or six chased after a ball that had come in my direction. I stopped it with my foot and waited for the boy to come near me. He looked up at me and without hesitation, I handed him the chocolate bar I had just bought. If nothing else, I hoped that he would remember that an American GI had been kind.

Unfortunately for them and for me, just a day or two after arriving, I received my new assignment. Fifth Army, First Armored Division, Sixth Armored Infantry Regiment, 1st Battalion, Company B,[22] under the command of Major General Ernest Harmon. This was a combat unit. Yet, for two days, despite my new assignment, I was on kitchen patrol serving food and cleaning up in the officer's mess hall for Company B's supply depot, several miles from the front.

In the afternoon of January 4th, the 6th Armored Infantry began its attack on Monte Porchia. This was a relatively small, rocky hill compared to the green mountains surrounding it, and its elevation of just 700 feet above the plain, made it simple for the German defenders to easily target attacking infantry. Any assault on it would be suicidal. Despite this, taking Monte Porchia was critical because whoever controlled

---

[22] A company has 100-200 soldiers while a battalion has 500-800 soldiers.

it also controlled Highway No. 6. This highway passed next to Monte Porchia, cutting across its lower northern slopes, then past Monte Trocchio, then across the Rapido River at the town of Cassino, and continued north all the way to Rome. The mountain with the same name, Monte Cassino, was the ultimate target of the Allied attack because at its summit was an impenetrable Benedictine Monastery in which the Germans had taken up positions. The road to Rome was impassable as long as the Germans remained on Monte Cassino, but to get there we had to take Monte Porchia first.

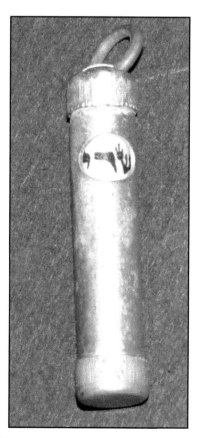

The mezzuzah that I wore with my dog-tags.

On the evening of the initial assault, after finishing up in the kitchen, we were ordered to appear before two Army doctors, one white and one black. The black doctor examined me. "Where have you been?" he questioned. I answered that until now I had been an office worker in North Africa. He grasped my dog-tags to record my name, but before he let them drop back against my chest, he examined the small charm attached to the chain from which they hung. It was a tiny, cylindrical mezzuzah. Inside was a rolled scroll of parchment and written on it was the Hebrew declaration of faith, the 'Shema,' stating that there is only one G-d. On the outside of the scroll were three Hebrew letters and these could be seen in the oval opening. It was one of the Hebrew names for G-d - Shaddai. "Step aside!" commanded the doctor. His reason: my throat appeared irritated. He ordered me to rest for 24 hours. Quietly he added, "Your people have suffered enough."

That order probably saved my life. During those 24 hours, other replacements were sent to the front to Company B, which had been engaging the Germans on Monte Porchia. Company B consisted of just 175 men. After the first 24 hours of the assault on January 4th and 5th, only 25 men returned to combat. The rest were either killed or wounded.

During the second 24 hours of the assault, on January 6th, I was standing with 20 to 30 other men in the back of a truck, a combat infantryman in Company B, being driven to the headquarters that was set up about two miles from the base of Monte Porchia. As soon as we arrived, an officer ordered each of us to pick up a case of ammunition and set off in the direction of Mt. Porchia.

We spread out and briskly walked towards the base of the low mountain. I walked at a distance from the other men. We made our way along the muddy embankment of a small creek in order to avoid mines. If we were shelled, we could jump into the water. As we neared the mountain, men killed in the previous nights' battle lay as if asleep. I walked right past them. Others stopped to look at the hands of the dead soldiers. They were looking for rings on their fingers. If the hand wasn't swollen, they just pulled the ring off the finger. If it was, they cut the finger off with a knife. I pretended not to notice, yet the image burned itself into my brain. What type of person would do such a thing? To lower oneself to such depravity for a useless piece of gold or silver? I continued walking and somehow we joined up with the remnants of Company A at the foot of the mountain. As soon as we dropped off the ammunition which we had brought with us, another soldier and I were ordered to carry a wounded soldier back to the headquarters from which we had just come. We picked him up and put him to sit on top of a rifle carried between us. His right leg was hanging at the knee. Shrapnel had hit it, cut through the flesh, and snapped the bone. There was a blood soaked tourniquet wrapped around his leg to staunch the bleeding. There was no gentle way to carry him back. He screamed out in considerable pain while we retraced our steps. I tried to calm him. "Don't worry...you're going home now. The war is over for you. You're lucky." I said it again and again, my voice straining to pierce the sound of the constant gunfire and explosions, until we reached headquarters and brought him to the field hospital. We were immediately ordered back to the mountain. I hoisted a case of C rations onto my shoulder. The other GI followed my lead and did the same, and we both started back. Each way was about 2 miles.

As soon as I dropped the case of C rations at B company, I was ordered to the eastern edge of the mountain to watch for any enemy movement. Walking along the southern edge, I made my way to a outcropping of rock. I lay motionless on my belly, rifle in front of me, watching, waiting, alert for any movement. I lay there silently while our artillery shells exploded in the distance in front of me, and German artillery shells exploded behind me. The hard ground beneath me made me keenly aware of the rise and fall of my chest. My exhaled breath was visible before me in the cold air. Despite being warm, bundled inside a thick, lined combat uniform, I had no gloves. My fingers became numb. I longed for a baked potato to warm my hands like the ones I carried with me to school in Polyán.

Hours passed before I was relieved. I stiffly rose from the ground, hardly able to move. At that moment, my weapon would have been useless had I needed to fire it. My hands were stiff from the cold. Although it was the middle of the night, there was no such thing as sleep now, just moments of rest. I was sent to another observation post. This time, I was ordered to the mountain's peak. The terrain was rocky. There were no trees, and no shrubs to speak of. Unlike the mountains in the distance, Monte Porchia was mostly barren. There was always the risk of sniper fire, so I made my way through the patches of nearly frozen ground to a crevasse near the top to avoid being targeted. I sat behind the crevasse looking out at the terrain, a flat expanse of land between Monte Porchia and the larger Monte Trocchio, but I couldn't see anything. Further in the distance, and much higher, was Monte Cassino, and on its peak, the Monastery.[23]

The German soldiers were out there somewhere, regrouping, perhaps readying their counter-assault. I sat there watching until I was relieved, but that only meant switching observation posts. We kept alert for any enemy movement. We saw none. During the next day we were motionless, taking cover behind rocks while mortars and artillery flew overhead. At night, the German infantry tried to retake the summit, and they came very close, but we were able to repulse their attacks. The

---

[23] http://www.history.army.mil/books/wwii/winterline/winter-fm.htm

bombardment continued day and night until January 14. The Germans had retreated from their positions on Monte Trocchio, and the Allies, surprised by this, began their attack on Monte Cassino. Company B was pulled back to Capua to reassemble and prepare for our next assignment. Anzio.[24]

My little black book's calendar for 1944
January 6-14 indicate Monte Porchia.
January 30-31 and February 1 indicate the first heavy fighting in Anzio.

---

[24] The 6th Armored Infantry Battalion, an element of the 1st Armored Division received the Presidential Unit Citation, Streamer embroidered Monte PORCHIA.
http://www.history.army.mil/html/forcestruc/lineages/branches/inf/0006in002bn.htm

Forward observers on Monte Porchia after it was occupied by the Allies.
https://www.ibiblio.org/hyperwar/USA/USA-MTO-Salerno/img/USA-MTO-Salerno-p309.jpg

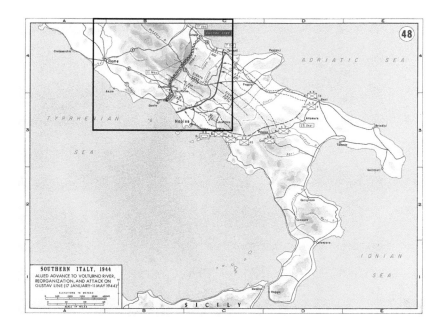

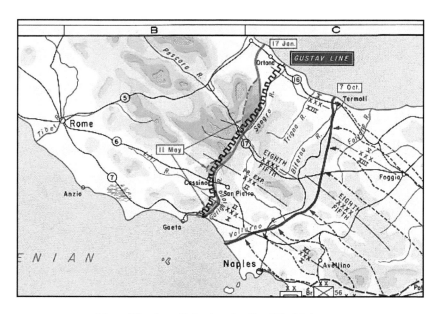

Map of Southern Italy showing the Allied Advance.
http://www.jewishvirtuallibrary.org/map-of-allied-advance-to-volturno-river-january-may-1944

Above: Looking south from Highway 6 towards Monte Cassino, Monte Trocchio, and Monte Porchia.
Photo taken: July 2017

Below: Looking north towards Monte Porchia. Photo taken: July 2017

MT TROCCHIO

MT LA CHIAIA

HIGHWAY NO 6
MT. PORCHIA

S. VITTORE

Above: Looking northwest. Monte Porchia is on the left. 1944
http://www.history.army.mil/books/wwii/winterline/p095.jpg

Below: Looking north towards Monte Porchia, 1944
http://www.dalvolturnoacassino.it/asp/raccolta_image_view.asp?id=3639

C Co Sector

B Co. Sector

A Co Sector

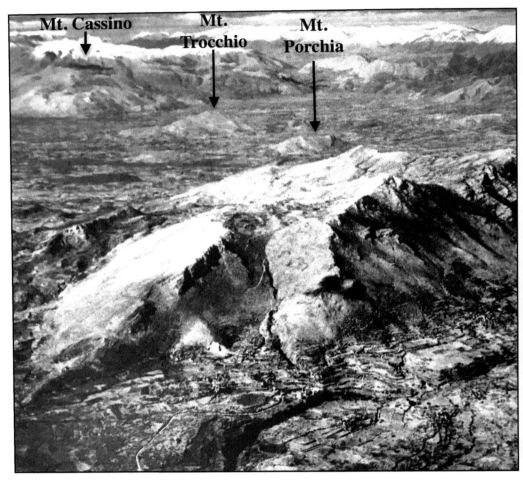

Looking northeast towards Monte Porchia.
Battle History of the First Armored Division, George F. Howe
Combat Forces Press; 1st US Ed edition (1954)

Town of Cassino, Italy, 6 February 1944. The castle is on the small hill in the foreground and the Benedictine monastery is on the summit.
http://history.amedd.army.mil/booksdocs/wwii/woundblstcs/chapter8figure265.jpg

The Benedictine Monastery at the summit of Monte Cassino
http://ifthenisnow.eu/sites/default/files/null/pre_bom_monte_casino.png

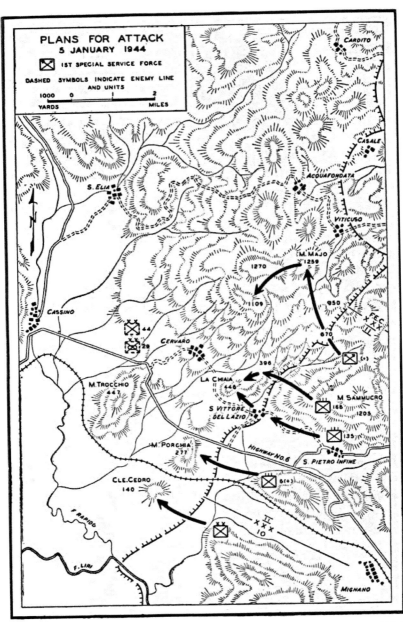

Battle Plans for the attack on Mount Porchia, Cedro Hill, and Mount La Chiaia.
German positions here barred the Allied advance along Highway 6.
http://www.history.army.mil/html/books/100/100-9/CMH_Pub_100-9.pdf

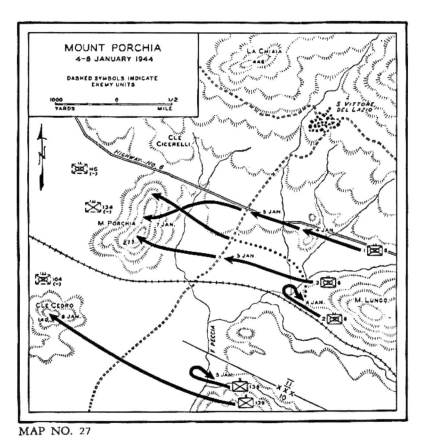

MAP NO. 27

Battle for Mount Porchia - January 4-8, 1944
http://www.history.army.mil/books/wwii/winterline/winter-drive.htm#m27

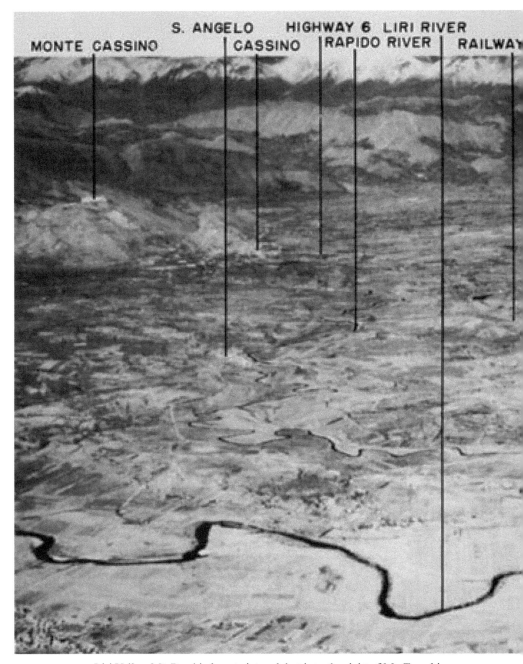

Liri Valley. Mt. Porchia is not pictured, but is to the right of Mt. Trocchio
https://www.ibiblio.org/hyperwar/USA/USA-MTO-Salerno/img/USA-MTO-Salerno-p311.jpg

**The battle for Monte Porchia from the pamphlet
"Fifth Army at the Winter Line"
by the Center of Military History**

On the left wing, II Corps' offensive involved taking Mount Porchia, just south of Highway No. 6 (Map No. 27, above). Task Force A was given the assignment of attacking this isolated hill.

The 1st Battalion, 6th Armored Infantry, moved on the afternoon of 4 January to secure its line of departure. The battalion encountered difficulty in clearing two small rises on either side of Highway No. 6, just north of the end of Mount Lungo, which were vigorously defended by the 5th Company, 134th Grenadiers. Losing his positions by 1930, the enemy counterattacked. Heavy mortar fire met the 2d Battalion as it tried to move west astride the railroad. Until noon of 5 January, the Germans fought hard to stop the drive short of their main defenses. Mauled severely by fire of our artillery, tanks, and tank destroyers, they were forced to withdraw toward prepared positions on Mount Porchia.

At 1515, after an artillery preparation of thirty minutes, the 3d Battalion of the 6th Armored Infantry led an attack that reached the north-south road in front of Mount Porchia. *At dawn of 6 January the 1st and 3d Battalions were ready to resume the effort toward their objective; the 2d Battalion came into the center of the line to join the assault, which began at 0700. Little progress was made during the morning, though tanks attached to Task Force A finally reduced the machine-gun nests in stone houses and pill boxes. Early in the afternoon, after another artillery preparation which included smoke to cover the north flank of the zone, parts of Companies A and B reached the crest on the north end of Mount Porchia. The combat strength of the 1st Battalion had been reduced to 150 men. At 1800 the 48th Engineer Combat Battalion (attached to Task Force A) was committed to the attack as infantry, with companies attached to each of the battalions of the 6th Armored Infantry. An enemy counterattack was launched at 2210 from the northwest by three infantry companies of the Hermann Goering Panzer Division which had been rushed from reserve positions, six miles west of Cassino, to help defend Mount Porchia. The Germans reached positions behind American units on Porchia and caused considerable confusion, but the reinforced 6th Armored Infantry held its gains.*

Despite the enemy efforts, the entire hill fell on 7 January. During the morning the Germans continued to resist from positions near the summit and the southwest edge, but all three battalions of the 6th Armored Infantry succeeded in fighting their way to the crest all along the hill by noon. At 1500 the enemy counterattacked and was beaten off; strong artillery support helped the 6th Armored Infantry hold Mount Porchia. After one more effort to take the hill that night the Germans withdrew.

An alternate account of the battle is recorded in "The Battle History of the 1st Armored Division" by George Howe.

To force its way into the Liri Valley, II Corps had first to clear the route along Highway No. 6 by taking Mts. Porchia and Troccio, south of the highway, and another group of hills and high ridges on the other side. The 1st Armored Division was to provide the elements of a force to defend Mt. Lungo until the attack began, and then to assault Mt. Porchia...II Corps (General Keys) designated a special Task Force Allen for the attack on Mt. Porchia instead of giving the job to the Division command. The force was to combine the 6th Armored Infantry (Col. Paul Steele) with the tanks of two separate armored battalions which were not a part of the Division - the 753d and the 760th - but was to include Division Artillery and the 701st Tank Destroyer Battalion. The 1108th Engineer Combat Group (48th and 235th Battalions) were to give engineer support. Brig. Gen. Frank Allen Jr., of Combat Command B, 1st Armored Division, was to command this force...Allen's plan of attack sent two battalions of the 6th Armored Infantry attacking abreast, the 1st Battalion with elements of the 753d Tank Battalion on the north astride Highway No. 6, and the 2d Battalion, supported by tanks from the 760th Tank Battalion, on the south astride the railroad line. To reach the line of departure for the assault on the hill, the force had to cross more than two miles of open flat, cut by tributaries of the Garigliano. This ground was mined, and well surveyed by enemy artillery. Two low knobs on the northern flank in the path of the 1st Battalion gave the enemy high ground from which heavy machine guns could sweep the valley floor with enfilading fire.

Allen recognized the necessity of crossing this area under the cover of darkness. Although artillery and air attacks on specific targets were to be provided during the two previous days, no special preparation was scheduled for just before the attack, in the hope of achieving surprise. The line of departure was partly under the enemy's control and unlikely to be reached without a fight.

The two assault battalions came down from higher ground and started out across the flat at 1930, 4 January 1944. Ahead of them with mine detectors were men from Company A, 16th Armored Engineer Battalion, who had been parceled out among the infantry companies. Deffenbaugh's 1st Battalion quickly met heavy resistance, and took a long time to reach a phase line while under flanking fire from the two low knobs. Ringsak's 2d Battalion therefore waited at the first phase line for the other battalion to advance abreast of it. There it was struck by an overwhelming volume of deadly accurate artillery and mortar fire.

The troops soon dropped back, leaving scores of casualties on the field. Medics and stretcher bearers were taxed to the utmost by the large numbers to be evacuated...

The enemy counterattacked on the morning of 5 January with infantry and tanks but American artillery drove him back. By 1515, after an artillery preparation, Task Force Allen resumed its approach to Mt. Porchia. The depleted 2d Battalion had gone into reserve. The 1st Battalion shifted southward and took up the attack along the railroad, while the 3d Battalion left the nose of Mt. Lungo to attack along Highway No. 6. The enemy there had been worn down and all but isolated, but the 3d Battalion still had a slow time of it under heavy artillery fire. They got as far as the north-south road from Taverna, on the highway, to Rocca d'Evandro, on the railroad. *From that line of departure, the assault on Mt. Porchia finally started at 0700, 6 January.*

The enemy had been awaiting for an attack for weeks, and gave this one a hot reception. He had put out many mines, including the new Schü mine now first encountered by the attacking force. His pillboxes had withstood the artillery bombardment. The stone houses near Mt. Porchia were used as machine-gun nests. German artillery and mortar fire was heavy. Tanks of the 760th Tank Battalion, leading the deliberate advance, blasted the houses and pillboxes and were aided by elements of the 235th Engineer Combat Battalion. Early in the afternoon, 2 officers and 20 enlisted men of Companies A and B, 6th Armored Infantry, reported that they were on the crest at the north end of Mt. Porchia. They sent back almost as many German prisoners taken there. But the enemy sent in reinforcements from reserve positions west of Cassino; three companies of the Hermann Goering Division counterattacked at dusk and recaptured the top of Mt. Porchia.

At 1800, the 48th Engineer Combat Battalion dropped work along the railroad and entered the fight as infantry, one company to each battalion of the 6th Armored Infantry. The 1st Battalion in turn drove the enemy off the crest during the night, reporting at 0300 to Colonel Steele that they held it again.

The other two battalions mopped up the lower slopes of Mt. Porchia during the morning of 7 January, and dug in along the ridge with the 1st Battalion. The enemy kept them under artillery fire. At nightfall, they awaited the enemy's next and, as it turned out, his last, counterattack on Mt. Porchia. It began at 0100, 8 January, and was a failure.

After four more days, Colonel Steele withdrew the regiment upon its relief by the 141st Infantry. The regiment bivouacked near Bellona on 13 January. Casualties reported then, with later adjustments, were very high. The 6th Armored Infantry had lost 7 officers and 106 enlisted men killed, or died of their wounds, 328 wounded and evacuated (including Colonel Ringsak of the 2d Battalion), and 71 missing in action. Losses in other units brought the totals to 139 killed or died of wounds and 402 wounded by 10 January. *Several hundred replacements came to the regiment during the battle. They had pitched in as ammunition and ration carriers, and were assigned to the companies to restore their total strength.*

V-Mail I sent to my brother Dave on January 14, 1944, after I returned from the front on Monte Porchia. "I was in combat." V-mail correspondence was written on 7x9 inch letter sheets that would go through mail censors before being photographed and transported as thumbnail-sized images in negative microfilm. Upon arrival to their destination, the negatives would be printed. The final print was 4 1/4 by 5 1/4 in, about the size of the image above.

Chapter 17

שתשכביני לשלום ותעמידני לשלום

"she-tashkiveni le-shalom, ve-ta-amideni le-shalom"
Allow me to lie down in peace and let me rise up again in peace.

Soldiers disembarking an LST at Anzio
Source: National Archives (111-SC-192681)

ON JANUARY 22, 1944, the Allies launched a surprise amphibious invasion at Anzio, a port north of Monte Cassino. The mission was to seize the high ground about 20 miles inland and take control of Highways No. 6 and No. 7 cutting off the Germans atop Monte Cassino. The Germans hadn't expected the flanking maneuver and the area was only lightly defended. The Allies, afraid that the weak response was a German trap, consolidated the beachhead and landed more than 36,000 soldiers. Within two days, the Germans regrouped and amassed more than 40,000 troops to oppose the invasion.

In the early morning of January 25th, Combat Command A of the 1st Armored Division sailed from Naples to Anzio, and I was standing on an LST (Landing Ship, Tank) heading for that beachhead. I was tense, not knowing what to expect when the LST's bow would open. I began to focus on the rocking of the LST in the waves. For a moment, I was home in Polyán.

Dezső was late again and the front door was locked. He often went out with the non-Jewish townspeople to dance the csardas, a Hungarian folk dance played by the local Gypsy violinists. He did this against our father's wishes, and he enlisted me to help him sneak back into the house without our father finding out. I was perhaps ten years old and didn't know any better. I idolized my older brother and would have done anything for him. This time was different though, since Marie had joined his escapade for the first time. Until then, Dezső had paid a dance teacher to come to the house to teach Marie how to dance. After a few lessons, she became very good, but even so, my father would never have given her permission to go out dancing.

After our father went to sleep, Dezső convinced her to go with him. He didn't have to argue with her very long, and they went. Now, in the wee hours of the morning, his light tapping on the window pane woke me. I hadn't been sleeping deeply because I excitedly knew that Dezső was relying on me to help. I quickly and quietly tiptoed to the door and unlocked it for them. Marie smiled sheepishly at me, and silently came inside. Dezső's hair was disheveled, his shirt unbuttoned, and his shirt cuffs folded up. He patted my head and said softly, "Thanks, little brother! Remember, not a word to father! Now get to bed and I promise, I'll take you fishing with me in the morning!" I obediently did as I was told, because the promise to go fishing was an excellent bribe, however I didn't get much sleep. Fishing! I could hardly wait!

I awoke at the first sign of daybreak, got out of bed, prayed, and woke Dezső. After all, he promised! He was bleary eyed from his late night antics, but he kept his word. He dressed

Sherman Tanks from the 1st Armored Division being unloaded from an LST.
Anzio, April 27, 1944.
http://liberationtrilogy.com/books/day-of-battle/historical-photos/slideshow/

Soldiers disembarking from an LST at Anzio
http://www.historynet.com/last-ride-at-anzio.htm

quickly, and without praying, grabbed his hat. Together, we walked to the far end of the backyard, where the Latorica River flowed. Dezső helped me into the small rowboat that we kept tied at the river's edge, handed me the rope that tied it to the shore, and then he climbed in, too. The current wasn't very strong and we drifted gently along as Dezső used the oars to steer.

When we reached a "good" spot, Dezső prepared a fishing line. Since he was confident that we would catch some fish, he took his watch off his wrist and gave it to me to hold so that it wouldn't get wet when he would take the fish off the line. I felt so proud that he trusted me to hold his dear watch for him. I put it on my own wrist, even though it was too big. We waited patiently. I looked into the still water, hoping to see a fish swim by and grab the hook. When one did, I got so excited that Dezső's watch went flying into the air. Time slowed down as I watched in horror as the watch splashed into the water. I glanced towards my brother. Dezső was busy with the fish and hadn't noticed. Quickly, I leaned over the edge of the boat, and reached as far as I could, hoping to grab the watch before it sank out of sight. Instead, the boat tilted and I went head first into the chilly water. Not knowing how to swim, I panicked. My arms flailed and I started to swallow water. Suddenly, a hand grabbed me by the shirt and pulled me into the boat. Dezső saved me from drowning. I was wet, cold, and scared. I expected him to take his fury out on me for dropping his watch into the river. Instead, all I saw was tender worry in his face, and relief. He rowed us back to shore with just the one fish, without exchanging even a word. When our father asked what had happened, Dezső merely replied, "The little boy fell in..."

A shell exploded off to the side of our LST and the thunderous noise quickly drew my attention back to the present. However, my daydream reminded me that Dezső had sent a tiny bottle of Scotch in the care package I received from him. I took a small swig to calm my nerves. It helped. Surprisingly, it was quieter than I expected as we approached the shore. There was shelling directed to ships at sea and a lone German aircraft was flying overhead. The LST brought us into the harbor. The giant doors opened, the half track's motor started, and it began to move slowly out over the ramp that had just been extended to the land. We followed the half track off the LST as its tracks kicked up dirt and its exhaust spewed smoke. It was good to be on land again.

The Germans were targeting the landing craft. As more men and equipment poured onto the crowded shore, we waited for orders. Again, hurry up and wait. It was all very surreal.

Everyone thought that we should be moving out, and yet, there we were, waiting for more tanks and halftracks to be unloaded. Only afterwards did we move out to the bivouac area. My first assignment was to patrol the perimeter while the others began to dig in. Rumors spread. Some thought we had taken the Germans completely by surprise, others thought that it was a trap. At any moment, the German counterattack would begin. Yet, as the sky brightened, there wasn't any return gunfire where we were. We began to move inland. The 6th armored infantry's 1st battalion consisted of companies "A", "B", and "C." Company A had tanks and had moved on ahead of us. My company, Company B, had both heavy machine guns and halftracks. We moved out, but the going was slow. The ground was soft and muddy and the tanks and halftracks got bogged down.

A typical American halftrack.
https://www.pinterest.com/pin/461970874259201744

Rather than continue, we began to pull back. We were ordered to dig in. Most of the guys immediately took their shovels from their packs and started digging their foxholes, deep holes in the ground that we would use as shelter. I hesitated momentarily to survey my surroundings. Company A had dug in among a large grove of trees, while Company B was ordered to dig in not far from them in an open plain. Pfft. Thud. Pfft. Thud. The rhythmic sound of shovels slicing through the earth, followed by the gentle thuds of dirt tossed aside punctuated my thoughts. I concluded that when the Germans began shelling us in earnest it would be safer to dig in under the roots of a huge tree at the edge of the woods. An airburst might destroy the tree above, but I would be safe below its roots. So, defying my Sergeant's orders, I took my shovel from my pack and began digging my foxhole.

"Hey, Private, this area is company A only," the sergeant called to me. "Company B is there..." He pointed to the open area just a few yards away.

"I'm digging in here...it's safer." I thrust my shovel into the dirt, let go of the handle so that it stood upright in the ground, turned, and faced him.

"I don't care what you think. Go dig in with the rest of Company B. That's an order!" he barked. I had already made up my mind that I wasn't moving. The Sergeant saw this and raised his weapon, threatening me.

"Try it," I said calmly, drawing my own weapon. "I'll blow your head off." He thought for a moment, gauging me. After what seemed an eternity, he withdrew. I had no idea how long I would be in that foxhole under the tree, but for now, it was mine.

The relative quiet of the first day turned into constant bombardment on the second. Shells began falling like raindrops. One of them exploded above the tree that I had chosen to dig my foxhole under. Branches were destroyed, GI's nearby were killed, but I was safe under its roots. The explosion shattered one of the lenses in my glasses. I picked up the large pieces of the broken lens and put them, along with the frame, into a pocket. I couldn't see clearly without them and for the foreseeable future, everything would be a blur.

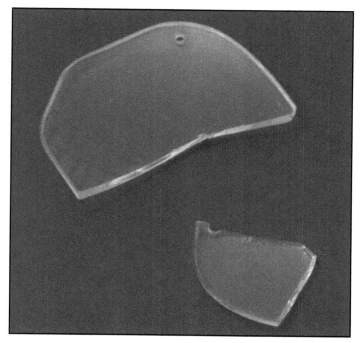

The remains of the broken lens from my glasses that shattered at Anzio.

From that point on, time itself came under attack. Some nights lasted for weeks, while some days lasted mere minutes. If not for the dates I marked in my black book, I would not have known how much time had passed. It all seemed like one long, unending nightmare, one in which you could neither fall asleep nor wake up. Each night, 30 of us would go out on patrol. Each night, ten would return. The rest were dead or wounded. The guys in my unit agreed that I should never give the password when we returned. My English was much better, but I still had a heavy foreign accent. I didn't want to be mistaken for a German soldier and risk getting all of us shot at and killed by friendly fire. We repeated these patrols every night using hit and run tactics to probe the enemy lines. When company A was able to make a break in the German lines, we would be sent to that position by foot as reinforcements. The halftrack was too noisy, and would attract German fire. Once, while walking on the side of the road, we came under heavy attack. All we could do was dig in, using whatever we had to get our heads below the crown of the road for protection. I used the spoon that I ate with as a shovel. Somehow, we managed to pull back. We took cover anywhere we could: under bridges, in the mud and muck of a riverbed, anywhere.

Misery loves company, even at the front. The first few days after we landed, Buddy, a friend of mine from Company A, would come back to my position to find out how I was. His nickname was easy for me to remember, and his given name, Adolph, even easier. After we had been pulled back from Monte Porchia, he saw me writing to my family, so he asked me to write a letter on his behalf to his wife, and I did. We enjoyed talking. I shared the pogacha cookies that my sisters sent in their care package to me, however, I didn't share the small bottles of "medicine" that Dezső continued to send! He asked me to visit him at his position. I never did. I didn't want to take unnecessary chances, even for friendship. I often imagined sending him a message with a homing pigeon, like I had done as a child at home, but even birds knew better than to be on that beachhead.

After our first engagement with the Germans, Buddy stopped coming. He had been killed. The 6th armored infantry may have had the same name, but it was never made up of the same men. Someone was killed every day.

It wasn't just through good luck that I was able to survive. You needed to be alert. I learned quickly that some activities invited death. Our British allies, who also participated in the invasion of Anzio, insisted on having their tea, and the Germans pinpointed the light from their fires. Teatime never ended well. Similarly, Americans loved their cigarettes. However, smoking at night was inevitably bad for your health. The Germans pinpointed the reddish hue of the puffed cigarette. It was usually a man's last.

Every activity associated with life, like eating, sleeping, or bathing became synonymous with death. I used to go to the rear area to eat at the chow line. The chef's last name was Nagy, and his family was from Hungary. We used talk in Hungarian and he would give me plenty of food to eat. I wrote to his parents for him because he wasn't able to write well in Hungarian. He shared his letters from his parents with me. They even invited me to visit when we got home because they were so thrilled to get a well-written letter from their son in Hungarian.

One morning, I spent a little more time in the dugout brushing my teeth with my finger. I just had a bad feeling about going to the chow line. I waited in the dugout, near the halftrack, and this random decision saved my life. The chow line was shelled, and whoever was standing there was killed. The difference between life and death was just a matter of seconds. From then on, I ate cold C rations from the can, just potatoes and meat, alone. I avoided anyplace that people congregated, which included latrines, laundries, and showers. The only way to clean clothing was with gasoline and the only showers available were cold ones. Neither appealed to me and I decided it was better to live in my dirty uniform than to die trying to be clean. As for the toilet, I relieved myself like an animal.

Since company B was often held in reserve to reinforce any attack on the perimeter, one could say that I was lucky. However, there were some men who were luckier than others. There was a soldier named Wenzel who found his way into the basement of a farmhouse near the 'Factory,' an area near the railroad station in Aprilia, a town not far from Anzio. He found some wine, got drunk, and slept there for a few days. It saved his life. Some of the fiercest combat took place in the 'Factory' during the days he was in that basement.

Someone else's luck had run out. I was assigned to replace a man killed at a radio position just a few miles from the German lines. The position was well dug in and heavily fortified with sand bags. The job was to operate the main switchboard responsible for routing calls between different positions. Wires ran from our forward position to others both in the front and in the rear. The ends of each wire came into the switchboard and we sat in front of it answering and connecting the different calls. When a call came through, a jack lamp would light up. I would plug a wire into the corresponding jack and find out who was calling and who they wanted to speak with, and then I would plug in another wire to make the connection. It was the right place to be if you wanted to know what was happening along the front. Knowledge was not always a good thing. One day, a call came through asking to be patched through to Major Deffenbaugh, the battalion commander. I patched it through, only to hear an explosion on the other line. The explosion killed Major Deffenbaugh.[25]

---

[25] Lyle Deffenbaugh had been a Lt. Colonel and received both the Silver Star and the Distinguished Service Cross. He was also the battalion commander at Monte Porchia. He was killed on May 28, 1944.
http://iagenweb.org/wwii/WWIISurnamesC_D/
DeffenbaughLyleJ.html

A soldier operates a switchboard at which field lines from division headquarters and lines to artillery and batteries terminate.
Army Signal Corps photograph. Photographer: J. P. Johnson. 22 March 1944
http://www.ww2online.org/image/soldier-operates-switchboard-which-field-lines-division-headquarters-and-lines-artillery-and

One of the guards at the switchboard's dugout was an imposing man who stood nearly seven feet tall. He had a habit of twirling his pistol around his finger. He also had a habit of letting me know how he felt about me.

"How'd a coward Jew like you get picked for a job like this? I thought all you people stayed in the rear?" I ignored him.

"You know, the only good Jew is a dead Jew..." his pistol stopped spinning and the barrel faced directly at me. He started laughing. "Ah, Gluck, I'm just kiddin'. You know that, right?" I didn't, but I chose to focus on my job and not give him the attention he seemed to crave. "Ok, Gluck, you have everything under control, I'm going out for a smoke." The dugout was set so deeply into the ground that the walls of the entrance gave him room to stand.

No sooner had he stepped outside, then a shell exploded. The ground shook and dust blew into the dugout through the hole where the wires entered. I was certain that he had been killed. When the dust settled and the ringing in my ears began to subside slightly, he walked in, covered in dirt, but alive. Despite his earlier antagonistic remarks, I couldn't have been happier to see him standing in one piece in the doorway. From the expression on his face, he was relieved to see me alive, too. All the communication lines had been blown out. We were both just plain lucky.

One particular day, I thought that my luck had finally run out. We were out on patrol when we came under heavy fire. There was a farmhouse in the distance, and although nobody had given an order to take the farmhouse, somehow I became determined to get there. The crater left behind from an exploded shell was several yards in front of me. I thought it would be a safe place to take cover. I ran to it, and jumped inside. A German sharpshooter stationed in the window of the farmhouse saw me and opened fire. I buried my head just under the edge of the crater. I could hear shouts from behind me. "Gluck, keep your head down! Don't move!" I didn't. The bullets kicked up the dirt beside my head. Fffft. Fffft. Fffft. The dirt went into my eyes, my mouth, my ears...I was pinned down. Fffft. Fffft. Fffft. The slightest twitch would have cost me my life. I had to survive. My sisters would be devastated. "Don't move! We're setting up the machine gun! Stay put!" Rattattat. Rattattat. With our machine gun providing cover, I heard the shouts of GIs from my unit as they made their way closer to the farmhouse. I heard our mortars rain down and explode upon the roof and then I heard the explosion of our grenades. With my head frozen in the dirt, all I could do was listen intently to the sounds I had come to know so well, and think. I was furious with myself. How stupid! I knew better than to believe that I, one soldier, could singlehandedly change the tide of a battle, and win the war. I swore, then and there, that I wouldn't make the same mistake. I'd let the heavy weapons do their job.

Finally, after what seemed like an eternity, the sharpshooter who had been targeting me stopped his fire. There was relative quiet in my direction, but I didn't dare move until I had convinced myself that the Germans had abandoned their position in the farmhouse and pulled back. When I did, I took a chance and jumped up from the crater and ran back behind the mound I had originally climbed from in order to take cover and regain my composure. Eventually, I joined up with the rest of my unit where we regrouped, took a head count, and made our way to a waiting truck that brought us back to the bivouac area. A rumor began to circulate that a German sharpshooter had been captured wearing a woman's dress. I wondered if it was the same one who had targeted me.

Chapter 18

Ruppemi l'alto sonno ne la testa un greve truono,
sì ch'io mi riscossi come persona ch'è per forza desta;

A heavy thunder broke the deep lethargy within my head so that I jumped,
Like a person who is wakened by force;
Inferno (Canto IV), Dante Alighieri

THE SCREAMS OF THOSE CONDEMNED TO HELL would be no match for the screams of the German rockets that cried out over our heads. We called them "screaming mimis." These shells were fired eight or ten at a time, and as they flew overhead, they gave off a shrill piercing sound. Punctuating these shrieks was the sound of German artillery shells with rocket-assisted boosters built into them. The Germans fired them from huge guns mounted to railroad cars. They would roll the gun out of its hiding spot to fire its rocket, and then roll it back again making it extraordinarily difficult for it to be targeted by our aircraft. There was always a second explosion when the rocket assist kicked in. That sound was a blessing, though. If you heard it, it meant that the rocket was continuing overhead to hit the rear area or beyond to the ships ferrying supplies to the beachhead. If you didn't hear the rocket assist, you were finished. Someone nicknamed the railroad gun 'Anzio Annie.' [26]

Aerial dogfights were our entertainment. The engine roar of the German Messerschmitt 109's was distinct from that of our P-47's, and theirs was distinct from our B-17's, B-24's, and P38's that flew above us daily. Often I could see the parachute of the losing pilot as he floated peacefully out of the heavens towards our hell. In mid-February, one particular aerial assault made heaven, earth, and my own little portion of hell shake

---

[26] http://samilitaryhistory.org/vol133lw.html

with thunderous fury. Overhead passed hundreds of Allied aircraft, relentlessly bombing the German positions in Cassino. I thought we would be moving out at any moment. However, the bombardment made no difference at all. Our position stayed the same, but I later learned that the monastery at Monte Cassino had been destroyed that night.

Monster Krupp K5 280mm railway gun captured by the Allies in Citaveccia, Italy. The class included two guns, which the Germans named Leopold (pictured) and Robert. Nicknamed "Anzio Annie," both shelled the beachhead.
http://waralbum.ru/wp-content/uploads/2012/04/K5_Leopold_1944.jpg

Four months passed in this way. Day in and day out. Night after night. Bombardment. Shelling. Airbursts. Tracers. Anti-aircraft. Mortars. Planes. Machine gun fire. Flares. Those who believe hell doesn't exist know nothing. Those who believe hell is below us are wrong. Hell was there, right upon the Earth, and six feet below it, too. A buddy of mine and I dug down deeply and made ourselves a house underground. It was the safest place to be when we weren't on patrol, and although we would sweat inside, it was better than being outside. Sometimes, I'd sit at the entrance and write a letter with only a small candle to light the page. If a German plane flew overhead, I'd blow the candle out, and like a groundhog, clamber back into my underground "home." I had been there so long that I began to think that we should have just kept digging because we'd have gotten to Rome a lot faster.

In order to remain hopeful, I kept before me an image of my sisters back "home" in Ohio, figuratively and literally. Since basic training I carried pictures of them, and they sent new ones with their letters. In the year that I was gone, their faces had aged from worry. They needed me. They were praying for my safe return. They were my reason to survive. Although I was hopeful that somehow, with G-d's help, I *would* survive, the reality of the situation was that survival was not a foregone conclusion. The urge to leave something of myself, something tangible, some marker that would be proof of my very existence and of what I had been through became a pressing concern. I decided to use my knife to engrave my history onto the side of my chow cup. I began by carving out the emblem of the first armored division, which was a tank pierced by a lightning strike enclosed by a triangle with the number one in the vertex. Above the triangle, I carved the word "Ohio" with the year 1940 beneath it. That was the year I had arrived to my adopted homeland. Beneath the triangle I carved out the words "6th Armored Infantry." To the left of the triangle, I carved my name and to the left of that I began a list of all the places that I had been. First went my birthplace, Czechoslovakia, split over two lines. Beneath it, Hungaria, Yugoslavia, Germany, Italy, Morocco, Gibralter, Portugal, Lisbon, Spain, N.Y., Ohio. Alongside these places I carved "1938-1940." Of course, there were mistakes in the spelling. It didn't matter. I began another column. Africa. Oran. Naples. Cassino. Anzio. I became determined to add the name of every place I was in until I returned to the U.S.A. If I didn't survive, anyone finding my cup would know *where* I had been, and more importantly, that I *had* been.

April arrived. There was a lull in the fighting and I had an opportunity to go to the rear and try to get my glasses replaced. I met a Jewish pharmacist in the field hospital. "I'll tell you what," he said, giving my jacket an admiring look. "Give me your combat jacket, and I'll see what I can do to help you." I took it right off, even though I still could have used it, and gave it to him. I hoped he would be able to help me in some way. Although he didn't get me glasses, he did something even better. Seeing that I was exhausted, he contacted a doctor he knew. I was examined and reclassified for a non-combat position. It didn't help, at least not yet. I was sent back to the front.

By the end of May, after finally breaking through the German lines, we began moving north. It was stop and go. Since we were still held in reserve, we had to wait for the front to advance before we continued. Our halftrack passed the bodies of dead German soldiers that lay on the side of the road. During the night of June 4, the 1st Armored Division liberated Rome and continued north in pursuit of the retreating Germans. 132 days after I landed at Anzio, I carved the word "Roma" on my cup. The battle of Anzio was over.

Photos of Hermine (left) and Marie that I carried with me.

The Pine Woods—a 6th Infantry mortar squad cleans its weapons.

I remember this photo of my squad being taken.
I was just outside the frame on the right side, next to Wenzel, the GI smoking.
The Story of the First Armored Division, Army Booklet

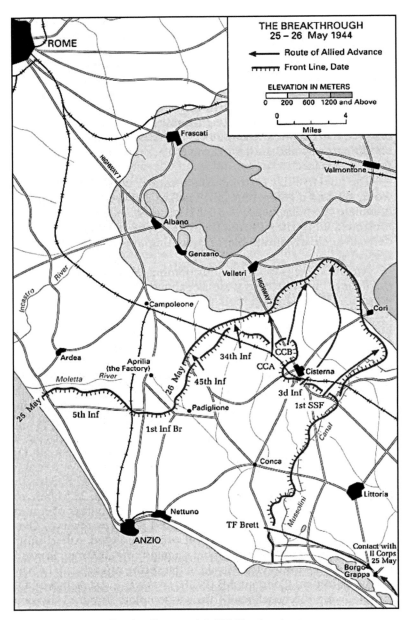

Combat Command A (CCA) at breakout.
http://www.history.army.mil/brochures/anzio/map4.JPG

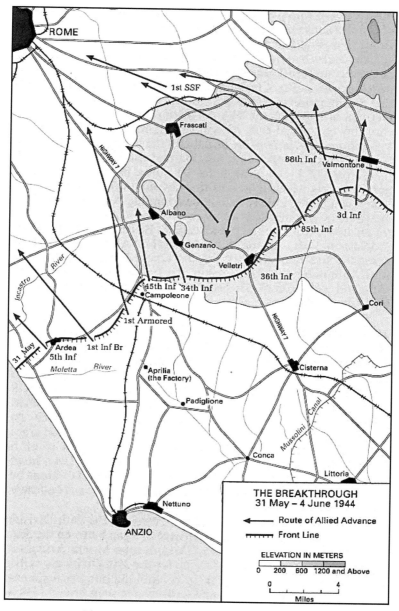

The 1st Armored Division races north to Rome.
http://www.history.army.mil/brochures/romar/map3.jpg

AFRICA
ORAN
ITALY
NAPELS
CASSINO
ANZIO
ROMA
LEGHORN
FLORENCE
PISA
1943-44
FRANCE
MARSEILLES
DIJON
NANCY
PARIS
GERMANY
WORMS
HEILBRONN
LE HAVRE
U.S.A.
O-HI-O
19-40
IRVING
1
1943
1945
ARMORED INFANTRY

THE CROSSES GROW ON ANZIO

Oh, gather 'round me, comrades; and
listen while I speak
Of a war, a war, a war where hell is
six feet deep.
Along the shore, the cannons roar. Oh
how can a soldier sleep?
The going's slow on Anzio. And hell is
six feet deep.

Praise be to G-d for this captured sod that
rich with blood does seep.
With yours and mine, like butchered
swine's; and hell is six feet deep.
That death awaits there's no debate;
no triumph will we reap.
The crosses grow on Anzio, where hell is
six feet deep.

. . . Audie Murphy, 1948

Opposite page: My chow cup...hand engraved with my knife.

Following page: Fifth Army Organizational Chart
https://history.army.mil/books/wwii/winterline/winter-conclusion.htm

1ST RANGER BATTALION
Commanding Officer
Lt. Col. William O. Darby

3D RANGER BATTALION
Commanding Officer
Lt. Col. Herman W. Dammer

4TH RANGER BATTALION
Commanding Officer
Lt. Col. Roy A. Murray, Jr.

---

10 CORPS (BRITISH)
Commanding General
Lt. Gen Sir Richard L. McCreery

46 DIVISION
Commanding General
Maj. Gen. J.L.L. Hawkesworth

128, 138, 139 BRIGADES

56 DIVISION
Commanding General
Maj. Gen. G.W.R. Templer

167, 168, 169 BRIGADES
201 GUARDS BRIGADE

23 ARMORED BRIGADE
Commanding Officer
Brig. R.H.B. Arkwright

II CORPS (U.S.)
Commanding General
Maj. Gen Geoffrey Keyes

36TH DIVISION
Commanding General
Maj. Gen. Fred L. Walker

141st, 142d, 143d
REGIMENTAL COMBAT TEAMS

3D DIVISION
Commanding General
Maj. Gen. Lucian K. Truscott, Jr.

15th, 7th, 30th
REGIMENTAL COMBAT TEAMS
(18 November-29 December)

1ST ARMORED DIVISION
Commanding General
Maj. Gen. Ernest N. Harmon

6th ARMORED INFANTRY REGIMENT
1st, 13th ARMORED REGIMENTS
(17 December-14 January)

1ST SPECIAL SERVICE FORCE
Commanding Officer
Col. Robert T. Frederick

34TH DIVISION
Commanding General
Maj. Gen. Charles W. Ryder

133d, 135d, 168th
REGIMENTAL COMBAT TEAMS
(From 24 December)

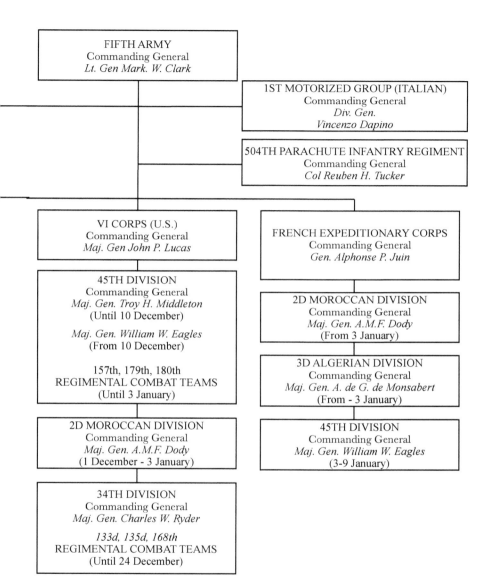

A brief description of the 6th Armored Division's activity in Anzio as related in http://www.a-1-6.org/regulars/RegHist.htm

Before the end of January, the 1st Armored Division split in two parts -- Division HQ and Combat Command A were at Anzio -- 1st and 3rd battalions were part of that group. Combat Command B was left in an area south of Cassino -- 2nd battalion was with this group.

On the night of 21-22 January 1944, the attack on Anzio began, against minimal resistance. Combat Command A was still in the Naples Staging Area. Units began moving to the assembly area about 4 miles north of Anzio 24-28 January.

On 29 January, 1st Battalion attacked, while 3rd battalion remained in reserve. Thick mud bogged down the vehicles, and the 6th Regiment got no further than the ridges near the rail track. On 31 January, another attack was planned, but called off. The enemy there was in too great strength, so 1st and 3rd battalions stood down.

During the night of 31 January to 1 February, units moved back to the staging area north of Anzio. All units dug in in the Padiglione woods, including vehicles. The enemy kept up a barrage on the entire beachhead, making extensive use of air-burst artillery shells.

On 8 February, 2nd battalion rejoined the regiment on the beachhead, arriving in time for heavy bombing.

On or about the night of 18-19 February, a task force including 1st and 3rd battalions conducted a raid toward Carroceto. 3rd battalion was on one side of the road, about half-way to Carroceto, when the attack was halted. Some of the enemy positions were destroyed, and some enemy were taken prisoner. Then enemy conducted a counter-attack the next day, but it was stopped by artillery fire. After this raid, the regiment spent some time in a reserve role. The months of March, April, and May were a stalemate, although soldiers were still killed or wounded during patrol activity, or from artillery fire and bombardment.

For two weeks in March, the 6th took over part of the line from the 45th Division.

In the middle of March, Mt. Vesuvius erupted south of Naples.

Through March and April, replacements continued to arrive, various tank units trained with the regiment, and parts of Combat Command B began to rejoin the regiment at Anzio. By May, mosquitoes from the marshes made life miserable.

On 23 May 1944, after artillery preparation, Combat Command A and Combat Command B began to attack. 1st and 3rd battalions were with Combat Command B. Tanks, in the lead, continuously hit mines and suffered blown treads. 3rd battalion bypassed the tanks and moved ahead, although after a while, some tanks were able to catch up. Some enemy guns were taken out, but fire from German artillery and tanks began to fall on the Regiment. Friendly counter-fire took out the German tanks and artillery, but the Regiment was unable to cross the railroad tracks before dark. During the night, a defensive perimeter was formed along with the tanks.

On 24 May, with less opposition, 3rd battalion led the attack across the railroad tracks to the high ground on the other side.

Tanks and infantry combined to knock out infantry and gun positions in the woods. Several enemy prisoners were taken. Again, the 3rd battalion out-posted with the tanks that night until relieved by the 34th Division.

On 26 May, 1st battalion, with another task force, advanced in the direction of Velletri. Artillery fire struck the area. One concentration hit the battalion command post, killing the battalion commander, LTC Lyle J. Deffenbaugh. About this time, COL Steele was relieved and replaced by LTC Edgar C. Doleman.

On 29 May, Combat Command A and Combat Command B began to attack further west. 2nd battalion was with Combat Command A. Attached tanks bypassed strongpoints, while the infantry, following, caught the brunt of the fire and suffered casualties. 1st battalion reinforced Combat Command B the next morning. For its efforts on the beaches of Italy, the 6th earned Battle Streamer - ANZIO, WITH ARROWHEAD.

On 3 June 1944, the 6th Infantry Regiment, less the 2nd battalion which was in reserve, assembled for the drive up Highway 7 in Italy. Anti-tank resistance and blown bridges slowed the advance. Units had to leave the highway to use secondary roads, but entered into Rome from the south at dusk. Combat Command B proceeded north, through Rome, toward Lake Bracciano and beyond. Following relief by the 36th Division on 10 June, the Regiment returned to Lake Bracciano and became the reserve.

On 18-20 June, the Regiment assembled near Grosetto. 2nd and 3rd battalions were with Combat Command B, with the 1st battalion now in reserve.

On 22 June, the Regiment began an attack which lasted until 10 July. The attack advanced along secondary roads through the hills to Massa Marittima and Pomerance to Ponsaco and Pontedera. At the end of June, the Regiment reached the Cecina River north of Pomerance, and most of the division headed for Bolgheri. For its operations throughout the Rome-Arno Campaign, the 6th was awarded the **ROME-ARNO** Campaign Streamer. [27]

---

[27] For more reading on Anzio, see the following:
http://www.history.army.mil/brochures/anzio/72-19.htm
http://www.history.army.mil/html/books/100/100-10/
CMH_Pub_100-10.pdf

BUY VICTORY WAR BONDS STAMPS

WEATHER
Warm, showers tonight; Tuesday cooler.
Yesterday's high, 89 at 2 p. m.

Columbus Evening Dispatch

OHIO'S GREATEST HOME DAILY

Associated Press News, Features, And Wirephotos
International News Service

VOL. 73, NO. 341. *** Telephone—MAin 1234 COLUMBUS 16, OHIO, MONDAY, JUNE 5, 1944 (Entered at Columbus, Ohio, Post Office as Second-Class Matter) 18 PAGES PRICE

ALLIES PUSH NORTH FROM ROME

Romans Cheer Liberators--Some Die for Freedom; Indian File Yanks Encircle Duce's Empty Balcony

By DANIEL DE LUCE

ROME, JUNE 5.—(AP).—Mussolini's balcony hung empty in the gauzy mist of moonlight as Fifth Army soldiers in Indian file encircled the former dictator's office at the Palazzo Venezia last night and thousands of Roman Partisans fanned the fires of liberation.

De Luce

Behind a screen of Partisan volunteers who wore hammer and sickle armbands, waved red flags and brandished old firearms, American forces drove to the Tiber river through futile German resistance in the streets—resistance that was real despite the German pretense that Rome was an open city.

Some Romans died in the fight for freedom, cigarets between their lips and cheers in their throats. Some were lying across the German machineguns they had tried to seize barehanded.

"Why were you so long in coming? We expected you four months ago," said some of the Partisans.

Others in unwhimpering silence, asking no questions, waited for their wounds to be bandaged.

Thousands of the people of Rome marched jubilantly in impromptu parades with the occupying forces. They waved flags and red banners, splashed through water from broken water mains to grasp the hands of the troops, almost smothered the liberators with roses and kisses.

They shrieked curses at blinking German prisoners, cried at the sight of a dying American soldier. With shrill cries they warned of hidden anti-tank guns and machinegun nests.

Mothers held up their children to be kissed by the grimy, bearded doughboys, in sight of dying German scout car crewmen.

But the doughboys just swung along in a tired shuffle in the face of all this demonstration, awestruck by the famous avenues that had been their goal for nine long, dangerous and wearing months.

At a police station near the Forum officers said all was quiet in Vatican City and that the last Germans were fleeing from their rendezvous near the Colosseum.

Wherever the Americans moved forward today against hit and run Nazi armored forces they found Italians—of all ages and degrees of poverty—ready to die for "the liberation."

I saw a 10-year old boy carrying ammunition for his elder brother on sniper patrol. A stubbly-bearded, gray-haired peasant in his middle fifties begged to be put into action. A dark-haired girl with a bandolier insisted "me Partisan, too."

By military standards the battle for Rome was merely a heavy skirmish with the objectives temporarily being to secure the Tiber bridges. From just behind the leading tank, however, I found the struggle as hard on the senses as getting hit between the eyes with brass knuckles.

Several tanks and one heavy self-propelled gun held up our armor for seven hours at a point five miles outside Rome. But the Allied commander accepted unusual risks rather than bring down a devastating fire on areas where civilians might be sheltering or cultural treasures harmed.

As the final push sent General Sherman tanks clattering through Centocelle's alleyways and green fields, their machineguns drove scores of German snipers from cover. Italian Partisans rode the American tanks or preceded them like game beaters.

"I'll bet there are enough Fascist party badges in the Tiber today to make the fish sick," said one officer.

Near the San Lorenzo railyards in Rome the Partisans shrilly warned of a German 88 about 200 yards behind the next corner. Light tanks swerved and hit it from the rear while weeping mothers murmured blessings, kissed the hands of the tank destroyer crewmen and lifted up their children to be kissed on the cheek.

Within a few seconds after the first tanks crossed under the arch of Porta Maggiore, one of the gates of Rome, the avenue ahead was filled with what seemed all of the population of Rome. Crowds in order to clasp our hands waded through water from a water main broken by the Germans in destroying a Fiat factory.

As we passed the Basilica of Santa Maria Maggiore, Romans from upper apartment windows shouted a warning that a German scout car was head.

We were proceeding down the Via Nazionale in front of the Bank of Italy—one block from the Roman Forum—when a German heavy machinegun suddenly began firing. My driver, Pfc. Kenneth Kopplin, of Huron, S. D., headed straight into the entrance of a big store. When the shooting stopped we saw the wrecked scout car ahead with two Germans dead and another dying with blood gushing from his chest.

By EDWARD KENNEDY

ROME, JUNE 5.—(AP).—Rome, shining brightly in sparkling sunlight and spared almost entirely from the ravages of war, today gave Fifth Army troops a welcome which turned the Eternal City into a near carnival.

The city is virtually intact. The Germans, last of whom slinked from the capital last night like beaten dogs, limited their demolitions to a few installations of no artistic or religious importance.

Bricker Slates National Radio Talk Saturday

Following a four-day campaign tour of eastern cities, Gov. John W. Bricker arrived back in Columbus Monday where he will make preparations for a radio address over a nation-wide hook-up from New York Saturday night.

The Governor announced in New York that he will also address the Seventy-Eight Club, composed of "freshmen members" of Congress, in Washington on June 14, and probably participate in a nationally broadcast radio forum while in Washington at that time.

Upon his arrival here Monday morning, the Governor went at once to the home of John Galbreath, chairman of his campaign committee. Mr. Galbreath has been ill.

Mr. Bricker's "barnstorming" tours probably will be few from now on, since the Governor expects to go to Chicago on June 19, a week before the Republican National Convention, to lay plans for his battle on the convention floor and in the caucus rooms.

Friends Among Delegates

The Ohio Governor was believed to have made many friends among the Connecticut delegates whom he addressed Saturday at Hartford. Although pledged to Gov. Raymond E. Baldwin, the Connecticut delegation adopted a resolution stipulating that no one should "bind" the delegates of that state to vote for any candidate for President other than Baldwin until and unless the delegation meets and takes such action.

At Hartford Mr. Bricker reiterated his belief that the GOP convention is going to be a "deliberative" one, explaining that the action of the Indiana State Convention in refusing to instruct its delegates to vote for Gov. Dewey reflects the sentiment of the Mississippi Valley.

Sentiment Indicated

Another indication that sentiment is shifting in the mid-west came in an editorial in The Tulsa

Continued on Page SIX, Column THREE

OHIO WAR CASUALTIES

KILLED IN ACTION

JACKSON — Shipfitter 2c Eugene Hayth.

MISSING IN ACTION

MARION—Maj. H. T. Hill, Austria.

BELLEFONTAINE — S/Sgt. John F. Boone, Germany.

WOUNDED IN ACTION

WILMINGTON — Pvt. George A. Benlehr, Italy.

PRISONERS

COLUMBUS—Lt. Franklynn V. Cetner, AAF, 25, 2140 Cambridge Blvd, and 2nd Lt. Oscar Iezman, AAF, 26, 543 E. Fulton St, Germany. (Both previously reported missing.)

Scene of Allies Fighting in Rome

In this radiophoto of the actual fighting in Rome, Allied infantrymen are pictured dashing along a street apparently under fire as a German tank burns. Allied tanks in the background spearhead the advance. This (AP) Wirephoto was furnished by the U. S. Signal Corps.

Hitler Says Rome Abandoned To Keep City from Being Destroyed

LONDON, JUNE 5.—Adolf Hitler acknowledged the fall of Rome belatedly last night with declarations that the German fighting front had moved to the northwest of the city and that a proposal had been made to the Allies to regard the Italian capital as an open city.

Two special German communiques—the first word in many days from the Fuehrer's headquarters—were broadcast after Allied troops had liberated the eternal city.

The fight in Italy will go on, said the first announcements, "to force final victory for Germany and her Allies. The year of the invasion will bring Germany's enemies an annihilating defeat at the most decisive moment." It declared German troops had left Rome "to prevent its destruction."

The other announcement asserted Field Marshal Albert Kesselring had given the Vatican proposals that Rome be made an open city, and asked they be conveyed to the Allied command.

The conditions offered by Kesselring, said the German radio, proposed that the open city of Rome should be:

"From San Paolo, except for a railroad line to the north, up to Piazza Maggiore, then from Piazza Maggiore following the railway line and the station Tiburtina to the last of the Villa Chigi.

"The railway line and Tiburtina station shall be outside the open city area from Villa Chigi up to the Tiber bend one and a half kilometers (nine-tenths of a mile) south-southeast of the race course of the Torre Des Quinto, from where the line shall run south of the Tiber to Ponte Mil-

Continued on Page SIX, Column FOUR

Well, They Never Knew What Benito Meant, Either

NEW YORK, JUNE 5.—(UP).—The Allied entry into Rome received its crowning touch today when a soldier stood with one of his comrades on the marble balcony overlooking the famous Palazzo Venezia where Mussolini used to harangue the Italian people and made a speech about the fallen dictator, NBC said.

A cheering crowd of Italian men, women and children stood below and although they didn't understand a word he said they laughed and cheered and waved flags.

Bulletins

Swimmer Saves Self

Carl J. Kueffner, 36, of 796 Mohawk St., was caught in the underflow while swimming near the dam north of the Greenlawn Av bridge in the Scioto River about 1 p. m. Monday, but managed to make his own way to shore before emergency squadmen, called by youths who saw the swimmer's difficulty, arrived on the scene.

Insurance Is Interstate

WASHINGTON, JUNE 5.—(UP).—Overruling a decision that has stood for 75 years, the Supreme Court held today that insurance is business in interstate commerce, and is subject to the Sherman Anti-Trust Act.

Rome Food Aid Planned

WASHINGTON, JUNE 5.—(UP).—Undersecretary of State Edward R. Stettinius said today that prompt measures are being taken to relieve food shortages in Rome.

Resistance Ends In City; Troops Cross Tiber, Pursue Foe

By LARRY NEWMAN

NAPLES, JUNE 5.—(INS).—Allied mechanized columns forced the Tiber River and streamed through the streets of liberated Rome at breakneck pace today in pursuit of disorganized German forces seeking to make a new stand somewhere far north of the eternal city.

(A Berlin military spokesman said that the "great battle in Italy is continuing with undiminished fury after the Allied occupation of Rome." Two centers of present fighting, Berlin said, are the sectors northeast of Rome and the southern slopes of the Sabine Hills. "Fifth Army attempts to overtake the withdrawing German troops were frustrated," the broadcast alleged).

Official announcement that the last vestiges of enemy resistance inside Rome had come to an end was made at 12:08 P. M. today (6:08 A. M., E. W. T.) by the headquarters of Sir Henry Maitland Wilson.

Before this time, it was possible only to say with absolute truth that American and British forces had consolidated themselves strongly only on the right flank, while enemy troops on the left had continued rear-guard resistance in an effort to protect the mass withdrawal to the north.

An official communique formally announcing the city's liberation revealed the Tiber River already has been crossed in some places by the Allies, making it manifestly impossible for the Germans to offer any further organized resistance within the capital.

WASHINGTON, JUNE 5.—(AP).—President Roosevelt will address the nation at 8:30 p. m., Columbus time tonight, to discuss the fall of Rome, in a 15-minute broadcast to be carried by the four major networks.

"Leading elements of our Fifth Army troops have passed through the city and are now across the Tiber in some places," Gen. Wilson's statement said.

The triumphant Fifth Army troops liberators of the first Axis-dominated capital in Europe to return to civilized influence, scarcely paused in their drive through Rome.

Except for essential forces left behind to maintain order, the bulk of the Allied army swept out of the redeemed city to the north, continuing in relentless pursuit of the harried Germans.

It was evident the Nazis would attempt to establish a new line somewhere south of the Po River valley.

The extent to which German armed strength was smashed in the crucial days preceding first Allied penetration of Rome's borders yesterday afternoon was shown by the fact that 337 enemy prisoners taken at Velletri had been thrown together from 50 different companies.

Throughout the day, planes of the Allied tactical air force flew more than 900 sorties in the Rome area alone.

ROME, JUNE 5.—(INS).—King Victor Emanuel today turned over his crown to Prince Umberto in conformance with a recent statement that he planned to retire as Italy's ruler as soon as Rome fell to the Allies.

Meantime the government of Marshal Pietro Badoglio was in another political crisis because his cabinet is clamoring for another reshuffle of the ministry in order to place more civilians in positions of power.

Six hundred enemy vehicles, part of the parade of routed German strength streaking to the north, were destroyed. Another 600 were damaged.

The roads north of the capital were jammed with wrecked and burning vehicles. Tanks filled with German dead littered the streets.

Allied infantry and tanks meanwhile continued to advance on the whole main front south and east of Rome, capturing Fiuggi and the neighboring town of Acuto. Fur-

Continued on Page SIX, Column ONE

Time Table of Allies' Advance from Tunis to Rome

Airmen Make 29-Day Trek Through Enemy Land

It was a short war so far as two Columbus members of a Liberator crew based in Italy are concerned.

Chronologically, the overseas service of S/Sgt. Merle A. Neff, 21-year-old son of Mr. and Mrs. Frank Neff, 983 S. Champion Av, and Sgt. William Park, 27, son of Mr. and Mrs. Harvey E. Park, 2180 Sale Rd, goes like this:

On March 4, they climbed into "My Aching Back" at Salt Lake City, Utah, and flew to Italy.

On April 12, with three engines of their B-24 gone, they bailed out over enemy territory, their mission uncompleted.

On May 11, they reported back to a base of the 15th Air Force and the intervening 29 days must remain a "blackout."

On June 2, they landed in New York City, two days less than three months after they had gone overseas.

On 13th Mission

Sgt. Park was on his 13th mission and S/Sgt. Neff on his seventh on that ill-fated April 12. They were within half an hour of their target when two engines went out, disabled by anti-aircraft fire.

"We had dropped out of formation and were losing altitude fast as we tried to get into the clouds for protection in case enemy fighters came along," Sgt. Park said Monday.

"Then as we were trying to get over an 8000-foot mountain, the third engine went out," put in S/Sgt. Neff.

The two Columbus men watched the parachutes of five others of the crew float down toward the treetops in stair-step style and then Neff joined them. Park was the last to jump. The pilot, co-pilot and bombardier stayed with the ship and their fate is not known.

Within five hours the seven were united and then began a 29-day trek over mountains and through woods. They slept in haymows and ate scanty rations.

"The eats weren't too good but we didn't go hungary," they both agreed.

S/Sgt. Neff celebrated his 21st birthday in enemy territory and Sgt. Park wasn't too sure he'd live to be 28 next month. Even now their feet aren't fully recovered from that long hike through country that was rugged, to say the least.

50-50 Chance

Fliers who land in enemy territory have a 50-50 chance of getting back safely, they feel, and luck has a lot to do with making the most of that chance. Later this month both of them will report to the AAF Redistribution Center at Miami Beach, Fla., and it's not likely they'll return to combat duty in the area from which they have just returned.

S/Sgt. Neff, a truck driver for the Cussins & Fearn Co. before he entered the service in January, 1943, was radioman-gunner on the Liberator and Sgt. Park was engineer-tail gunner. He worked at the Ohio Malleable Iron Co. before joining the AAF in October, 1941.

S/SGT. MERLE A. NEFF AND SGT. WILLIAM A. PARK

Wickard Addresses Otterbein Class

The postwar choice of an expanding economy to promote the security of the nation, or a shrinking economy and lower standard of living, was placed before graduates of the 1944 class at Otterbein College, Westerville, Monday morning, by Secretary of Agriculture Claude R. Wickard, who made the commencement address in the college church on the campus.

At the same ceremony the cabinet member received the honorary degree of doctor of humane letters, in company with three other men who also received honorary degrees. Fifty-six seniors were in the 1944 graduating class.

Dr. J. Ruskin Howe, president of Otterbein, presented the degrees. Other recipients of honorary degrees were: The Rev. Charles M. Bowman, Westerville, superintendent of the Southeast United Brethren Conference, and the Rev. Elmer A. Schultz, general director of Christian Education, U. B. Allegheny Conference, both doctor of divinity degrees, and a doctor of education degree to Harold L. Boda, assistant superintendent of schools, Dayton.

Emphasizing that the present-day graduate faces more challenging problems than peacetime graduates, and that

Continued on Page SIX, Column THREE

— BUY WAR STAMPS —

That's a Big Help

NEW YORK, JUNE 5.—(INS).—The Japanese official radio comment on the Allied occupation of Rome declared today:

"We have received the news with great sympathy."

— BUY WAR STAMPS —

COOLER DUE TUESDAY

Columbus residents who have been taking the heat wave in their stride, will welcome Weatherman George Mindling's forecast of somewhat cooler weather Tuesday.

Columbus Evening Dispatch, June 5, 1944

Chapter 19

As part of the 1st Armored Division, the 6th armored infantry continued north as we pursued the Germans. Company B was usually in reserve, assisting Company A as needed, and escorting prisoners to the rear. It was stop and go the whole way. At intersections, we stopped, looked, and listened; not for traffic, but to be on the lookout for the low rumble of remote controlled mini tanks[28] that the Germans packed with explosives, or their telltale wires extending across the roadway and into the woods.

[28] The SdKfz. 302 (Sonderkraftfahrzeug, 'special-purpose vehicle'), called the Leichter Ladungsträger ('light charge carrier'), or Goliath, carried 60 kilograms of explosives. The vehicle was steered remotely via a joystick control box connected to it by a 650-meter cable attached to the rear of the vehicle. Goliaths were used by specialized Panzer and combat engineer units on all fronts where the Wehrmacht fought, beginning in early 1942. Goliaths were used at Anzio. https://en.wikipedia.org/wiki/Goliath_tracked_mine

As we captured German soldiers, I had a chance to talk to a few of them. Some were real Nazis, indoctrinated with hatred, while others were Polish or Czech, regular guys who had been conscripted by the Germans to fight, and who claimed that they had been threatened with being shot if they didn't. I didn't feel sorry for them, just like I didn't feel sorry for the Italians that I saw as we advanced. From my observations, the people in the cities had suffered, while the farmers living in the countryside seemed to have plenty of food. All of them complained that the Germans had taken everything. My only thought was that they brought this misery upon themselves by supporting Mussolini in the first place. With my knife I inscribed into my cup the cities of Leghorn (Livorno), Florence, and Pisa. Finally, during the first week of August, my unit[29] was taken off from the front line, and I was sent back to a replacement depot north of Naples. I had been overseas as a soldier longer than I had lived in the United States.

My mail finally caught up with me and I received a letter from Buddy's wife. She had only just learned that Buddy had been killed. She wrote me to share her tragic news and to find out how he had died, but what more could I tell her? In Anzio, I had been surrounded by death. It was my constant companion.

Dear friend Irving,
I hope this letter finds you well. Received your nice letter July 5, which you wrote June 16. It is nice to hear from you again after so long a time. I hope you are getting along fine. I hope this war will soon, very soon, be over. Let me tell you, I know what you and all the other fellas are going through. It is hell. It

---

[29] The 6th Armored Division was reorganized 20 July 1944. The 1st Battalion became the 6th Armored Infantry Battalion. The 2nd Battalion became the 11th Armored Infantry Battalion and the 3rd Battalion became the 14th Armored Infantry Battalion.

is a dirty shame, but it can't last forever. Each day that passes means one day less of fighting and brings us one day closer to the end of this awful war. Another thing I want to tell all of you fellas, is that you are doing a wonderful job! We here at home are very proud of all of you. Irving, I have something to tell you, so if you are not sitting down, please do so. I think it will be a shock to you. Buddy, my beloved husband, was killed, somewhere in Italy on January 30th. That is what the War Department said in the telegram that I received from them on the 18th of March. Somehow Irving, I can't believe it. I feel that he is alive and oh, I pray with all my heart that he is. I don't know where in Italy it happened, or how, all I know is what the telegram said. I wish there was some way of finding out, some way of securing such information, but I was told I would have to wait until the war is over or someone who was with Bud would be sent back to the States and they would get in touch with me. Irving, I have four pairs of wool socks and a pair of wool gloves that I bought and sent to Bud. They were sent back to me. I have no use for them and would be very glad to send them to you. Please write and ask for them. I can't send anything overseas without a written request. Write, so that I can send them and if you can't wear them, perhaps some of the other boys can. If you would like some cookies or candy, write and ask for them please. I would be very glad to send you candy and cookies. Irving, as I write this letter, I have Buddy's letter with me with yours, and I noticed the similarity of handwriting, yours and my Buddy's look so much alike. The letter is the last I received from Bud. It was written January 17, 1944. Well, Irving, I will close for now.

Good luck, and G-d keep you safe and well for those who love you. Write again please.

Sincerely,
Mrs. Marguerite Hunecke
4517 Tower Grove Place
St. Louis, Missouri

I had to laugh because she had noticed the similarity between Buddy's handwriting and mine, but didn't put two and two together to realize that I had indeed written both letters that she had received! Although I wanted to share with her what little I knew about Buddy's death, it was impossible. Letters from the war zone were censored, and I knew that anything I wrote about where we were or what we were doing, even though it had happened so many months ago, would be blackened out by the censors. She would have to live with her misplaced hope, and for any details about Buddy's death[30] until the war's end. I on the other hand, had to remain optimistic for the future despite knowing the answers that she longed to hear.

---

[30] "Private Adolph Frederick Hunecke, son of Mrs. Georgianna Hunecke, 4626 Tower Grove Place, was killed in action Jan. 30 in Italy, the War Department revealed yesterday. Pvt. Hunecke, 32 years old, was the husband of Mrs. Marguerite Hunecke, 4517 Tower Grove Place. A former welder at the Gimlin Engineering Co., 1133 South Seventh Street, he was inducted into the infantry in February 1943 and was sent overseas four months ago." St. Louis Post-Dispatch, March 19, 1944
https://westnewsmagazine.com/2015/06/23/59468/return-to-sender

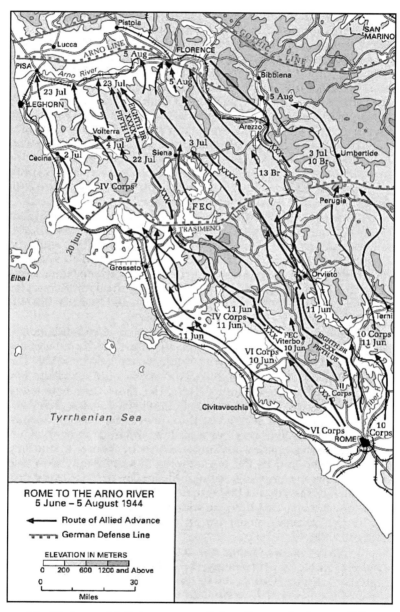

The 6th Armored Infantry moves north from Rome to Leghorn and Pisa
http://www.history.army.mil/brochures/romar/map4.JPG

The 1st Armored Division in the Italian Campaign

Life in the replacement depot was an upgrade from the life I had lead in combat. I had a tent to keep me dry from the summer rains, which were occasionally quite heavy, and I was able to attend the "synagogue" in the camp. Although I had missed saying kaddish for my mother since I had been at the front, now I was able to say Yizkor[31] on Rosh HaShana. We broke the Yom Kippur fast with cheese sandwiches and coffee. It would have been nicer to attend a real synagogue in Naples, but I was thankful nonetheless because I was safe. For now.

By mid October my reclassification as a non-combat soldier in exchange for my combat jacket came through, and I waited in limbo to be reassigned. Like everything else in the army, it was "hurry up, and wait." On October 23rd, I was given a job at a post exchange, a PX for short. It was like a grocery store, but we also distributed the weekly rations to our battalion. The hours were long, but running it was simple. I worked only three or four days a week, enjoyed taking inventory and filing requisition forms, and had plenty of candy and chocolate. Most importantly, I was in the rear and didn't mind staying there. I needed the rest. The only thing that could have been better was if the war would have ended, and I would have been home.

Being in the rear gave me plenty of time to write letters home. In fact, I tried to write home every day. This actually meant writing at least two letters, one to David in California, and one to my sisters and brother back in Ohio. I did so happily until I received a letter from my cousin Arthur. He was an educated man having studied philosophy at the Ohio State University, and I admired him. However, his letter dealt two

---

[31] Yizkor is the prayer said during the three pilgrimage holidays, (Sukkot, Shavuot, and Passover), and the New Year, reaffirming that despite the loss of one of our closest relations (a parent, child, or sibling), we still have the hope that the world will become a kinder, more idyllic place.

blows to the image I had painted in my mind of the situation back home. Until that point, my sisters wrote that everything was fine and they were all in good health. Arthur's letter shattered that truth: Hermine had had an acute case of appendicitis and had been operated on at the University Hospital. He reassured me that she was fine, but I was hurt nonetheless. Why hadn't she written me herself? Why had none of my siblings written me about it? What could I believe when she eventually would write me? My mind raced, and I longed to be home to comfort and help my sister. That was still an impossibility. Arthur also wrote: "You may even be able to go into Hungary and Czechoslovakia and it will be a great adventure to visit with your father. Moreover, if it would work out, you should take in all of the historic sites. It isn't very likely that after the war you'll be able to soon take a pleasure trip to see the old war area and while you get a chance to take in ancient historic places, you should do so." His own words demonstrated his ignorance! That anything now would be called a "great adventure" or that a visit to the combat zone would be part of a "pleasure trip" was absurd! I should visit all the historic sites in Europe? For all his education, he was clueless, his imagination wandered in the high clouds of an ivory tower, and he was blinded by them. An adventure? Is that what the folks back home thought I was having? I considered writing something scornful to Arthur, but thought better of it, and of writing something that expressed my disappointment to my siblings, but even that, after more consideration, I didn't do because I understood that they were just trying to keep my spirits high. I did take a short break from letter writing though, because I received new orders.

After combat in Italy. Notice the mustache!

Waiting for reassignment.
This picture was taken in Piazza Mazzini, Santa Maria Capua Vetere
North of Naples, Italy. Fall 1944

A greeting card for the Jewish New Year.

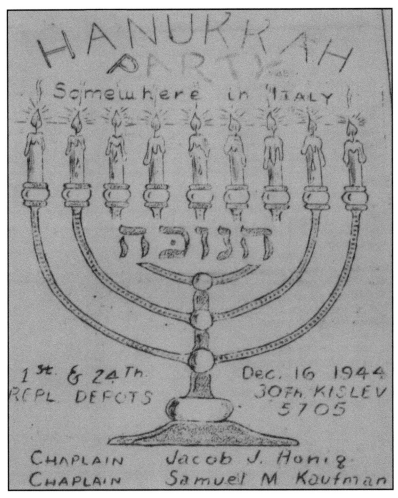

The cover of a greeting card that I sent home while at the replacement depot in Naples.

I was put on a ship from Naples heading to Marseilles, France. I arrived safely on February 20th. From there, I was sent to Dijon, near the border with Switzerland. I was stationed in a small farmhouse. After two weeks and a few days rest in an actual cot, I was attached to the 67th Military Police[32], given a sash indicating that I was a military policeman and was ordered to patrol, by motorcycle, the streets of Dijon, Toul, and Nancy. Patrol simply meant to monitor vehicular traffic for driving infractions, keep the peace among the townspeople, be on alert for any mischievous behavior by American GIs and to look out for German stragglers. Being an MP suited me. I was no less determined to keep the pleats of my uniform sharp and my shoes shined as I had been to keep the corners of my bed tight so many months ago during basic training in Texas. I took my job seriously. So much so that I was even willing to give a speeding ticket to a vehicle driven by a French official, despite his vigorous protestations.

The meals we ate were prepared by German prisoners outside of the town of Nancy. They were housed in a long, one-story home. Although they were prisoners, they were not very heavily guarded, but needed to remain inside the home. Whatever they made, they served us, and we would go outside of their "mess hall," sit on the steps of the house, and eat. One of the cooks was an older German who also happened to be a carpenter. He lived in a small room that was off to one side of the room that was used as the "mess hall," and when he wasn't cooking, he was doing woodwork in that room. Since I could twist Yiddish into German, I approached him and explained that I wanted a small box to hold a few mementos. In just a few days he had crafted a wooden box from the remnants of supply containers. He made hinges for it out of scrap metal. I

---

[32] The 67th Military Police Company was awarded the Meritorious Unit Commendation for its service in France and Germany.

was amazed at his handiwork and brought the box back with me and filled it with whatever items I had accumulated since leaving the U.S.A. two years earlier. Not everything fit. I burned most of the letters I had received from home.

Although I'm sure many GIs fell in love, one of my assignments was to patrol lust. Since time immemorial, soldiers on leave seek out women. Many GIs were getting sexually transmitted diseases, so the US Army saw fit to protect its soldiers by sending medical units to the local brothels to examine the women, and the soldiers who frequented them, and ascertain the source of the infections. I was assigned to one of these units. My job was to knock on the door of the brothel, gain access and secure it, and to stand guard outside to protect the doctors while they made their "house calls." During this time, no one was allowed to enter or leave.

My wooden box, crafted for me by a German prisoner in Nancy, France. Inset: Hinge detail

Above: Eating near Dijon, France
Below: Somewhere in France. I'm standing in the back row, first soldier on the left, holding my chow cup.

On patrol in Lyons, France. I'm on the right.

Chapter 20

ON MAY 7, 1945 GERMANY SURRENDERED. It was the long-prayed for V-E Day. Many people celebrated. I wasn't one of them. I felt nothing. It meant nothing. The war was over, but only if you had enough points. The only difference for me was that the army stopped censoring my mail, and I was able to write home to America freely. Soon after, I was able to send mail again to my father and brother in what had been Czechoslovakia. I hoped I would get a reply from them quickly and that somehow I would be able to visit them.

In the meantime, there was work to be done. The 67th moved into Germany to transport German soldiers who had surrendered and been taken prisoners. We stood guard as hundreds of them were packed into cattle cars, then we rode on the outside of the train, watching. Alert for anything. The train stopped once or twice to let the prisoners out to relieve themselves. We stood a good distance away from the train, watching in every direction for any attempt on their part to escape. Our orders were to shoot to kill if anyone tried. Thankfully, nobody did. The trains continued into France, all the way to Paris, taking the prisoners to work as laborers to clean up the areas decimated by the fighting. We hardly slept. After transferring the prisoners, there wasn't much time to enjoy anything. I was immediately sent back to Germany as an MP and was stationed in a private house in Mannheim.

Mannheim had become the headquarters for the US command. Several of us were directed to occupy a vacant house and set it up as our headquarters. The house was a large residence on a main street. with its entrance at ground level.

Inside, we found that the German homeowner had left in a hurry and many of their belongings, including furniture, bedding, and books had been left behind. I found a spot to call my own and began to look around the house. As a book worm, I was naturally drawn to the bookshelves. A large book caught my attention. It was a soft covered coffee-table book entitled "Der Parteitag Des Sieges" honoring the German Reich, its Army, and the Nazi regime. The pictures included photos of the German Army listening to their leader give a speech, soldiers marching, and many of the leaders in the upper echelons of the German government. It was astonishing to see the number of soldiers that were assembled to listen to him speak. However, more interesting to me than the fold out page showing a wide angle shot of his speech, was a single torn page in the middle of the book. One individual's picture had been intentionally and carefully torn out. I assumed it must have been the owner of the house. I took the book and put it with my belongings in the bottom of the box made by the German prisoner in Nancy. It would make for an interesting souvenir.

There were six or eight other MPs in this house with me. I was glad to be able to wash my clothing for the first time in months. We dipped the clothing into a large five-gallon bucket filled with gasoline. Because we didn't use water, the pleats in the pants remained crisp even after they'd dried out.

Above: The six frame fold-out from the end of the book, "Der Parteitag Des Sieges" that I took from the house in Mannheim in which we were stationed.

Opposite: A close-up of the center of the fold-out.

The page with the torn picture from the book, "Der Parteitag Des Sieges"

Der Führer begrüßt Kultus-
minister Rust
(von links nach rechts: Koch,
Rust, Bürckel, Grohé, Terboven)

Hauptmann v. Pfeffer, der
ehemalige Oberste SA-Führer
mit
Staatsminister Adolf Wagner

Oberstleutnant Kriebel,
ein früher Mitkämpfer der
Bewegung

My new assignment was to stand guard outside the private quarters of Major General Arthur R. Wilson. He was the commander of the US forces in Germany, and lived in a private house in Mannheim, near the US Army headquarters that had been established in Seckenheim. No one was permitted to enter the house without his authorization and my assignment was to make sure no one did. Since I was a mere Private, it was unacceptable for me to interact with the General in any way other than to salute him whenever he entered or exited the house. I had never looked as neat as I did then, nor did I ever salute as smartly. One day, as General Wilson was coming out, he stopped, and for whatever reason, spoke to me.

"At ease, soldier!" I lowered my salute and stood with my hands behind my back, feet slightly apart, feeling very much ill "at ease".

"Where are you from, Private Gluck?"

"Columbus, Ohio, sir!"

"No, no, before that? You have an accent..."

"Czechoslovakia, sir!"

He asked me further about my history and I told him how my sisters, brother, and I had left Europe and come to America, how I had volunteered to fight in Europe, and where I had been.

"Your sisters must be mighty worried about you...give me their address. I'm leaving tomorrow for Washington and I'll be sure to drop them a note to tell them that you're well."

"Thank you, sir!" I didn't think he would really write my sisters. Weeks later, when I was reassigned and my mail caught up with me, Hermine wrote that sure enough, he had. Knowing it was impolite, but embarrassed by her still limited English, she never replied to him. Nonetheless, my sister wrote to me that she was proud of her little brother and asked that G-d bless me. He already had.

Major General Arthur R. Wilson, U.S.A.
COMMANDING GENERAL CONAD

22 May 1945

Misses Herminia & Marie Gluck
50 Linwood Avenue
Columbus, Ohio

Dear Misses Gluck:

When I left Germany for a short trip to the United States I asked members of my staff to give me any messages they would like delivered. Private Irving Gluck asked that I write you and let you know he is in good health and feeling fine.

Lack of time and press of work prohibit a personal telephone call so this greeting will have to suffice.

Sincerely,

ARTHUR R. WILSON
Major General USA

am I can say
that is the
zone

After Major General Wilson returned to the USA, I was assigned to the 6996th Guard Company. Each day I went out with another MP on patrol throughout Mannheim, Seckenheim, Iggelheim, Worms, and Speyer. Our schedule would change often. Some days we patrolled during the daytime, and on others we patrolled at night. Sometimes we patrolled using a jeep, sometimes we went by motorcycle, but mostly we were on our feet for twelve hours a day, walking the streets. It wasn't quite as bad as being up at the front in Anzio, but it was exhausting nonetheless. Many areas had suffered extensive bombing by our air force, and I hoped that after so much destruction, the German people had finally learned their lesson.

One particular day while on foot patrol in Iggelheim, I and another MP named William Chapman from Spencerville Maryland, stopped in front of a small, unremarkable house. It was two stories tall, with a red tile roof and dirty white walls. The address on the door was Schillerstaße 18. A little girl was playing out front and her golden hair caught my attention. She was quite young, perhaps four or five years old, and she bore a remarkable resemblance to my brother Lajos' daughter, Lenke. When she saw the two of us walking down the narrow road, with the innocence that only a child of that age could have, she waved to us and smiled. Having nothing to give her, I simply returned her greeting. We would have continued on our patrol except the front door opened. The girl's mother cautiously called her daughter inside without being seen, but as we were already in front of her, she opened it widely, smiled politely, and greeted us good morning in German.

"Guten Morgen!"

"Und guten morgen, fräulein!" I replied. She looked at me quizzically.

"How is it that you speak German so well?" she asked me, still in German.

I hesitated in answering. "I studied a little in school," I finally replied.

"Where do you come from?" she pressed.

Again, I hesitated. I wanted to conceal the fact that I was Jewish. Rather than lie, I looked at her daughter, and remarked how she reminded me of my niece. I turned to continue the patrol, when she asked my name. "Irving Berlin, from Ohio," I replied. I gave her the first name that came to mind. Obviously, it was a bad choice. I hoped she wouldn't realize that this was the name of the famous composer, or that he also happened to be Jewish.

"Pleased to meet you, Irving Berlin! My name is Ruth," she called out as we began walking away.

When I returned to the house we were staying at, Chapman, who had been with me on patrol, told the other MPs how we had stopped to talk to Ruth and her daughter. Of course, there was some good-natured ribbing about flirting with the enemy, but everyone quickly understood that it was the young girl, rather than her mother, that got my attention. They understood that she reminded me of my niece and how much I missed my family and was worried about them.

Paul Imhoff, who happened to be from Cincinnati, was another MP I often went out with on patrol, thought he had a wonderful idea.

"Look, I bet if you request it, we could get permission to take motorcycles and ride to Czechoslovakia. You could check on your family, and I could get some beer! We can stop in Pilsen on the way! Wha'd'ya say, Gluck? Shall we go?"

Despite Paul's enthusiasm, and I must admit my strong desire to visit home and to see my father after so many years, I was hesitant. After all, the war had barely ended and I had no interest in becoming a target in the middle of what had very recently been enemy territory. I couldn't imagine that everyone would welcome two American GIs with open arms, especially when one was a Jew. Nonetheless, with my sisters' encouragement, I asked for permission to leave my unit and travel to Czechoslovakia. This being the army, I knew I would have to wait until my request was approved. All I could do now was wait for the army's permission or my father's reply to my letter.

In the meantime, I patrolled the streets of Iggelheim regularly. It was my habit while on patrol to keep my pistol locked, unloaded, and in its holster at my side. There was no reason to do otherwise, after all, I had no intention of killing anyone. One day, as I began to remove the pistol out of its holster, it suddenly discharged. Someone had loaded it and unlocked the safety. Luckily, the bullet missed my foot. Perhaps whoever tampered with my gun was jealous of how diligently I carried out my duties. Maybe they just didn't like me. Perhaps it was something else. I was puzzled by it, but never figured out who loaded it or how the safety had become unlocked.

Upon hearing that I would no longer be patrolling Iggelheim, Ruth, for no other reason than friendship, invited me over to talk about the war and the situation worldwide and introduced me to her elderly parents that lived with her. Her husband was not home yet—he was a German soldier, but she had no idea whether he was dead or alive. I enjoyed the conversation and we exchanged addresses. Ruth promised to write to me, that is to Irving Berlin, in Ohio. I doubted if she would, especially if her husband returned home safely. The irony of my sincere hope that her husband had survived was not lost on me.

Standing with Ruth Balbach outside her home at Schillerstraße 18 in Iggelheim

Secondheim, Germany. I'm on the right. The little girl reminded me of my niece Lenke.

On patrol, Mannheim, Germany

On patrol, Mannheim, Germany

On patrol, Germany

Outside of CONAD (Continental Advance Section), 67th Military Police Station, Germany

On patrol, Mannheim, Germany. I'm on the left.

In an apple orchard, somewhere in Germany

Pass, 67th Military Police Company

Bill Mauldin cartoon poking fun of MP's.
"The Stars and Stripes," Volume I, Number 95. July 8, 1945

Chapter 21

85 POINTS. THAT'S ALL I NEEDED to go home. Just 85 points! We got one point for each month of service and another for each month overseas. Five points for each award and another five for each campaign star. I did a quick calculation. I was very close but needed to wait to find out if I was to be sent to the fighting in the Pacific or if I would finally be sent home. During wartime, I also needed to have 32 months overseas and I only had 24. Some guys who had been in infantry units were being sent home, while others were being sent back to their units. I had no idea what my future would hold, but I held onto my faith in G-d, that He had gotten me this far and that he would continue to help me. I was reassigned to a replacement depot near Paris and finally had a chance to take in some sites. I was one of the lucky ones because only five soldiers from my unit were given permission to go to the city at a time, and I thought I would never get a chance. It was something that everyone wanted to do.

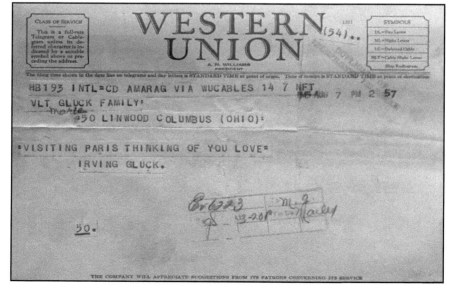

Posing triumphantly before the Arc de Triomphe
I'm the first person standing on the left. Paris, August 1945

At the replacement depot, we were told that we'd soon be on our way home. I signed the separation papers thinking everything was completed and I'd soon leave for the Promised Land. However, this was the Army. One day they said one thing, and the next day they did something else. I no longer believed anything until after it happened. I waited. Time stood still, and nothing changed. We were told once again that we were on our way to America. Soon everybody realized that we were from the same region: Ohio, Indiana and Pennsylvania. That seemed auspicious. Finally, my new orders came in, but like everything else in the army, it was hurry up and wait. Boy, did I wait. I was sent to Camp Lucky Strike near Le Havre, France and from there we would continue on to the good ole USA. Eventually. Dover lay just across the English Channel. My new home was an army tent. My new bed was a cot. My new pastime was boredom. With what little money I had, I purchased a radio for $50 (it included a battery from a jeep to make it work) and I tried to pass the time by listening to the news, or to whatever music was playing.

LUCKY STRIKE EXCHANGE
The bearer is authorized to purchase not more than two gifts at the gift shop.

There was no point in listening to the weather. The camp was enveloped by fog as thick as pea soup. It was so foggy that you couldn't see a yard in front of your own face. It was like this for days at a time.

I began to wander around the camp looking for something to do. One day, I happened upon a group of men standing around a makeshift craps table.

"Come on lucky seven! Come on!" The shooter threw two red dice onto a canvas board. "Four and three! We have a winner!" the dealer exclaimed, and happily handed over a few coins and a dollar bill. "Come on fellas, who's next? Try your luck! Ten cents to play!" I stood off to the side and watched as one GI after another took a turn throwing the dice. It seemed to me that the only one who was winning was the dealer. After all, if you wanted to play, you had to pay! However, the more I watched, the more I realized that there was more to this game. Before the shooter rolled the dice, the dealer put a dollar in the pot and four or five GIs would put in at least ten cents to play. The shooter could keep throwing the dice until he threw a winner, that is, a seven or an eleven or a loser, that is, doubles. A winner meant that they won all the money in the pot. A loser meant the dealer won it all. After a shooter won, the dealer put another dollar in the pot. That would get the guys interested in playing some more. After all, they were bored just the same as I was. The odds of throwing a seven were pretty good, but throwing an eleven was much harder. There was only one combination that would get that, so more often than not, the dealer would win. I had become so bored sitting around doing nothing, I too tried my luck. Days passed, and I won a few and lost a few, but it didn't matter. I would choose boredom over combat any day. After a few of weeks of this monotony, and the unyielding fog, it seemed like nothing would change. I couldn't have been more wrong. At the end of one unlucky day at the craps table, the dealer, whom I had gotten to know fairly well, made me an offer I couldn't refuse.

"Look Gluck, I'm shipping out tomorrow. I'll have no use for the craps table where I'm going. You take it! It's bound to bring you the same good luck that it's brought me! You can't lose...you're the house!"

The next morning, in the usual spot, I set up my newly acquired craps table. After all my observation, and all my playing, I knew just what to do. I threw not one dollar into the pot, but two, and sure enough drew quite a large crowd around me. By the end of the first month, I made more than $500!

Lady luck couldn't have smiled on me at a better time, and she kept on smiling for three more months. Every dollar I made, and I made almost $1,500, I sent home to my sisters and instructed them to freely take whatever they needed. Instead, they put it in my bank account and didn't take even a penny.

I'm the house at the "Chuck A Luck" table!
Lucky Strike, France, Fall 1945

Passbook 1 (top):

Ohio Federal Savings and Loan Association of Col[umbus]

IN ACCOUNT WITH

Columbus, Ohio

No. 11[...]

DATE	BY	DEBIT	CREDIT	BAL
APR 8 - 1940				
APR 15 1940				
MAY 8 - 1940				
MAY 27 1940				
JUN 11 1940				
JUN 1 [...]				
JUN 2[...] 1940			2	
JUL 3 0 19[...]			10	
JUL 1 - 19[...]				
JUL[...]				
JUL 3 [...]				
AUG 6				
AUG 21				
AUG 2 6				
SEP 3 - 194[...]				

Passbook 2 (bottom):

NAME ___ Irma [...] No. 1113

DATE	BY	DEBIT	CREDIT	
		AM'T FORWARD		
FEB 3 - 1943	G			
FEB [...] - 1943			20 —	
FEB 20 1943			2[...]	
FEB 27 19[...]			2[...]	
[...] 1943			20 —	
JUN 8 - 1943		20		
JUN 3 0 1943	Dr		50 —	
AUG 10 1943			13 59	
			20 —	
12-31-43 0[...]			14 75	
6-30-[...]			14 97	
DEC [...] 1944				
DEC 31 1944	Dr		11 5 00	15
FEB 3 - 1945	G		12 13	13
APR [...] 1945	G		80 —	1[...]
JUN 3 0 1945	Dep		23 20	16
SEP [...] - 1945			15 23	16
NOV 9 - 1945	V		23 20	18
NOV 2 [...] 1945		AM'T FORWARD	500 —	23
			7 00 31	3[...]

The fog of Camp Lucky Strike. I'm standing on the right.
Camp Lucky Strike, France, 1945

Chapter 22

"Patience is a virtue, possess it if you can..."

BACK IN JULY, I HAD HOPED I'D BE HOME IN A MONTH. I looked forward to celebrating Rosh HaShana (the Jewish New Year) with my family and even delayed sending out greeting cards until it dawned on me that I wasn't going to make it home in time. I knew the army's philosophy, hurry up and wait, but I was tired of it and their excuses. How could my ship be postponed when there seemed to be so many sailing home? It was now the end of October and I had been waiting in the replacement depot for three months and had twice signed papers that should have sent me on my way. There were rumors again that we would be reassigned. I wouldn't believe anything until it actually happened.

November 1945 came and finally, I was the lucky son-of-a-gun going home! I packed my belongings into my duffle bag, including a Walther P-38 pistol that I confiscated from a German prisoner, jumped on the truck, and couldn't stop smiling the whole way to the port in Le Havre. I was leaving the war zone. The misgivings I had about leaving Europe with no word from my father or brother were overpowered by the sheer joy of going home to my sisters and brothers in America. At the port, doctors examined us to make sure that we were well. Some unlucky ones were sent to the hospital because they had some illness or another. I passed with flying colors. How could I not after three months of rest? We boarded the 'Liberty' ship 'Frederick', a medium sized cargo ship and troop transport, and despite its drab Army gray colors, it was the most beautiful ship I had ever seen. With no one to say goodbye to or bid us bon voyage, we set sail packed inside like sardines, but it didn't matter. Like a baby in a cradle, the ship rocked me to sleep. I slept so peacefully that the ten-day voyage passed like a pleasure cruise. However, on the last day, when I knew we would soon be arriving in New York, I didn't sleep a wink. I waited outside on deck most of the night, knowing that at any moment, I would see her face again. Finally, she came into view. Her outstretched arm, with her torch lighting the dawn sky, was my first glimpse. Slowly, her crowned head grew larger and larger, until at last her face, unchanged in three years, greeted me, the early morning sunlight beaming upon it. I wept openly. I had never given up hope that I would see her again, but the pressure of three years of war had taken its toll. Lady Liberty. My Lady Liberty. The tears rolled down my face and mixed with the salty water of New York harbor. I was happier than I had ever been.

In a blur of excitement, we boarded a train headed for Indiantown Gap Military Reservation, near Harrisburg, Pennsylvania, in order to be discharged from the Army. I received a new uniform so that I would be presentable when I returned home. It included six stripes, each representing six months of service and the Meritorious Unit Commendation Patch for my service with the 67th MP's. I also received several medals to pin upon it: the Good Conduct Medal, the American Campaign Medal, the World War II Victory Medal, the European African Middle Eastern Campaign Medal with four bronze stars to indicate the four battle zones of the war that I served in, and most importantly the Combat Infantryman Badge to indicate that I had personally fought in active ground combat. The biggest surprise was that I had been promoted to Private First Class. Once the paperwork was finished, the commanders lined us up, saluted, and congratulated us on becoming civilians. It was nice to be called "Mister." It was November 7, 1945, just one week before my 24th birthday.

Discharged as a Private First Class
Indiantown Gap Military Reservation, November 7, 1945

177-15

Army of the United States

SEPARATION QUALIFICATION RECORD

SAVE THIS FORM. IT WILL NOT BE REPLACED IF LOST

This record of job assignments and special training received in the Army is furnished to the soldier when he leaves the service. In its preparation, information is taken from available Army records and supplemented by personal interview. The information about civilian education and work experience is based on the individual's own statements. The veteran may present this document to former employers, prospective employers, representatives of schools or colleges, or use it in any other way that may prove beneficial to him.

1. LAST NAME—FIRST NAME—MIDDLE INITIAL			MILITARY OCCUPATIONAL ASSIGNMENTS		
GLUCK IRVING			10. MONTHS	11. GRADE	12. MILITARY OCCUPATIONAL SPECIALTY
2. ARMY SERIAL No.	3. GRADE	4. SOCIAL SECURITY No.	3½	Pvt	Infantry Basic 521
35 633 941	PFC		7	Pvt	Rifleman 745
5. PERMANENT MAILING ADDRESS (Street, City, County, State)			4	PFC	Military Policeman 669
50 Linwood Ave Columbus			8	PFC	Duty Soldier III 590
Franklin Co. Ohio			6	Pvt	Telephone Oper. 309
6. DATE OF ENTRY INTO ACTIVE SERVICE	7. DATE OF SEPARATION	8. DATE OF BIRTH			
16 Mar 42	7 Nov 45	14 Nov 21			
9. PLACE OF SEPARATION					
Indiantown Gap, Penna.					

SUMMARY OF MILITARY OCCUPATIONS

13. TITLE—DESCRIPTION—RELATED CIVILIAN OCCUPATION

MILITARY POLICEMAN OCCUPIED TERRITORY : Main duties were as interpreter of German, Hungarian, Czechoslovakia, Polish, Italian, and French nationals. Guarded German prisoners of war in trains from Germany to vicinity of paris. Did regular patrol work in France and guard work of areas in Germany. Worked as leader and consulate for any foreign persons that may have reason to see American Commanders.

WD AGO FORM 100
1 JUL 1946   This form supersedes WD AGO Form 100, 15 July 1944, which will not be used.

Front of Separation Qualification Record

MILITARY EDUCATION

14. NAME OR TYPE OF SCHOOL—COURSE OR CURRICULUM—DURATION—DESCRIPTION

Army Projection Operators School in Italy about one week.
Study of projection and general repair work on projector.
Received US Army Projection Permit

CIVILIAN EDUCATION

15. HIGHEST GRADE COMPLETED	16. DEGREES OR DIPLOMAS	17. YEAR LEFT SCHOOL	OTHER TRAINING OR SCHOOLING	
			20. COURSE—NAME AND ADDRESS OF SCHOOL—DATE	21. DURATION
10	None	1937	Business School	

18. NAME AND ADDRESS OF LAST SCHOOL ATTENDED

Czechoslovakia

Studying English
in 1941 to 1942   1½ years

19. MAJOR COURSES OF STUDY

Academic

CIVILIAN OCCUPATIONS

22. TITLE—NAME AND ADDRESS OF EMPLOYER—INCLUSIVE DATES—DESCRIPTION

DUPLICATING MACHINE OPERATOR : Worked for Frey Yenkin Paint Co.
Columbus, Ohio for 3 years operating a multigraph machine making
labels for cans. Set type and names. Did repair work and kept
machine clean in good running order. Filled all types of orders from
small cans to large drums. Supervised and instructed in operation
of multigraph machine.

ADDITIONAL INFORMATION

23. REMARKS

Recieved Combat Infantryman Badge in the Italian Campaign

24. SIGNATURE OF PERSON BEING SEPARATED	25. SIGNATURE OF SEPARATION CLASSIFICATION OFFICER	26. NAME OF OFFICER (Typed or Stamped)
Sharing Glund		M. E. GOLDBERG, Capt., AGD

U. S. GOVERNMENT PRINTING OFFICE—O-657477

Back of Separation Qualification Record

I telephoned my sisters in Columbus to be sure that they had received the telegram I sent from France. I didn't want a hero's welcome, but my sister Hermine insisted that she was preparing the finest dinner for me to celebrate my return. I wasted no time and bought a ticket for the next bus to Ohio. With nowhere else to go, I waited at the terminal. As the departure time approached, I noticed that I had begun to feel very uncomfortable near the crowds of people that gathered. Apparently, I had left the war but the war had not yet left me. The crowd reminded me of the chow line and the day that it was bombarded. I felt anxious and tense. I needed to stand away from the crowd as much as possible. I was excited to board the bus even though I knew that it would take more than 15 hours. Despite my excitement, time dragged on as I sat looking out the window. The flatlands reminded me of Anzio beachhead and the mountains reminded me of Mount Porchia. My seat mate had fallen asleep next to me and his posture reminded me of the soldiers 'sleeping' on the battlefield. I too tried to close my eyes, but that didn't bring me any solace, just more memories. I hoped that this feeling would pass as soon as I arrived home to my family's welcoming arms. It wasn't like me to feel so anti-social and anxious.

Of course, I knew that some things had changed while I was away. After all, it had been more than three years! I knew, for example, that my brother Dezső had changed his name to David and moved to California in search of work. He had written me all about it while I was still overseas. As much as I wanted to see him, I knew that I wouldn't for some time. Instead, I sent him a telegram letting him know that I had arrived home.

My sister Hermine had moved to New York looking for better job opportunities and an expanded social life, and perhaps to find a husband, but she'd answered the phone when I called so I knew that she'd come back to Columbus just to see me. I didn't know when my bus would arrive, so there was nobody at the terminal to meet me. As I stepped off the bus, with my duffle on my back, the scene seemed surreal.

My telegram to David
Columbus, OH, November 9, 1945

Everyone was going about their business. There was a shoeshine stand with men sitting, faces hidden behind their newspapers. A coffee shop with waitresses busily serving customers. A newsstand. A Pullman pushing carts laden with baggage. The tick-tick-tick of the digits quickly changing on the arrivals sign, which sounded like the rat-tat-tat of a machine gun. Latecomers rushing to catch a train. "Last call, on track..." The announcer's voice muffled by the din that filled the station. Business as usual. It appeared the same as when I'd first arrived in Columbus five years earlier, except it wasn't. Or rather, I wasn't the same. Everything I saw was filtered through the lens of what I had seen in the war. Every sound startled. Honking. Doors slamming. Luggage falling. The taxis jostled for position to take their fares. I was one of them, eager to get away from the crowd, which I now equated with danger. Eager to get away from the hustle and bustle. Eager to see my sisters. Eager to go...home? The word came haltingly. Columbus didn't feel any more like home than did the foxhole in Anzio. A taxi pulled next to me. My duffle took the front seat and I settled into the back. At first, I savored the silence of the taxi ride, impatiently waiting for the driver to wend his way to my destination. Traffic. Intersections. Horns honking. Civilization. My head began to pound. The taxi finally pulled to the curb. I handed over the fare, grabbed my duffle, and bounded onto the sidewalk. In the front window on the second floor hung a small flag with a blue star.[33] Opening the door, the smell of browning onions and paprika drifted down the hallway straight to my nostrils. I rushed up the stairs of 50 Linwood Avenue knowing that at least one person was home. Marie must have heard my footfalls on the stairs, because even before I got to the top, her head was peeking out of the door, looking for me. As soon as our eyes met, she shouted out, "Oh, my little brother Irvingkém! Look, Hermine, Irving is home!" A head shorter than I, she buried her head in my chest and hugged me. "My dearest Irving!" she repeated over and over. Hermine came running from the kitchen and hugged me just as tightly. "My, darling little brother!" Herman could only grab my hand and shake it since my sisters would not let me go.

"Oh, Irvingkém, sit down, I have been busy all week making you something to eat!" Hermine said excitedly.

After all I had been through, I willingly obeyed my big sister. The smell of fried onions filled the air and my mouth watered

---

[33] The Service flag is an official banner authorized by the Department of Defense for display by families who have members serving in the Armed Forces during any period of war or hostilities the United States may be engaged in for the duration of such hostilities.

at the thought of home-cooked Hungarian style potatoes. I called out to Hermine, who was already back in the kitchen busily stirring the potatoes so that they wouldn't burn.

"When did you come back from New York?" I asked her excitedly.

"They gave me a whole week's vacation so I could be here to see you when you arrived!" she replied.

The "Blue Star Flag" that my sisters hung in their window.

She served the steaming plate of potatoes and went right back to the kitchen to bring some vegetable soup. This image, my sisters, waiting for me, needing me, was what sustained me throughout my three years in the army. It was their letters, their gifts, the very thought of them being alone that gave me the strength to continue. Now, here I was, finally home with my little family. My sisters were my home. I felt as if my heart was filling itself with life again. "What of our father? Have you heard anything?" I asked Marie. She reached over to a neatly arranged pile of letters. She thumbed through them and I recognized many of the letters as V-mail that I had sent. Others were unopened letters from America sent to our father in Hungary that had been returned and marked "undeliverable." There was a letter from Germany addressed to Irving Berlin. I couldn't help but smile. However, Marie pulled out an envelope that bore a Hungarian postmark instead. My heart skipped a beat as I took it from her hand. I didn't recognize the handwriting. It was addressed to Hermine Gluck. I turned the envelope over and looked at the return address: Schwartz, Emil. Király Helmec. Hungary. It was from Uncle Márton's son. The postmark was dated June 24, 1945. I took the thin, typed written page out of the envelope and began to read:

Dear Hermine, Marie, Herman, and Ignac.

Before I begin to write, let me introduce myself to you. My name is Emil. I am Márton Schwartz's son, your cousin. I remember you well because you came to our home to say farewell on the day you went on your way to America. I will now tell you about my dear parents and brothers and sisters. On April 4, 1944 they dragged us to a concentration camp.[34] We thought we would remain there together as a family. On May 10, they marched us to a railroad box car normally used for cattle. 94 of us were forced into it. The doors were closed, the air was stifling, and there wasn't any water. After traveling like this for four days, we arrived to Auschwitz, the famous [for nothing] concentration camp. They forced us from the train and immediately lined us up...it didn't take more than 10

---

[34] After the German invasion (March 19, 1944), about 4,000 Jews from Sátoraljaújhely were confined in a ghetto, joined by another 11,000 from nearby villages, all crowded 20–25 to a room. All were deported to the Auschwitz death camp between May 16 and June 3 in four transports. Only 555 survived. Encyclopedia Judaica. Using Emil's description, the yahrzeit would be the 21st of Iyar.

minutes before they separated us. As I looked back I saw my dear mother and the children were on one side and my dear father, my brother Hersu, and I were on another side. My poor sister Magda was crying. We never saw them after that moment. There wasn't even a chance to say goodbye. Within two days they took the three of us in a transport to Austria to a concentration camp. We worked there for three months and then Hersu [had an infection on his leg and] was taken with a sick transport. After that, there was no news of him. My dear father couldn't take it any longer and two days before Chanukah he died in front of my eyes. You cannot imagine how difficult this moment was for me. I lost my desire to live. I knew that my mother was put to death in the gas chamber and burned in Auschwitz. However, I was determined that someone from our family should return home. After that I suffered from typhoid fever and was bedridden. I was very sick and weak. I don't remember the exact date when we were freed. I was taken by the Americans to a hospital and within one month I recovered completely. With the first train, I came back home to Helmec. I am staying now with my cousin Zoltan Pollak, I'm sure that you know him. He is the only one from his family to survive. We were together with your brother Lajos in Auschwitz. There Lajos volunteered for masonry work and there's been no news of him since then. From Mrs. Lenkes family Hersu, Hentsu, and Jidesz survived. I do not have any more to write. I would ask one favor from all of you: if you can, please secure or send me a visa, because I am under 17 and have no one else. There are no other relations alive.
My birth information is as follows:

Emil Schwartz
August 13, 1929
Király Helmec

With a pure heart, love, and a warm embrace from your cousin, Emil Schwartz
PS. I'm enclosing two pictures of myself in this letter.

Uncle Márton and Aunt Ethel, Emil's parents, and Emil's younger sister Lilli, and brother Labele (Aryeh) in a photo from 1942. Márton Schwartz was drafted into the Hungarian Army, and was given his officer's rank that he earned in the first World War.

I read, and then reread, the letter, letting the full weight of Emil's story sink in. I thought I had gotten used to death. I had been surrounded by it for so long, but nothing prepared me for this. April 4. May 10. I was in Anzio. It never occurred to me that the lack of a reply to the letter I sent to my father from Lucky Strike meant that my entire family had been murdered. Where was Auschwitz? I didn't even know. I was orphaned, but not alone. My eyes, welling with tears, looked up to find some comfort in my sisters' faces. There was none. My brother stared blankly into the distance unwilling to reveal his emotions. Through her tears, Hermine took out a form from the International Red Cross and handed it to me. It was a carbon copy of a missing persons report. "Who knows..." said Marie. "If Emil survived, maybe one of Lajos' children did, too. I'm certain they did. I can feel it." Hermine chimed in, "And you know Lajos, he must have survived. He's strong. Emil doesn't know more than we do. They were separated, that's all." They genuinely looked hopeful. I looked at the unopened letters that lay on the table. One was addressed to my father, postmarked from Columbus on June 25, 1945 and the other, to my brother Lajos, dated June 26. Both were marked in English with the words "Service Suspended." I took a knife and carefully opened the thin, delicate envelope addressed to my father. I immediately recognized that Hermine's handwriting began the letter and Marie's ended it. I read to myself.

Dear beloved Father, Lajos, and Etelka!
We have been waiting for years for the moment that we would hear from each other. I hardly can find words to express what I feel at this particular moment. I hope that all of you are in good health. We thank our G-d that the war has ended. It is very difficult waiting for a reply from you, but as soon as we get one, we will do everything possible to help. How are you Lajos? Believe me there wasn't a minute that we didn't think of you because you may have been in the worst danger. How is

Etelka and those dear children? I wish to help them if G-d has helped them to live through this terrible war. How are our grandparents - Grandma? Grandfather?... And Uncle Márton and his dear children? What about his brother, Uncle Lajos and his wife, Aunt Etel? Write about everything! As soon as the moment arrives that we are permitted to send packages, we shall immediately mail them to you. I don't even know what to write to you. First, I'm well. I'm working for a telephone company in their office and Marie works in a hotel as a cashier. Herman is working in a factory. Ignac is an American soldier and is in Germany. He wrote that he would like to go to Polyán to try to help you if it's possible. We hope he'll succeed. We received a letter last week from him saying that he wrote to you, too. Thank G-d he is well. I wish he would be able to get through to you so that you, our dear father would see him...he's a handsome young man, "kanahare"[35]. Dave went to live in California. The climate there is always warm and he likes it quite a bit. We did not go because I, and the rest of us, want to help you to perhaps come to America. Bertha advised us that by staying here in Ohio, we would be able to get Arthur to help us to do that. They are well. How are Miksa Shon and Rezsi and their families? The Szurti relations? I will write again. Take care of your health for the children's sake and give our love and wishes for good health to everyone. I'm sorry that right now I cannot send a small package of food, but as soon as I can I will immediately!..... I wish Ignac would succeed with his plans to see you. It would be wonderful if everything turns out okay. Once again I ask that G-d give strength to all of us----- to sustain us in the aftermath of this horrible war. Please don't worry about us. We are well and in good health. Thank G-d, David is, too. Do you have food to eat? Are you at home? Write!! With love and kisses to you, our dear father, and

---

[35] Kein Ayin Hara ("no evil eye"): (Yiddish) "No evil eye!" Customarily added after praising another; expressing the wish that the evil eye should not affect the individual discussed.

to Lajos, Etelka, and little Emil, Lenke, Miklós, Gyula and Zoli.

Please send our love and kisses to Uncle Márton and Uncle Lajos and their families----- and also to our dear grandparents, Hermine.

Our address is:
Hermine Gluck
50 Linwood Avenue
Columbus 5, Ohio U.S.A.

Maria wrote her own letter at the bottom of the thin sheet of airmail paper.

Dear beloved Father, Lajos and Etelka,
I don't know how to start this letter. First of all we are well. We think a lot about you dear father, and the whole family, and about these terrible years that you had to live through. I hope that G-d remembered our dear family. We did not forget you, whom we have left behind, even for a minute. My dear father how are you? Please take care of yourself. We are going to try everything to help you as soon as possible. And you dear Lajos - how are you and your family? I can't even imagine what you had to go through. It is a miracle of G-d. And I hope that G-d did not forget to help you. How are our grandparents? Poor people - what they had to go through. How is dear Uncle Márton and his family, and Uncle Lajos and his family? We are waiting for the moment that we hear news from you. Our little Ignac is in Germany as an American soldier. We received a letter from him in which he tells us that he also wrote to you. He will try everything to help you. He is a very dear young man. I would be very happy if you, our dear father, could see him. I hope that this letter will find all of you in good health. And I hope to hear from each of you. I ask you all, my dear father and our family, to take care of yourselves and your

> *health. I'm sending you a lot of kisses always, your daughter and sister, Maria*

The second envelope was also from Hermine and Maria addressed to our brother Lajos. I opened it and scanned it quickly.

> *My dear beloved brother Lajos and Etelka,*
> *... It's a miracle of G-d if you are alive and well...*
> *...We would like to know that you have survived this horrible war...*
> *...those innocent children. How much they must have suffered by being hungry, too.*
> *...All of us, even Arthur, will try to do anything possible to help...*
> *...I know that nice words can't fill an empty stomach, but right now we can't do much more...*

I had gone to Europe to make a difference - to save my people. From 23 immediate family members, we had heard from only one: Emil. The world we had left behind, everything, everyone, had been destroyed. The freedom loving world had succeeded by winning the war, but I had failed miserably. The absolute trust that I placed in G-d was gone and I was shaken to the very core of my being. The simple, straightforward understanding of the Torah, and Judaism, that I had grown up with was unsustainable. It was impossible to reconcile my trust in Him with the loss of my family. I had believed with certainty that G-d protected me during combat because our cause was righteous and just, and I was a good, sin-fearing, G-d loving Jew. And yet, so were they.

Chapter 23

"You've got to be taught
To hate and fear"

South Pacific, Rogers & Hammerstein

Mr. Irving Gluck
50 Linwood Ave.
Columbus, Ohio

Dear Mr. Gluck:

I am happy to note that you have completed
your admission to Ohio State University.
From this time on you are a part of Ohio
State's ever-growing "family", whose members
now number many thousands. Just as we have
looked with pride upon the achievements of
students of other years, so we shall watch
with keen interest your progress in school
and after graduation.

With all good wishes as you start this new
and important part of your life's work, I am

Cordially yours,

Howard L. Bevis
President

The letter of acceptance to Ohio State, January 9, 1946

THE QUIET SOLITUDE OF HOME did nothing to quell my restless thoughts, which focused incessantly on the war I'd just been through and the contents of Emil's letter. In fact, it did the opposite. I decided that my only escape was to do what I knew best...to bury my head in books and study. With the opportunity provided by the G.I. Bill, within one week of arriving home, I took a general educational development test, and based upon my score, I applied to and was accepted as a full-time undergraduate student in the department of Commerce and Administration at the Ohio State University in

Columbus. My Cousin Arthur was proud of my choice, especially since he had endowed the university's Philosophy Department and created the Gluck Memorial Library of Philosophy in honor of his father Julius, or as we called him, our Uncle Jónás.

When classes began in January 1946, I tried to devote all my energy to studying, but there were constant interruptions. We began to receive replies to the letters Hermine had sent to our father's Gentile neighbors and our relations in Europe. Each letter was like a nail in the coffin of hope. The first letter to arrive after I returned was from the Klein family. Ignac, Manci, and Rozsi Klein were related to us by marriage. Their sister Etelka was our brother Lajos' wife. If they had returned, then there was yet hope.

1945 November 6
With love, dear Hermine and Marie,
I'm sorry that we have taken the letter you addressed to your family into our hands, but I believe regretfully that in America you know more about everything than we do here. We were taken in 1944 on the Saturday following Passover to Ujhely concentration camp. Poor Etelka from Helmec gave birth to a little boy there named Shemaya, but he died in Ujhely. It was a good thing for that little boy. As they were transporting us from Ujhely, your dear father and Patyu [Uncle Márton] along with Uncle Lajos were taken away together, but we remained there for a few days. It's a shame that we only saw each other at Ujhely. My dear Hermine, only those who came home were given strength by G-d to be able to survive one and a quarter years of misery. In the concentration camp at Auschwitz, they separated people that they considered to be strong. My sister Rohesi and I were together from the first moment. From there they took us to Nuremberg. While there we endured heavy bombing. In February, they brought us near Pilzen where we were freed on May 5 by the Americans. My dearest, I'm sorry to tell you that the only person from Polyán that

The book plate for books at the Memorial Library of Philosophy at OSU.

remained alive is Malvin. She is in Sweden because those that were weak were taken there to recuperate. Malvin writes to us that Aunt Lenke's two girls are there. Hersu is at home and Uncle Márton's son Emil, came home, too. The Pollak's girls all died from typhus and their brother Zoli is left alone. The Braun family has all died. Tuci Lefkovics is by himself and he married Edit Veisz. Medi, Mityu, and their father are at home. Etyu Moskovits has a relationship with one of them. Etyu is in Homonna. The three Slanger girls and Marie are living in Uncle Lajos' house. From the Frida family, Hetyu and Arsu survived. The two Stark boys are at home and of the three Stark girls, Lenke and Irene survived and are in Sweden, but Helen died. From the Reisman Family only Szerenyke and Miki are alive. Miki already got married to a Kaposi girl. Szerenyke is living in Karlesbad. As it is in Lelesz, there are only 22 Jews left. Majsu Frolinger survived, but Berti and his son died. Lili is also in Sweden. We have received several letters from the two Klein girls. I was flabbergasted that you did not write. The situation here is very bad. The non-Jewish people are very mean. They are not willing to return anything to us. For example, your father left a watch with Gerenyi and we asked for it and they replied that they'll give it only to Dezső because that is what your dear father instructed them to do. Therefore you should write to them. Ignac was named to take care of your properties. The fields were not seeded when we came home but now, Ignac has given them out to be seeded. The furniture is at Ivany and Ragany. They took it. There is no judge to make legal decisions. In our house we found only the furniture. Everything is very costly here, so no one can be considered poor, just unhappy, because very few of us remained alive. My dearests, it's impossible to write down what we have gone through. The Feuerisen girls, with the exception of Nelly and their parents, returned. Little Majer is missing. Zseni did not write yet. My dear Hermine, even though little Lenke died after the liberation I still believed that at least little Emil would come home. In other words, the

elderly, the children, the pregnant women, no longer exist. This is German culture. Here is a new sidre [chapter]. My dear Hermine, now I know how strong a person can be and how much one can tolerate. I have no patience to write any more. To all of you with kisses and love,
Ignac, Manci and Rohesi

The first letter to arrive from our neighbors was from Mrs. Deakne. She was a very good friend to our family and her daughters went to school with my sisters.

12/19/1945
My dear children!
Please do not be insulted by my salutation, but it happens to be a wonderful feeling to say the word, 'children', because I cannot tell that to my own because they aren't alive. My dear children, I received your letter and it found me in good health and I hope and wish to G-d that you are, too. I regret that I can't answer your question. The situation is so sad that it is impossible to write it down. My dear children, I will tell you that your dear father, along with the whole Jewish community, were told by the Germans that within one week's time they were to report to them. Every family member should take along one pair of underwear and clothing, shoes, and food for themselves. The Germans did an inventory of everything that remained at home. They took them to Helmec and from there, all the Jews of the whole district were taken to Ujhely. We took them food during the week after they were taken there. After that, they were gone. While they were there, they wouldn't let us in, not even into the street where the Jews were held. We didn't see them after. Shon came home once for food and we collected about eight loaves of bread, eggs, and bacon. He couldn't talk to me when I was there, but he wrote a letter from Ujhely to me. Shon expressed his sorrow that he could not meet with me. This was the last thing from there. We did not hear anything more from them. In Lelesz, many people came home. Ignac Klein and his two sisters and Veisz's daughter

came back. There are more men that came home in Lelesz. It is a shame that the people from our family have not returned. Malvin Lefkovics is in Sweden and wrote that she should be coming back home in the spring. She's in touch with Ignac Klein. There are still others returning, but as of now I think that your father certainly went to your place in America. We hope and trust G-d that Shon will return home. And G-d forbid, if they do not come home, then they may have been destroyed. I beg you to accept G-d's will because you can see that you were taken away from these destructive hands and he took care of you. Love each other as brothers and sisters and ask G-d to help you and keep you from all misfortune. My dear children, you can't know or imagine the destruction that we have lived through. We have often envied the dead. From day to day we don't know what tomorrow will bring us. The men were taken by the Russians and they are still there. It's already been a year since some of them came home and many others have been killed. From 70 men only one third came home and they weren't soldiers, just civilians. There are some families that lost three members. We have had bad things happen to us, but more likely we deserved it. We behaved badly and were unwilling to improve. My dear Hermine, you asked me about Marie and Anna? They're well. They weren't frightened no matter how bad the situation got. In three years I have buried six that have died. My dear mother in one year and then my Grandfather and then Icsa, the next. In November, two years after I buried my mother and my daughter Annuska. On February 16, I buried Anus, and just a week later on February 25, Marie. I had to struggle with all of this. The mother has to bury all her children and now I am alone in this miserable world, waiting when the wind will grab me also. You can imagine how orphaned I am. I continue to trust in G-d that he will watch over me, for if not for him, I would also have been destroyed. He arranged to bring me a small thing that I can lean upon. My nephew's wife passed away and left five children. Two years ago my nephew brought me his four year old little daughter and now she is six. With G-d's help, I will be able to raise her, and then at least I would have someone to speak to and won't be alone. Our situation is certainly very difficult and I hope that G-d will help me.

My dear children, don't be angry that I write to you about myself and my problems, but I did so that you could learn from me that you too should accept what G-d has brought upon us. I ask you to please write to me and tell me a lot about yourselves. I have not heard anything from my relatives.

I'm closing these lines with kisses to all of you and may G-d be with you, Deakne.

PS. The furniture from your house is at Ivanyo.
Puskan lives in your house.

At almost the same time, we received several letters from our sister-in-law Etelka's siblings with more details from home. Our letters had crossed in the mail. The description they gave of our neighbors made it very difficult for us to even consider helping Mrs. Deakne, or anyone else who asked.

1946 January 15
With Love to you Dear Girls and Ignac,
Your precious letters brought happiness. I have already written to you a long, detailed letter describing everything. Did you receive it? I got your address from the letter you addressed to your dear father and I took it from the postman, Smojak. Dear Hermine, I don't have the strength to write about our suffering. I would like to forget everything. I said it many times that those that died are better off. All three of us came home. Here we hoped we would slowly become more like ourselves, we wouldn't have to worry, and we would be able to live. My dearest, at home we found nothing else except the furniture. Imagine, being there one and a half years living just on beet soup while our bodies require good food to have energy and to feel well. We can get everything here, but we don't have money.

We had received American help, but now we don't get anything. My dearest, I'm cooking kosher. We received from Rezsi Klein a package with food weighing 2 kilograms. Dear Hermine, if you are able to, please help us monetarily. Rozsi will continue this letter. I'm awaiting your reply. With kisses and lots of love to you all. Manci

Dear Hermine and Marie!
I was very happy to receive the letter. I was by myself when the postman delivered it. I began to read your letter and I burst into tears crying. Dear Hermine, if you could have seen those precious children as they were waiting for you to send things to them. It is heartbreaking what has happened to those poor children and to my poor sister, after all the suffering. How she brought them up so well and lived every moment for them, and especially now, she would have enjoyed them. What could have been is like a dream before us.
Manci has already written to you about us. Now I'm going to write to you about our relatives. We went together with Uncle Lajos. Your grandfather died here at home in 1942. It was a good thing because at least he was buried. Your grandmother and my mother were together in Germany, but they do not have a tombstone. Marie, you ask about Uncle Márton from Helmec. His little son is at home and he lives with Zoli Pollak in Helmec. His name is Emil, and in Hebrew his name is Avruham. He is a beautiful, big fellow like your Ignac. He comes to visit us. And Zoli takes good care of him. Mrs. Lenke's son, Hersu, is also alive. This is all I have to write about the relations. As far as I know, no one from Shon's family exists. There are two girls from Szürte at home. I do not know them. Hermine, why didn't you write about Dezső and Herman? Are they soldiers? Our Ignac is writing to you about the problems in Polyán. Dear Ignac I wish you would have come home to visit. Dear Hermine, I would ask your help. Do you remember Tuci from Asvany? His father lives in New York. We don't have his address. Perhaps you could advertise in the

papers that his nephew survived? He's a very gentle young man and he's by himself. He doesn't have their address and the poor thing came home alone. You are asking about Lenke Schwartz and Moric and Lenke Slager. They are at home. I'm writing this with a broken heart, Marie, but nothing will heal it. Regretfully, we are poor and unhappy. Please write to us about everything. With lots of love and kisses to all of you, your loving relations
Rokcsi

Dear, beloved Hencsu and Mariska,
We were very happy to receive your letter. Unfortunately, I can't write anything good to you, after all this horror. Dear girls, I can only write about the family. Whoever hasn't given a sign about their life until now, unfortunately no longer exists. Dear girls, you asked about the home and the land. The home is in bad shape. There is a poor peasant that lives in it and I rented the land out. Your dear neighbors stole everything from the home, and even from the barn. They stole everything. They even want you to send them dollars. They would have taken the house too, if it would have been on wheels. Unfortunately, nobody came home to Polyán. Malvin is in Sweden already. I sent to her already to write to you. Dear girls, you asked me what do I live from. Unfortunately, there is nothing to do and I have no money either. Dear girls, I bought two horses in the past. I helped Lajos out. So, I'm asking you now to please help me out so I can buy two horses for myself, in order to succeed, because now I'm very poor. I live together with the girls. They unfortunately don't live, they only eat. Unfortunately, we have neither clothing nor shoes. I have nothing, so please, if you can help me out, I will never forget. Dear girls, the Gentiles have taken all of the furniture. They don't want to give it to me, so please do me a favor and send me a letter of authorization so they will give it back to me. Not even a pillow is left. Nothing. They took everything. Your best neighbor, who you would not even think of doing this, the Simon family, are very

nice. They stole plenty from you. Pista Ivanyi isn't better and about the Csarosz family, I can hardly write to you what bastards they are. They would kill us too, if they could. They can hardly stand it, that a few people came back. They would have been happy if nobody came home at all. Believe what I'm writing in this letter. I don't even have enough money to mail it to you. So, if you could, please help me out. If you could, it would come in handy for me, because now I'm here without anything. Why didn't you mention [anything] about Dezső, only Ignacz? I will not write more, I'm waiting for your response.

I will stay with love, your relative, Ignacz

Soon after these letters from Etelka's brother and sisters we received another letter from Emil.

1946 January 24

Dear Hermine.

I received your letter and I'm replying at once. The last time I wrote a letter, I put the wrong number on the address...instead of 50 I wrote down 59. I hope you will receive it. In your letter you asked about your father. We haven't received any news from anyone and he must have perished like my parents. In my last letter, I wrote to you and told you how this great catastrophe happened. Thank G-d, I feel fine. I'm here with my relation Zoli Pollak. I'm sure you know him. He takes care of me like a father. I have everything I need: clothing, shirts and underwear. Thank G-d I'm well and in good health. I sent you a picture, as a memento. It appears that you didn't receive it yet. I know everyone who is in Lelesz. Unfortunately from Uncle Lajos' family, no one survived except Etyu from Paloc, probably you know him. Please do not send any packages because I have everything. I would like to see you very much. Did any of you get married? I remember you all. Since you did not receive my previous letter, I introduced myself and explained how I know you. Tomorrow I will be traveling to the former Germany and from there to Palestine. I hope to get there with G-d's help. Please write to the following address, they will forward your letter to me. Once I get to Palestine, I will write you again with my new address. I genuinely thank you very much that you have not forgotten me. With a pure and true heart and with love and kisses to all of you, your cousin Emil.

ZOLTAN POLLAK
KRALOVSKY HLUMEC
CESKO-SLOVENSKO

PS. As I wrote above, Zoli will forward the mail to me. When I get to my new place I will give you my address. Write me often. I'm very happy that you did not forget me. Once again, if and when I'll be in Palestine, I will let you know and will write you a lot. Hermine, I send kisses to you separately, because I always loved you when you were at our place. In my last letter I sent you two pictures, but I'm not sure whether you received them, so I'm enclosing another one.

In February, I received a reply from the American Red Cross regarding the inquiry I had made about my family back in October 1945, while I was still in Europe. "Family Schön and Glück don't returned from the concentration camp. All news about family thinks given Belo Friedman Kralovsky Chlumec Slovakia." This was only the beginning of many official letters from the Red Cross that would come, out of the blue, with names similar to those in our family, but bearing different birthdates or birthplaces. Unfortunately, they brought good news, just not for us.

These letters were heartbreaking, mostly because there was so little that we could do. Hermine and Marie prepared packages of food and clothing, anything extra that they could, and they sent them as soon as we were allowed. Emil wrote again in May. After four months he was still at home in Király Helmec, not Palestine. His reason for not having left, painful feet, seemed odd given the enthusiasm of his previous letter. I

GLUCK.   new   INQUIRY

                    AMERICAN RED CROSS   FEB 14 1946
                       in France
            INQUIRY FOR MISSING RELATIVES (Civilian)

Surname for Missing Person_   SCHON
First Name_____   Miksa
Date of Birth (or age)_____
Place of Birth_____
Nationality & Religion_____
Last known address   Bodrogmezo, Polany. Post Leleaz
                      by Kiraly-Helmec.
                      CZECHOSLOVAKIA. (Hungaria)
Name & Address of Persons abroad able to give informa-
tion Family Schön and Glück dont returned
from the concentration camp.All news about
family thinks give Belo Friedman Kralovsky
Chlumec Slovakis

Name of Inquirer_____   GLUCK. Irving. Pvt.
Address of Inquirer_____   Civilian War Relief.
                               AMERICAN RED CROSS IN FRANCE.

Nationality of Inquirer____   American
Relationship_____   Cousin
        Object of inquiry and short account of Inquirer's
welfare__WELFARE AND WHEREABOUTS REPORT.

                          Date of Inquiry__23.IO.I945

No. 513   S.G.   M & I

Home address
   50 Linwood Ave
   Columbus, Ohio

          GW 6223

wondered if it may have had to do with his cousin Zoli getting married, which he also mentioned in his letter. He thanked us for the packages Hermine and Marie sent, although he also cautioned them to seal them more carefully. The package had been opened, the envelope containing five dollars found, and the money stolen. He also enclosed a letter to our cousin Arthur in the hope that Arthur would send an affidavit for him to come to America.

We also began to receive more letters from our neighbors that, recalling how "fond" they were of us when the Hungarians took over in 1938, were insulting at best. They had taken our belongings for "safekeeping." They had used our land and our properties. They wrote as though they had no complicity in what had happened. It was as though Cain was once again asking, "Am I my brother's keeper?" The answer was still the same unequivocal "Yes!" Why had they done nothing to help save at least our brother's children? Mrs. Istvanne Toth, a former employee that used to work for us on our farm milking cows and helping out with whatever needed to be done, wrote us to explain her "terrible" situation. Yes, it was terrible, but she was alive, in her home, on her land with her seven children.

1946 March 26

My sweet and beloved Marie and Hermine. How are you? Thank G-d we are well and in good health and we hope you are also. I don't know how to begin this letter, my sweet Hermine and Marie, because I always felt you were part of my family. I mailed you a letter in January and you have not answered me. I don't know whether you have received it or not. Sweet Marie and Hermine, in my last letter I wrote to you that when the Germans came, they occupied your home, filling it with soldiers. They baked and cooked and they wanted to use the furniture for firewood, but my daughter Ilan told them that she would bring them firewood from our stock, because she

*was very sorry to have them use the furniture as firewood.
From then on, every day, we gave them firewood. They needed
it to do their washing. After they left, we brought the furniture
to our home, both the beds and Etelka's mirror. If you would
have seen them today, you would have destroyed them. As you
know, due to old age, they are full of holes. So that you
understand, Ignac [Klein] came and wanted to take the
furniture away. I felt very sorry for him, but we guarded it and
I thought that someone may come home from your family, so
that they should have it, but Ignac wanted to sell it to Puskar-
Eknak for a calf. My dear Hermine and Marie, if you believe in
G-d, tell Ignac not to take it away from us. The furniture has
no value. He is not as desperate as I am. As you know, when
you needed anything, I helped. I went to your place without
any hesitation. Whatever I had to do for you, I did. My dear
sweet Hermine, I would ask one more thing, if you can help,
please send us some used clothing for men or women.
Everything is good here, but you can buy only bacon, fat, and
flour, and we don't have even that because a very sad thing
happened to us. On February 25, my husband Pista, suddenly
died. At two o'clock in the afternoon he came home from the
village and wanted to lie down because he had pain in his legs.
He fell asleep and in the evening at eight o'clock he was dead.
This situation is so difficult with seven children, no less. The
burial cost me 1000 Kronin. I don't know what will I use to pay
for it, and because of that, my dear Hermine and Marie, if you
can afford it, and if you believe in G-d, do something good for
me because G-d will repay it 1000 times if you are kind to a
poor, old woman. Margit got married in October near
Kisvarda. She also said that if I write to you, I should tell you
that you should send her baby clothing because they can't buy
anything there and she's expecting in July, and she needs it.
Please write to me, tell me if you received my letter. If not, then
I will write you again, explaining everything I wrote
previously. I should have mailed it to you via airmail, but I
didn't have enough money. My dear, if you believe in G-d, do*

*good and please leave the two beds for me. They appear to
show their age and they're weak because they're already 50
years old. Perhaps one day one of my children will go to
America and will pay you for them.*

*My sweet Hermine and Marie, write to me about the boys.
Were they soldiers? I would like to see you. I'm very bitter
because your father gave me your album with pictures and I
watched over it as if it were my own child. I wanted it to
remember you all. Once when I was away in Helmec, Ignac
took it. If I would have been at home, I would not have given it
to him - those precious pictures! I will end this letter here. With
respect from my whole family.*

Reply immediately if you can,

Istvanne Toth

How could I feel sorry for her and her seven children? What about our nephews and nieces? Miklós and Gyula, the youngest, were most likely murdered by the Nazis. Lenke died after liberation. And we had no information about our nephew, Emil Gluck. In a village of 100 families, couldn't our "dear" neighbors have hidden four Jewish children?

As far as our land and property, what could we possibly do from America? I wrote a letter to Pál Lengyel. He worked in the district offices as a notary and our father knew him well. They had been very friendly and we hoped that he would be able to do something, if he was still alive. Mr. Lengyel's reply was only somewhat reassuring.

1946 June 6
Lelesz
Republic of Ceskoslovenska

> *Mr. Ignac Gluck*
> *50 Linwood Avenue*
> *Columbus 5, Ohio*

*In reply to your letter, I wish to advise you that the 'Gluck
properties' were given to Menyhert Torok of Polyán and they*

became his property during the years he used it. He paid the rental fee to the War Office and accordingly, you can't get them back now. When the government changed ownership of the properties that were left behind, it then gained control over them and declared someone to manage them. The manager turned out to be Ignac Klein. Since he was the closest living relative here, he was declared manager. He has no right to change the property's ownership, just to maintain it and he must account with the income from it. You needn't worry because he can't sell the property. Also, you don't have to worry that he will pocket the income because he has to report it. He has the properties but you should relax and don't worry. As American citizens, it will be very easy to have the properties returned to you. Please contact the Czechoslovakian consulate. If you're not happy with things as they are now, you could also change the management to anyone you want, but you must send a letter authorizing that. If you wish to get copies of the property records from the official book you can. It is very costly, but since you know approximately what properties you had, it will be easier. The properties include all the land your family owned when you left to America. If you intend to sell the properties, then you need a copy of the official property records. If you trust me, I would get them, but you must send me money to cover my expenses and then I will be glad to obtain the records and mail them to you. I will do it gladly because your father and I were very good friends.

I also wish to advise you that the main building is very neglected and the barn was destroyed by a strong gust of wind. I'm sure that Ignac Klein will write to you in detail about this and that you can trust him completely. He has also suffered quite a bit in the concentration camp and doesn't want to create any problems. He was declared as a manager by the Királyhelmeci district office and he doesn't get paid to manage the properties. I believe that I've given detailed information about the properties and if you need anything else, please ask me, and I will be glad to help with everything.

My best regards to all of you wholeheartedly

Sincerely,

Pál Lengyel
Lelesz.

Marie sent a letter to David summarizing the many letters we had received, especially this one about the property. She was busy preparing to move to New York to join Hermine.

August 14, 1946
Dear David!
We finally received the letter from you that we were waiting for, thank G-d that you are well. We are, too. There is nothing new here. Our little brother just received a card from the University that if he continues to do as well as he has been doing, then he can qualify for a scholarship. He is a very good student. If he receives this honor a few times then he can get a year of education for free. There aren't many who receive this honor. Right now, the courses that he's taking are difficult. However, he hasn't yet decided what would be best to study. You asked about Europe. We wrote the American consulate and they gave us information, but they themselves can't do anything. We also wrote to the district office in Lelesz a few weeks ago.

Marie repeated in detail Pál Lengyel's advice, as well as the news from their former neighbors, and then continued:

I mailed his [Lengyel's] letter to Hermine and maybe she will talk to the consulate and they can take care of the situation. As it is, one doesn't know how to begin. We wrote to Gerenyi. They replied and complained, and hoped to receive some packages from us. All of them complained because Ignac

[Klein] wanted to take back our property from them. We weren't in a hurry to send packages to Mrs. Gerenyi since she did not write to us first. Perhaps you should write to them without mentioning anything, however you should ask them what happened to the watch that our dear father gave to them. And that you would very much like to have it. Then you would hear what they have to say. Mrs. Gerenyi said that Manci asked for the watch. It would be better if Manci had it instead of the people that antagonized us. David, perhaps they won't lie to you and I don't believe that they'll ask you to send them packages or a lot of money. They all want something. We wrote to them that we have many people that we must help, but we are unable to help even them. We will mail some packages to Manci Klein and to Uncle Márton's son, Emil, who lives in Helmec. We sent a package to Lipot in Budapest. He lives there with his wife and two daughters. We don't know anything about the others, more than likely they don't exist. I'm going to end now since I have written you a lot. About myself, I don't know what to write. Right now, I'm at home. I don't know how to get ready to leave Ohio because our little brother is here and I don't feel like leaving him. I hope everything will turn out well.

Please take care of yourself, regards, love and kisses, Maria.

Herman, like before, is not interested in writing and best wishes from Irving.

By Rosh Hashana in October 1946, Marie had made up her mind and was on her way to New York, leaving me and Herman alone in Columbus. Like Hermine before her, Marie would stay with Bertha for a short time to get adjusted to life in New York and to find a job. It would have been nice if she could have stayed with Hermine, but Hermine could only afford to rent one room in a two bedroom apartment. The rent was $12.50 a week. The other tenant, an old woman, allowed her to cook in the kitchen since they both kept kosher. Hermine shared the news with David that Marie would soon join her in New York and chided him for not writing. She added,

> *"Hey David, if you have any old clothing that you don't need mail it to Uncle Márton's son, Emil. He lives in Helmec...We also received information that the youngest daughter of Sarolta from Szatmar is alive. I will write you once again in the near future, however I would also like to receive a reply.*
>
> *With kisses and with love, Hermine*

From Left to Right: Hermine, our cousin from Romania, Sarolta Klein, Marie, and Bodrog, our dog. I'm standing in the background. Circa 1936.

At the same time, we appointed a lawyer in Czechoslovakia, Balo Fenicky, to represent us to try and protect our property rights. It would take almost a year before we heard anything more from him about our property. His reply indicated that there had been a turn of events and that it would be a very difficult journey to recover anything, if at all. The Soviet Union was exerting its influence and Czechoslovakia had become a socialist republic and a part of the Eastern Bloc under the USSR's sphere of influence.

1947 September 3
Kral-Chlumec,C.S.R.
Balo Fenicky,

> *MR. IRVING GLUCK*
> *50 Linwood Avenue*
> *Columbus 5 Ohio. U.S.A.*

Dear Sir! I acknowledge that my reply to your dear letter is somewhat belated. You must know that in Europe after this horrendous, holocaust, Jewish life is somewhat more difficult, and earning a living as a lawyer is also. Due to the situation I do not have any time for letter writing. I want to advise you that everything I could have done up to now I did on your behalf. However, your relation Ignac Klein from Lelesz, has created a difficult road and I want to take legal action against him because his methodology is filled with deception. As of now he has not paid any taxes. Any money that comes in he keeps for himself. He deals with the property until he sees an income, but then does not repair the building. I want to inform you that I want to sell my own property, because only a person that works on the property himself can maintain it. So I would advise you that the best thing you could do is to sell yours, too. Andras Hornyak from Lelesz is willing to buy it. He's offered 9000 Czechoslovakian Kronen for one hectare. Here in Hungary, land is not valuable because people are waiting for the Hungarian government to take control of it. My advice is that one of you should return to Europe soon. I would be more than happy to help you with your legal affairs. Accordingly, while you're making a decision, I will be glad to help you. I'll do my best with the time I have available, but I can't commit myself, because I have too much work to do already, and I could not wholeheartedly do justice with your property, as I would like to do and as I did in the past. I would be very glad to extend my services to you as though I were your brother, but without a personal interest at stake. However, I must warn you that nothing can be finished here. I would like to ask you to please write to me regarding Emil and Lenke Gluck's relationship with you. Please give our hearty regards to the rest of your family. Please also write to me that all four of you are United States citizens. My advice to you is to sell the properties. As I'm writing to you I did the same with mine. Whatever decision you make is up to you. Please let me know. My heartfelt regards to all of you - Fenicky

Our father had transferred money and property into Lajos' children's names (Emil and Lenke Gluck) and David, as their godfather, was the custodian of their estate. What did it matter though? None of us had any intention of going back to Europe. So much time had passed since we had appointed Mr. Fenicky, and it seemed that he had done very little. We still hoped that something could be achieved from America, so we withdrew our authorization for him to act on our behalf, and I contacted Pál Lengyel again. I apologized for not answering his previous letter because of my studies, advised him that we had submitted papers in Bratislava to protect our property rights, and that we had given his name as a contact in the event they required additional information about our properties. We anxiously awaited his reply. Thankfully, he wrote back within a month.

Lelesz, November 15, 1947
Dear Mr. Gluck and family,

I have received the letter which you sent me. I have not received any information from Bratislava yet. However, if I do then I will take care of anything you want. The property tax assessment report does not indicate that the property has been confiscated. I am very surprised that by now, you don't know a great deal about your properties. As I wrote you previously, your property was registered as having "missing property owners" and the National Administrator authorized Ignac Klein to administer them because he is a relation of yours who has returned from Germany. Bela Fenicky was never officially authorized to act on your behalf by the National Administrator. This national guardianship lasts only as long as you decide to act otherwise. If you want to end it, mail a letter to the district office and you can assign your own administrator. I have spoken to Ignac Klein and he will write to you. He asserts that he is handling the properties. He rents them out and keeps the income. This shouldn't be a problem for you knowing the difficulties that the returning Jews face. Many come back with nothing, and since commerce has not resumed, they must live from something. He will reimburse you eventually. He also claims that he has an interest in the Gluck properties. and that he has communicated with you without any result. It would be a shame to go to court. If it's true that his sister's dowry was invested in your property, the judge would rule in his favor. It would be important to repair the house because of its current condition. If it isn't, it will collapse. I believe that in this short letter, I have enlightened you. It is up to you to act in your own behalf. If it becomes necessary for you to make decisions regarding the properties, I will give you additional information. Until then, best regards,

Pál Lengyel, District Notary Officer

In December 1947, misfortune struck again. A pre-dawn fire caused by a faulty water cooler destroyed our cousin Arthur's factory on 2176 South 3rd Street in Columbus, the home of his business, Bonded Building and Scale Manufacturing. Arthur estimated the damage to the building to be $80,000 and the loss of materials inside to exceed $400,000, an astronomical sum of money by any standard. This included belts and bearings for mining equipment, 400 electric motors, 80 tons of welding rod, as well as two brand new power saws used to cut steel that he had just bought for $7,000 each. Although his fifty employees were temporarily out of work, none were injured. Arthur vowed to rebuild the concrete block building, replace the lost machinery, and start again. Unfortunately, he thought it would take more than a year to do so.[36]

Fire Sweeps Bonded Scale; Loss Estimated at $350,000

Defective Water Cooler Blamed; Firm to Rebuild

---

[36] Arthur rebuilt his factory and ran it until his death in 1973. His son Samuel eventually sold the company. Arthur's obituary reads: "The Department of Philosophy of the Ohio State University regrets to announce the death of Arthur Gluck, on January 23, 1973. Mr. Gluck, a Columbus industrialist, endowed the Julius Gluck Memorial Library of Philosophy at Ohio State, and contributed to the philosophy libraries of several other institutions. A constant supporter of philosophy since his graduation from Ohio State in 1920, Mr. Gluck was founder and first president of the Ohio State Philosophy Club and established the Bingham Award for excellent undergraduate work in philosophy at Ohio State."

In the meantime, I pressed on with my studies. Language often proved to be a complicating factor since each class I took used different terminology. Not only did I need to know the definitions of specific terms used in class, but I also needed to know the definitions of the words used to define the terms. The dictionary soon became one of my best friends. However, my ability to speak Yiddish and German came in handy. Not wanting to waste time in an introductory class, I went to the head of the German department to find out how to get credit for my language skills. Naturally, I spoke to him in German. He was so impressed at how well I spoke, "even better than I do" were his exact words, that there was no need for me to even bother sitting for any of the German language classes the university offered. However, he did suggest that I take a German theater class. Little did I know, it was actually an acting class, and I was expected to perform on stage!

In costume for my role in the German play "Ein Mann muss heiraten" - (A man must marry)

In February 1948, in a coup d'état, the Communist Party of Czechoslovakia, with the backing of the Soviet Union, took control of the government of Czechoslovakia. This considerably complicated our efforts to regain control of our property, and to claim the money set aside for Emil and Lenke, but we were determined to keep trying.

As I progressed in my studies, my interest turned to the field of economics and I declared it to be my major. It seemed to me that bad economic policy was a major cause of war and I thought that by studying economics and understanding its theories, I could find some way to prevent another generation from suffering the way mine had. I was strongly influenced by Wendell Wilkie's book "One World" and by the writings of John Maynard Keynes. I associated with the brightest students and studied with them daily (one of whom, Herbert Baum, received his Doctorate in Economics from the University of Chicago in 2006 at the age of 79, the oldest person ever to receive the degree from that University).[37] When asked what we needed to know in a particular course, our professors admonished us to know the book cover to cover, and to study the index, only then would we be prepared. Being older than many of the other students by at least 6 years often worked to my advantage. I was serious, appreciated the opportunity that I had been given, understood the importance of a good education, and worked hard to graduate.

---

[37] http://www-news.uchicago.edu/releases/06/060821.baum.shtml

My yearbook picture after graduating from Ohio State University
June 1949

I received my BA in Economics in 1949 and began studying for my Master's degree. Unfortunately, one of my professors discouraged me from completing it, though. Rather than direct and guide me, he instead told me that I was naïve for wanting to work to create world peace, and that I needed to experience life among the people of the United States to see what their lives were really like before I continued my thesis about the economics of health care. I foolishly followed his advice and withdrew from the Master's program to seek employment. Among the many places that I sent out job applications, were the newly created United Nations and the US State Department, hoping to have some influence on world affairs, but they wanted translators, not economists. Of course I could translate, but my dreams were far grander than that. I wanted to do whatever I could to prevent wars from happening again. The economic reality however was that there were many more workers, returning soldiers and capable women who had filled the vacant positions left by the soldiers, than there were jobs available. I had to settle. My first job out of university was a simple clerical position as a record keeper at the Pollock Paper company, which manufactured paper for bread wrappers. After this, I worked in another factory performing time studies of their manufacturing processes to lower their production costs. I was stationed above the factory floor to observe the various stages that the workers performed. I didn't stay there very long because the smoke and fumes from the machines below made their way to me at my observation perch. The smell was noxious and I decided that the job was not for me.

Marie had joined Hermine in New York, so eventually Herman and I packed our belongings and moved there, too. We found an apartment in the Bronx and rented it together. I quickly found employment with Peter Kiewit, an engineering and construction company, as a purchasing agent and expediter, to procure materials for the construction of civilian airfields in Africa. As it turned out, General Wilson, whom I had been guarding as an MP in Germany, worked on the floor above mine. For some reason, I was intimidated and never went up to say hello. After one year, the project was finished and I received my pink slip on a Friday at 4:30 and was told to leave by 5pm.

I searched for another position and was soon hired by Atlas Construction as a purchasing agent to procure construction materials for a gas diffusion plant that they were building for the US Department of Energy in Portsmouth, Ohio. It was a good opportunity, and I didn't want to pass it up even if it meant leaving New York, and my family. Relocating was made somewhat easier because my sister Hermine had accepted a marriage proposal from a new suitor. Until that point, she had been close friends with Louis Schwartz, a Hungarian speaker from Youngstown, Ohio. They had corresponded with each other while he was stationed overseas in Iceland throughout the war, and we assumed she would marry him. However, as a Zionist, he wanted to move to the recently reborn State of

Israel[38] and Hermine was unwilling to uproot herself again, a feeling we all shared, so she refused his offer. Soon after, she was set up on a blind date with Eugene Solomon, a hard working Hungarian speaking immigrant from Romania in the grocery business. After dating him for eight months, they agreed to marry. Aunt Jennie, whom we had stayed with the day we arrived to America ten years earlier, sent out the invitations and Hermine married Eugene on March 5, 1950.

During this time an opportunity opened to file claims under the International Claims Settlement Act of 1949 against the Communist government for illegally expropriating our land. After repeated requests by the American Embassy in Prague, the Czechoslovakian Ministry of Foreign Affairs furnished the following report about our property on October 3, 1950:

"The real property owned by Ignac, Hermina, Herman and Maria Gluck, located in the cadestral area of Polány, District of Kralovsky Chlumec, consists of 7/9ths of a house with yard and of landed property covering an area of approximately 3 hectares. Since the year 1945 this property has been administered by one Ignac Klein, a resident of Leles, on the basis of an authorization given him by the Local National Committee under Ref. No. 1946/45 of November 15, 1945. Ignac Klein is using part of the property himself and collects the rent for the use of the remaining part of the property."

---

[38] On May 14, 1948, David Ben-Gurion proclaimed the establishment of the State of Israel as British rule in Palestine came to an end. The United States immediately recognized the new state. The next day, the armies of Egypt, Iraq, Jordan, Lebanon and Syria invaded. The Israelis, though poorly equipped, managed to fight off the Arabs and seized key territory, such as the Galilee, the Palestinian coast, and a strip of territory connecting the coastal region to the western section of Jerusalem. In 1949, U.N.-brokered cease-fires left the State of Israel in permanent control of this conquered territory.

At least we had an official acknowledgement regarding the current status of our property. They mentioned nothing about the monies held on behalf of Emil and Lenke. However, the government of Czechoslovakia had no intention of settling any claims against it, and as Americans, we would need to wait for the American government to enact the International Claims Settlement Act. For the moment, it seemed as if we had reached a dead end regarding our property. We didn't know what else could be done.

Taking the job in Portsmouth meant leaving Herman alone in the apartment. No sooner had I returned to Ohio, Herman broke his ankle when a wall of shelves collapsed on him at the warehouse in which he worked. Luckily for him, Marie, who was working as a cashier in Ratner's, a kosher restaurant on 2nd Avenue in Manhattan, was there to help him recover. At the same time, he was called in for jury duty. While serving, he met a group of men who were amateur investors in the stock market. They influenced Herman to take his hard earned money and try his luck "working" in the market. Since it took quite awhile for his leg to heal, Herman had plenty of time on his hands to "invest." To me, it seemed more like gambling than investing, and Herman's newfound enthusiasm for stocks didn't rub off on me. I preferred to earn money the "old fashioned" way.

Within a year I returned to New York because the project in Portsmouth was finished. I found a job at Eastern Precision, a company that manufactured resistors used in the electronics industry. It wasn't until the end of 1951 that Emil, in a letter written from Yafo, Israel, finally explained his long delay in leaving Hungary and emigrating to Palestine.

1951 November 1
Beloved Hermine,
Your long-awaited letter has arrived with a check on October 27. I can't remember when I was so happy. I was happy for

both the letter and the check at the same time. I'm surprised that you haven't received my previous letter or my New Year's card. I mailed them to you about two months ago. I hope that since you wrote your letter that you have received them. Did you? I can't cash the check immediately because there are hundreds of people receiving checks at the same time. Everyone gets a number and then needs to wait. It takes about two weeks before I can receive the cash. After 10 days I'll go to the bank and by then, my number will come up. Concerning this, it's much better if you send me a package because here they ask me to pay twice as much as what it costs you there. I know this because my neighbor gets packages weekly from her uncle, either a check or a package. Here our fellow Jews work according to the black market. Therefore Hermine, if you shop there for $15 then you could send me almost double what I could get here. The only difference is that the check comes in fast, whereas the package comes very slowly. Hermine, I hope that I may reply sincerely to your question regarding the beddings? If I'm too forward with my letters you should tell me that I am being rude (you have the right to tell me). I am sorry to tell you, but it's best that I tell you the truth about my bedding situation. If you saw me, you wouldn't believe that Uncle Márton's son is dressed so poorly. I don't want you to misunderstand me, so I'm going to explain why I don't have anything decent to wear. I'm not happy to write about this, because I would like to forget this embarrassing incident, however, I would like you to understand why exactly I'm in this predicament. As you know Hermine, after the concentration camp I was freed and I was by myself. My cousin Zoli would have been my guardian because I was underage. My poor father, before he died, told me where he buried gold, silver, and dollars in a small place in the ground. When I returned from the camp, I found what he had hidden. I discussed everything with Zoli. At that time he was an upright individual (he was not yet married). We decided that we would convert everything I found into dollars and I'd put it away until the time comes *that I needed it. That's the way it was. As you know, I've studied dentistry and I was living from that money. I didn't have any need for anything from Zoli. As a young man, I felt completely relaxed because of my little wealth, but regretfully I trusted Zoli too much, and I had to pay for it. Zoli got married and he completely changed. It would have been of no concern to me if he would not have done what he did. Before my immigration to Palestine, I went to him and asked him to please give me my money because I would like to buy things before I go to the new country, where I don't have anyone, and a person should have some money with him. He replied that he was very sorry, but he can't give it back because there's nothing left. I thought for a moment that he was merely teasing me, but after he explained that he had to keep up his house and had other expenses I knew he wasn't teasing. He used a lot from mine and the money disappeared and he himself has only a little left over. I don't know what other people would have done, but I turned around and I left him. Consequently, I was penniless as I left home, and I know now what it means to buy every piece of clothing and bedding. This wouldn't be a problem if it wasn't so costly to buy it here. In Israel, everything is obtained according to points. I can't afford to pay the black market price. My dear Hermine, you can see that despite my situation, I am not envious. Don't take this that I'm complaining but it's somewhat true as the saying goes, that lightening always strikes the same place. Therefore, my dear Hermine, if you want to help me, I will answer your questions regarding sizes that I wear. They are the following: my shirt size is 39, my pants size is 44. I have shoes. My socks don't have a size marked on them. I don't know how it's called, but one wears it under the regular shirt, in America it may be called Trico. Here you can't live without it because it's very hot and this item will be excellent because it absorbs sweat. I don't know where to get it at the market here. I had to work up the nerve to ask you for all of this, and I'm ashamed of myself, but I want you to know it's a must to have it, what can I do? Also, if it's not too difficult for you Hermine, then if you really want to help me, send pillow covers and bed sheets. I can't over emphasize what it would mean to me. But you, Hermine, probably can see that I'm not asking for these things lightly. I will let you know what I bought with the check and how much money they gave in the exchange. I'm sure that you'll be interested to know. In advance Hermine, I am not hungry because I'm satisfied just by thinking of the good meat in the package that you'll send. It's time for me to end here because I think you will get tired of this long letter. Hermine I'm waiting impatiently for you to write. Please tell Eugene to write to me, even if it's only to send his regards, otherwise I'll think that I'm making trouble for him. Maria, I always put you as an afterthought in my letters, but please don't take it that way. I'm a little bit tired and I'm unable to concentrate for another letter so this letter naturally speaks to you, too! In any event, I am very grateful to you Maria, and thank you for the package and its contents, the good G-d should pay you! Kisses to all of you and true love, your cousin, Emil.*

Life wasn't easy for us, but from Emil's letters it was even more difficult for him. We each had each other, but he was alone. Despite the many hardships he faced there appeared a single strand of hope that he would find some happiness.

1952 February 21
Jaffa, Israel

Dear Hermine and Eugene!

Let me explain my long silence. About two months ago I received a letter from you Hermine and it arrived just as I had to report to military service for five weeks. Every year one has to go for army reserve duty. This causes problems because after you finish reserve duty, you lose your job because by the time you return they usually hire someone else. Therefore, I'm unemployed now and I'm looking for work every chance I get.

Unfortunately I haven't been able to find a job. I hope that in a couple weeks I will. If I don't get the job to drive a taxi, then I'll have to look for something else. This is what happens when you have a job, but you're not your own boss. The main thing is to stay healthy and everything will be okay somehow....

I almost became bitter because of my misfortune, but when your beautiful package arrived - I can't find the words for what you've done for me. My dear Hermine, you can't imagine it. First of all, everything, every piece, each item individually is beautiful and fits me perfectly. I need all that you sent as desperately as one needs a piece of bread. As I opened the package, I tried every item on. Each thing fits as if it was measured to my size. Hermine, I must mention the shoes separately. Whoever bought the shoes must have good taste. It has to be a man, most likely it was you, Eugene. I'm not trying to exaggerate, but everyone who saw them, admired them. For the bed sheets and pillow covers I made a separate holiday because I have been sleeping in a bed without any sheets. What I had has disintegrated. I don't want you to think that I'm exaggerating, therefore I'm not going to detail the rest of the items, but the fact is, every piece is very valuable to me. The economic conditions here in Israel make it impossible to buy anything like what you sent. If you can buy them, you have to be wealthy. For example, with the income I would receive from one day's work, I could not purchase even one necktie from the three that you sent me. I could not have purchased it here at all because it's impossible to find it here. If you could, you would have to work for a whole week, and then there would be no money left for food. Therefore one must give up the idea of even walking in these magnificent shoes...Unfortunately, it is very sad to be in this country now. I'm sure you know the situation. I don't know where this will lead us to. The only thing I'm certain of is that there's no future here. I don't know my dear Hermine, perhaps I'm in a bad mood, and because of that I'm writing everything! I only know that from day to day it's more difficult to make a living (not only for me but for everyone). Think of what it means to stay in line for a loaf of bread for hours before getting just one. I know that you won't believe this situation and I hope you'll never have to know what it means. We've become accustomed to not eating meat for months. Whatever we can get we are happy with and those that never ate anything good may think that I'm exaggerating. The situation is such that we don't know how to solve it. Every evening we wait for a miracle, but it just doesn't want to come. My immediate problem now is that I can't afford to get a room. They ask exorbitant prices for even a very small room that I'll never be able to buy. I take from my mouth a few pennies so that I can save, but this is not life for a young man. I would like to get married Hermine, because it will be easier for two people to get through this problem. As I wrote you before there is a young woman that I would like to marry, however as I just wrote you, I don't have a place to live and without one, we are unable to get married. This is the reality. Regarding this Hermine, I have one thing I'd like to ask you, and I hope you won't get angry at me. I'm sure you know how important it is for a man who wants to be a groom to get some gift for the bride to be. I would do it, but without money I can't buy anything. If you have something that you don't wear Hermine, like a white night gown, you know what ladies want. I hope I'm not making it difficult for you, but please do it for me. It would be a tremendous help. And if you have any nylon stockings, even if they have a run in them, they can fix it here. Even if it's used, it's no problem either, because whatever you have can be worn. This young woman is pretty like you. I'm asking you for used items hoping that it will not create a problem for you. If Eugene has any used clothing that he doesn't need or use, I'll be glad to accept it. Forgive me for being very forward, but this is due to necessity. To conclude, I have tried your patience with this long letter. I promise next time I will write a shorter letter. Hermine and Eugene, I want to thank you for your good deeds and G-d should repay you for them. I have been so occupied with myself I just discovered that I didn't ask how you are and how life is with you? I would like to hear some good news from you and the family. Please write everything about all of you. I'm waiting for your lines as soon as possible; Lots of love and kisses to all of you, your cousin, Emil.

It wasn't until 1954 that I had saved enough money to visit David in California. We hadn't seen each other since I went off to Texas for basic training eleven years earlier. When he first arrived there, David worked as a longshoreman. Later, he worked for the Navy helping to coordinate material deliveries for the construction of a Liberty ship, the USS Crittenden. For the first time, David felt like he had an important job. No material was allowed aboard the ship without his approval. However, the job didn't last forever and like in Europe, he wasn't content to work for someone else.

USS Crittenden
https://atlanticfleetsales.smugmug.com/Photography/APA/i-Vq2msZr/A

As soon as he could, he opened his own business, "Gluck's Fine Draperies." He soon added lamps and shades to his inventory. When that didn't work out, he opened a restaurant and pizzeria called Freddy's Cafe and Deli. Unsuccessful, he opened another restaurant and bar called "Freddy's Place" in Long Beach and finally considered himself established. After all, he was now married and with his wife Dorothy, an American originally from Chicago, he had a four year old son named Frederick. They lived in a small house perched on a steep hill. A long, winding road led down the hill to the road where the restaurant was located. I call it a restaurant, but it was more of a bar than a restaurant. Dorothy's cooking skills were self-admittedly limited, but out of braggadocio more than necessity David took me there and made me a large steak for my first breakfast. Freddy's Place advertised that it had 59 international varieties of beer on tap. I didn't count them, but it certainly appeared to be true. Although he loved to cook, especially Hungarian stuffed cabbage or goulash (a beef stew), he would never share his recipes, and if he did, there was always an ingredient that he conveniently neglected to include.

Even though David gave the appearance of being successful, he never seemed to have enough money to make ends meet. He had even written me to ask not for my blessing, but for $250 dollars so he could marry Dorothy. Astonishingly, David never forgot his debt to Jane, the postmaster from Lelesz, who had loaned him money to come to America. After the war, they continued to correspond. Although there was no way to send money to her, he sent her shoes, stockings, clothing, fabric, and anything else that was scarce in Czechoslovakia but readily available in California. He also asked Marie and Hermine to send packages to Jane on his behalf. For her part, Jane was astonished that he remembered her with such kindness.

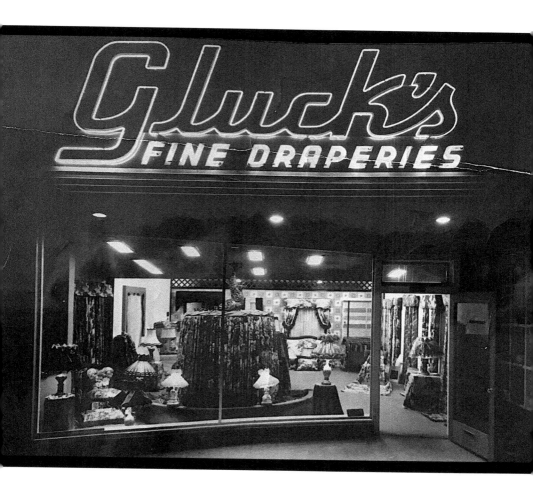

Above: David, standing on left, behind the counter at his restaurant, "Freddy's Cafe"
1741 Pacific Coast Highway, Lomita, California

Above and opposite: David behind the bar at his restaurant, "Freddy's Place"
promoting Asahi beer, one of dozens of imports, with the Asahi model.
240 Long Beach Boulevard, Long Beach, California

David (on the left) and me.

I flew by airplane from New York to California, a novelty at the time, but it had been a terrifying experience, and I decided to return by train. Since the return trip took longer than expected, I arrived back to New York one day late to find that I was unemployed. I had been fired. In combat, seconds determined your fate. In business, just one day.

I tried advertising in the newspaper to find a job. I mistakenly included the word 'single' to indicate my marital status. Rather than get job offers, I did get quite a few propositions from single women!

PURCHASING★ agent, 33, single, graduate business administration, experienced expediter, buyer electrical, elec-
tronic equipment, supplies, Government
contracts, seeks progressive firm. Will
relocate PR 8-1118. V609 Times.

Eventually I went into the vending machine business with my sister Hermine's husband, Eugene in New York. In fact, I had placed some of his machines at the electronics company where I worked before I had been fired. I continued to solicit new locations and to repair the machines when they needed servicing, but our business methodology often clashed. For one thing, I still enjoyed handing out free samples, like I did in Naples, a practice Eugene did not condone, so I decided to establish my own vending company. I traded the German P-38 pistol that I had brought back with me after the war to purchase my first machine. After all, I had no use for the gun. It wasn't exactly swords into plowshares, but it was close! It was such a wonderful feeling to be independent. For the first time, I was accountable to no one but myself. I made my schedule as I pleased and ran my business as I saw fit. My route grew as I placed dozens of machines at various locations in the Bronx and Queens, as well as in Nassau County on Long Island. Every day I serviced the machines by refilling them with candy or cans of soda, cleaning the coffee dispensers, or fixing a jammed coin mechanism, and my favorite part, collecting the money that the machines had earned for me. If not for the steady stream of income, I would have considered the long hours and the constant driving from location to location akin to slavery.

Sometimes however, just one machine placement could lead to unexpected results. I'd placed a machine at an A & P Supermarket warehouse in Elmhurst, Queens, and one of the managers there recommended that I place machines at the A & P bakery. Because I wanted to expand as much as possible, I went there and was able to place more than 20 machines. This became my largest and most important location.

No sooner had I placed the machines in the cafeteria, an interesting thing happened. While I serviced a machine, I usually gave its contents away for free: cups of coffee, candy, or

cans of soda depending on the machine I was working on.
This particular afternoon, there was just one man sitting in the
cafeteria while I was working on the coffee machine. "Would
you like to have a cup of coffee?" I asked. "Sure, why not!
Cream with extra sugar..." he replied. I pressed the appropriate
buttons on the machine and brought him his drink. We started
talking while I finished with the machine. Before I locked the
door, I took a cup of coffee for myself, walked over to the small
table and sat down across from him. We talked some more and
then he asked, "Do you know who I am?" I said to him, "No,
but it doesn't matter who you are!" "Well," he continued, "I'm
the President of the A&P Tea Company!"

Another time, while servicing machines at the A&P bakery, I
overheard a worker comment to another, "Well, the Jews never
did anything in the war. They were always in the back where it
was safe, and they could make money. They were never up at
the front. All they care about is money!" As I was in the act of
removing the coins from the machine, and therefore, his
comment was probably directed at me. He continued, "Here's
another one, grabbing every dollar he can. That's all they care
about." I couldn't contain myself. I closed the machine and
walked over to the two workers. "Really? The Jews were in the
back?" I reached into my pants pocket and took out my wallet.
I opened it with deliberate care and slowly withdrew my
discharge papers. I'd used a reproduction machine to reduce
the size of the original to fit in my wallet and had it laminated.
"Who wants to come here and read this?" I asked looking out
into the crowd. I handed the card to the loud-mouthed man's
friend and said, "Go ahead, read it!" I said it loud enough that
the 50 or more people eating their lunch in the cafeteria went
silent and a few gathered around us. He started reading.
"Gluck, Irving, Company B, 6th Armored Infantry Division." I
interrupted. "Louder, so everyone can hear!" He continued as
I ordered, "Military Policeman, occupied territory, M1 rifle, 30

caliber machine gun, Combat Infantry Badge, Naples-Foggia, Rome-Arno, Rhineland, Central Europe, Good Conduct Medal, American Campaign Medal, European African Middle Eastern Campaign Medal with 4 Bronze stars, World War II Victory Medal..." The crowd that gathered around us began to applaud. I raised my hand to silence them. "Do you know what those four bronze stars mean?" I paused. "Four stars mean four combat zones: Africa, Italy, France, and Germany. How about the Combat Infantry Badge? That's only for a soldier who was right there in the front lines! Now you know where I, a Jew, was...why don't you tell us where you were? What have you done?" He didn't have anything to say because he had never served anywhere. His coworkers booed.

Army of the United States

Honorable Discharge

This is to certify that

IRVING GLUCK 35 633 941 PRIVATE FIRST CLASS

COMPANY B 6TH ARMORED INFANTRY BATTALION

Army of the United States

is hereby Honorably Discharged from the military service of the United States of America.

This certificate is awarded as a testimonial of Honest and Faithful Service to this country.

Given at   SEPARATION CENTER
            INDIANTOWN GAP MIL RES PA

Date   7 NOVEMBER 1945

B J AMBROSE
MAJOR AC

Front of Discharge Papers

K171-12   ENLISTED RECORD AND REPORT OF SEPARATION

HONORABLE DISCHARGE

1. LAST NAME - FIRST NAME - MIDDLE INITIAL	2. ARMY SERIAL NO.	3. GRADE	4. ARM OR SERVICE	5. COMPONENT
GLUCK IRVING	35 633 941	PFC	INF	AUS

6. ORGANIZATION

CO B 6TH ARMD INF BN

7. DATE OF SEPARATION	8. PLACE OF SEPARATION
7 NOV 45	SEP CTR IGMR PA

9. PERMANENT ADDRESS FOR MAILING PURPOSES

50 LINWOOD AVE COLUMBUS OHIO

10. DATE OF BIRTH	11. PLACE OF BIRTH
14 NOV 21	BODROGMEZO CZECH

12. ADDRESS FROM WHICH EMPLOYMENT WILL BE SOUGHT

SEE 9

13. COLOR EYES	14. COLOR HAIR	15. HEIGHT	16. WEIGHT	17. NO. DEPEND
BLUE	BLONDE	5'11½"	150 Lbs.	NONE

18. RACE	19. MARITAL STATUS	20. U.S. CITIZEN	21. CIVILIAN OCCUPATION AND NO.
WHITE NEGRO OTHER *(specify)* X	SINGLE MARRIED OTHER *(specify)* X	YES X NO	1-25.125 DUPLICATING MACHINE OPERATOR

MILITARY HISTORY

22. DATE OF INDUCTION	23. DATE OF ENLISTMENT	24. DATE OF ENTRY INTO ACTIVE SERVICE	25. PLACE OF ENTRY INTO SERVICE
16 MAR 43		23 MAR 43	COLUMBUS OHIO

SELECTIVE SERVICE DATA ▶	26. REGISTERED YES NO X	27. LOCAL S. S. BOARD NO. 12	28. COUNTY AND STATE FRANKLIN OHIO	29. HOME ADDRESS AT TIME OF ENTRY INTO SERVICE SEE 9

30. MILITARY OCCUPATIONAL SPECIALTY AND NO.	31. MILITARY QUALIFICATION AND DATE *(i.e. infantry, aviation and marksmanship badges, etc.)*
MILITARY POLICEMAN OCCUPIED TER 669	30 CAL MACH GUN MRKM M1 RIFLE SS COMBAT INFANTRY BADGE

32. BATTLES AND CAMPAIGNS

GO 33 & 40 WD 45   NAPLES-FOGGIA   ROME-ARNO   RHINELAND
CENTRAL EUROPE

33. DECORATIONS AND CITATIONS

GOOD CONDUCT MEDAL   AMERICAN CAMPAIGN MEDAL   EUROPEAN AFRICAN MIDDLE
EASTERN CAMPAIGN MEDAL WITH 4 BRONZE STARS   WORLD WAR II VICTORY MEDAL

34. WOUNDS RECEIVED IN ACTION

NONE

35. LATEST IMMUNIZATION DATES				36. SERVICE OUTSIDE CONTINENTAL U.S. AND RETURN		
SMALLPOX	TYPHOID	TETANUS	OTHER *(specify)* TYPHUS	DATE OF DEPARTURE	DESTINATION	DATE OF ARRIVAL
26DEC44	24MAY45	26DEC44	21 APR 44	21 AUG 43	ALGERIA	2 SEP 43
				22 OCT 45	US	2 NOV 45

37. TOTAL LENGTH OF SERVICE						38. HIGHEST GRADE HELD
CONTINENTAL SERVICE			FOREIGN SERVICE			
YEARS	MONTHS	DAYS	YEARS	MONTHS	DAYS	PFC
0	5	3	2	2	12	

39. PRIOR SERVICE

NONE

40. REASON AND AUTHORITY FOR SEPARATION

AR 615-365 15 DEC 44 CONVN OF THE GOVT RR1-1 DEMOBILIZATION

41. SERVICE SCHOOLS ATTENDED	42. EDUCATION *(Years)*		
PROJECTION OPERATORS SCHOOL	Grammar School 8	High School 4	College 1

PAY DATA

43. LONGEVITY FOR PAY PURPOSES			44. MUSTERING OUT PAY		45. SOLDIER DEPOSITS	46. TRAVEL PAY	47. TOTAL AMOUNT, NAME OF DISBURSING OFFICER
YEARS	MONTHS	DAYS	TOTAL	THIS PAYMENT	NONE	$22.80	$33.35 MAHER JR
2	7	21	$300	$100			MAJOR FD

INSURANCE NOTICE

IMPORTANT IF PREMIUM IS NOT PAID WHEN DUE OR WITHIN THIRTY-ONE DAYS THEREAFTER, INSURANCE WILL LAPSE. MAKE CHECKS OR MONEY ORDERS PAYABLE TO THE TREASURER OF THE U. S. AND FORWARD TO COLLECTIONS SUBDIVISION, VETERANS ADMINISTRATION, WASHINGTON 25, D. C.

48. KIND OF INSURANCE			49. HOW PAID		50. Effective Date of Allotment Discontinuance	51. Date of Next Premium Due *(One month after 50)*	52. PREMIUM DUE EACH MONTH	53. INTENTION OF VETERAN TO
Nat Serv.	U.S. Govt.	None	Allotment	Direct to V.A.	31 OCT 45	30 NOV 45	$6.50	Continue Continue Only Discontinue
X			X					X

54.	55. REMARKS *(This space for completion of above items or entry of other items specified in W. D. Directives)*
RIGHT THUMB PRINT	LAPEL BUTTON ISSUED ASR SCORE (2 SEP 45) 75 INACTIVE SERVICE ERC FROM 16 MAR 43 TO 22 MAR 43

56. SIGNATURE OF PERSON BEING SEPARATED	57. PERSONNEL OFFICER *(Type name, grade and organization - signature)*
Irving Gluck	R F MAGUIRE CAPT MAC *B J Maguire*

Rear of Discharge Papers

Finally, in 1954 the United States enacted the International Claims Settlement Act of 1949. It authorized the Foreign Claims Settlement Commission ("FCSC") to consider claims of nationals of the United States against foreign governments, including Hungary and the government of Czechoslovakia for property nationalized after the Communist Revolution. Under the Foreign Claims Settlement Act, we first filed a claim against the Government of Hungary in 1955 for the loss of our property in 1938, that is the horses and wagons, when Hungary took over the Felvidék territories from Czechoslovakia. It was a long-shot, especially without any documentation, but we wanted justice. In 1957, this claim was denied because Polány, despite being under Hungarian control, "was not in Hungary within the meaning of section 303 of the Act."

Our claim against Czechoslovakia was more complicated. It required the complete description of our property: its exact location; the deed or the excerpt from the land register; a description of how the property was acquired; the dates of taking by the Czechoslovak government; the actual value at the time of loss, and more! Luckily, in 1958, assets of Czechoslovakia that were frozen by the United States were approved to be used to pay out successful claims under the Foreign Claims Settlement Commission and we began the process of collecting the required documentation. We authorized Pál Lengyel to access our records.

By 1959, David decided to join us in New York. He was in debt. Again. And he was certain that he was dying. In fact, years earlier in Europe he had been told by a gypsy fortune teller that he would die young. So when a doctor in California told him that he had cancer David believed him, partly because of the gypsy's prophesy and partly because it was an excuse to get out of paying his debts. However, the diagnosis was wrong. He was under pressure for sure, but there was no cancer. Nonetheless, the diagnosis, or rather the misdiagnosis was the impetus for his move. He, Dorothy, and Freddie stayed with Hermine's family until they found a home.

Once again, David reinvented himself. He bought a machine that made donuts and he sold them on a street corner in Manhattan. This didn't last long however, and for a short time he joined me in my vending business before starting his own, DJ Enterprises, a combination of his initial and our father's. He bought some machines, but because he couldn't afford the best quality machines made by the best manufacturer, he had trouble placing them. The vending machines soon ended up in his garage. As usual, David was undeterred and eventually opened his own retail clothing business. First he specialized in men's, women's, and children's clothing and then finally settled on women's undergarments. This he knew how to do! No matter the size, David always had the right bra in stock and wasn't reluctant to make sure that it fit correctly, much to the embarrassment of many a first time buyer.

At last, the small remnant of our family was reunited in New York. Herman had become an amateur investor in the stock market and had even made a nice profit from his investments. Yet, like many others, he had bought shares in various Cuban sugar companies. When Fidel Castro overthrew the American backed government there, Herman lost everything. Every hard-earned cent. Having been paid just ten cents an hour when he first arrived in America, this loss dealt him a severe blow from which he would never recover. Although he managed to live on his own, he was dependent on Marie to manage his affairs. Following our father's advice to take care of each other, she did.

After many years without any news from Pál Lengyel, we received a letter from him in early 1960 in reply to our requests for help in securing official documentation of our properties in Czechoslovakia.

March 9, 1960
My dear Hermine,

Don't be angry that I call you by your first name, however I only know you by that name. I would like to answer your letter completely, however, the land numbers for your properties that you requested cannot be obtained and mailed. You and your brother Ignac inquired about this back in 1945 and 1946 through the Foreign Ministry. At that time, I wrote about everything and mailed information about the properties to you. However, I am no longer working in an official capacity because I am retired. Even if I were still working, I would not be able to get information about everything because it's impossible to do so today. The district office as it was in 1950 has been dissolved. The properties have been given to the local communes in which they are located. This is the case in Polány. I have tried to get documents from there, but the local adviser would not cooperate. Therefore, I can only give general information regarding your property.

First, you must not dream about regaining your properties. Every Jew that left the country gave up their property. Those properties that belonged to American citizens, have been confiscated by the government. Therefore, in either case, all of your property now belongs to the government. The land, including the forage and grazing land, was given to the commune of Polány by the government, and the whole village uses the land and everything else as communal property. Private land ownership has ceased. The house has also been confiscated and it became government property. The government sold it to Sandor Puskar, who at one time planted your tobacco. I'm sure you knew him. The Polány properties are therefore communal agricultural property. Before this took place, Ignac Klein of Lelesz was guardian and rent collector. I believe that one of your family authorized him. Ignac does not live in Lelesz now, since he has remarried and left for Nagymihalyba, that is, Michalovcere, to live there with his

sister Rozsival. Regarding your father's securities, he [your father] withdrew it at the Lelesz security office and paid the debt to the credit union. He was lucky, because in 1945 the government confiscated all deposits, including bank deposits. I lost my deposits, too and I'm suffering now as a consequence. Finally, regarding [your grandfather] Samuel Schwartz's house in Lelesz. He sold it to D'Oczy his neighbor, and he attached it to his house. Since then, D'Oczy has also died. Finally, so that you know everything that happened during the time the Jews were taken away, all movable properties were auctioned. Things that were left over were stored. So don't have any hope about anything. If it happens that the American government would assist the Jews who are still alive, they would compensate them for local compensations. Then you would receive something in return. There must be an agreement between the two governments. Follow the local papers and if such an agreement is approved, declare your intentions. That's all I can write about. I have delayed writing because I have been sick almost a month. Now, I'm hardly able to write. Besides being sick, I suffer from high blood pressure. You were very lucky to have gone to America before the war and haven't felt the Fascist government in the second world war and the revolution that followed. I'm wishing that my letter will find you all in the best of health. May you all receive my luckiest wishes and heartiest regards.
Respectfully, Pál Lengyel

We couldn't help but be disappointed by this. As part of our claim, we needed to have the extracts from the land registry. Without them, we had no case. I know Mr. Lengyel was trying his best to help, and he was our only chance to get these documents. Nonetheless, it angered me that he wrote that my father was lucky to have withdrawn securities to pay a debt before all deposits were confiscated. My father had been murdered, and Mr. Lengyel was still alive.

In May, we received a second letter from Mr. Lengyel, this one included the records we had requested, and a request from Mr. Lengyel.

Lelesz, May 5, 1960
Dear Hermine, and all of you,

It has taken time to answer your second letter, due to the fact that I have been hospitalized in order to regulate my blood pressure. I was admitted for three days, and since then I haven't been feeling well. The doctors said I was lucky with this warning. I could have died. Since this doesn't pertain to the problem at hand, I am going to proceed to the present case.

It was difficult to secure these papers because the district office in Király Helmec has been closed and all official documents were brought to Terebesre [Trebišov], including the Land Registry. From there, I learned that these documents can only be issued through official channels and officers. Therefore I have to be satisfied with the papers and information that I could obtain locally in Polyán. Regarding this, I have made registration documents of the property, and they are enclosed. They consist of two pages containing seven registrars. I believe everything that is there that makes up your property. If this is not useful, then there is nothing left to do but to go through the Foreign Ministry, and officially ask for these registered documents. This will be easier now because you know the numbers. The final, official confiscation number is 50-1950.

To be sure, I would not have undertaken similar problems for anyone, since I had to put in a tremendous effort to fulfill your request. I am doing this for you because your dear father, Mr. Glück, was a very good friend of mine. We have on numerous occasions exchanged loans. For example, in 1938, I loaned him 500 Czechoslovakian korona of which he repaid 40 Hungarian pengős. Therefore figuring 40x7, that amounts to 280 korona, and the rest remains unpaid. Of which, it's beyond your own control, but he was unable to pay because he was taken away. Therefore 220 korona are still due me from you, *when you inherit it. If you can afford it, mail this amount to me, since my retirement pay is small. Here one dollar is worth seven korona. Therefore, I would request $32 from you. Of course, as you know, legally I cannot ask for this. As for the present documents I have paid for them, however I am not asking for payment on those unless you desire to do so. I would ask this of you, address the payment to my sister, Anna Lengyel Belane Bartko, because my sickness is such that although I'm alive today, I may be dead tomorrow. I've written to Ignac Klein in this matter so that he can help you, since he has used the property after the war. However, he didn't reply to my letter. I heard that he tried to hang himself, but they found out and saved him. Who doesn't have problems like this? We are very happy that you are in good health, even though you had a loss here, you found something greater to compensate for it.*

I believe in my previous letter, I have written more, therefore I do not want to repeat myself since there have been no changes since then. I send greetings to you as well as your family, brothers, and sister. I remain with best regards.

Pál Lengyel

Nothing could compensate us for our loss, and we would have given up anything to save our family, but that was "spilled milk." Nonetheless, David, Herman, Maria, Hermine, and I filed a claim for $20,000 against the Government of Czechoslovakia under title IV of the International Claims Settlement Act of 1949.[39] Mr. Lengyel was instrumental in identifying our property so that we could do so.

---

[39] In 1962, the First Czechoslovakia Claims Program was completed with awards totaling approximately USD 113 million for 2,630 claims. Ours was one of them. 8.5 million USD in blocked Czechoslovakian assets was initially used in partial payment for the awards. We were awarded $3,600 in a decision by the Foreign Claims Settlement Commission. The remaining $17,400 of our claim was denied for lack of evidence: we couldn't prove that Emil and Lenke were dead; we couldn't prove that Dezső was their guardian; and we couldn't prove that our belongings had been nationalized.

285 szám.   A./ Birtoklap   Teleiyva

Sor szám	Helyrajzi szám		Urbéri birtok		Kat.tér mérték	kat.t.jsz ta jöv.	Jegyzet
					h.hold.öl	Kor.f	
1		Az első számu betét A lapján bevezetett					
		közös legelőuöl járó 120/15090 rész					
2		A 2 számu betét A lapján bevezetett közös					
		erdőből 120/16650 rész					
		Ezen jutalék megfelel 6.3 legelőjognak					
		Ehhez tartozik még a Tibava községben fekvő közös erdőrész is					

3. Tulajdonilap

Sor szám							Jegyzet
25	a/.kisk.	Glück	Emil	3/22 részben			
	b/. "	Glück	Lenke	3/22	"		
26	c/. "	Glück	Hermina	4/22			
	d/. "	Glück	Mária	4/22	"		
	e/. "	Glüvh	Herman	4/22			
	f/. "	Glück	Ignác	4/22	"		

415   szám.   A./ Birtoklap   Polang

Sor szám	Helyrajzi szám						Kataszteri térmérték	Kataszt t.jöv	Jegyzet
							hold.öl	K. f	
1	114/2	Kert a beltelekben					634		
2	115/2	Ház és udvar a beltelekben					823		

3. Tulajdonilap

sorszám								Jegyzet
10	a/.kisk.	Glück	Hermina	javára	3/18-ad részben			
és	b/. "	Glück	Mária	"	3/18-ad	"		
13	c/. "	Glück	Herman	"	4/18-ad	"		
	d/. "	Glück	Ignác	"	4/18-ad	"		
	e/. "	Glück	Emil	"	2/18-ad	"		
	f/. "	Glück	Lenke	"	2/18-ad	"		

Land registry extract for Property Record Numbers 285 and 415.
This was sent to us by Pál Lengyel in 1960.

521 szám...

A./. Birtoklap   Polány

sor Nr. szám szám	...vol...	...rbéri birtok	...ttó...	Kat.tér- mérték K.hold	Kat. tiszta ... Kor...
1	3744	Rét az erdörejáró rétben	...Ártér	1 703	5.76

B./. Tulajdonilap

sor szám									Jegyzet
1	b/.	Glück	Látér	1/3- ad részben					
4	kisk.	Glück	Ignác	2/3-ad "					

522 szám...

A./ Birtoklap   Polány

or szám	Hÿ szám	...	I.		Kat.tér mérték Ha n-méter	Kat. t.jöved	Jegyzet
1	1458/1	Mocsár a Diószögben	Ártér		5149	–	
2	1549/1	Rét a Diószögben	"		1176	– 51	
3	1460/1	Szántó a Diószögben	"		3 9760	60.96	

B. Tulajdonilap

sor szám							Jegyzet
2 és 5	a/.	kisk.	Glück	Herman	javára	2/6-od részben	
	b/.	8	Glück	Ignác	" "	2/6-od	
	c/.	"	Glück	Emil	" "	1/6-od	
	d/.	"	Glück	Tenke	" "	1/6-od	

Land registry extract for Property Record Numbers 521 and 522.
This was sent to us by Pál Lengyel in 1960.

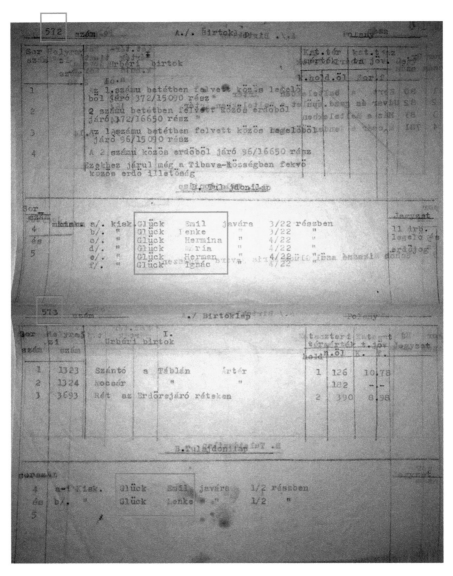

Land registry extract for Property Record Numbers 572 and 573.
This was sent to us by Pál Lengyel in 1960.

Land registry extract for Property Record Numbers 170.
This was sent to us by Pál Lengyel in 1960.

A few months shy of my 39th birthday, I married Barbara Nagel, a dynamic, vivacious, elementary school teacher, my junior by 16 years. Although I had waited until I was firmly established financially before even considering marriage, ours was a whirlwind romance. We were set up by Selma Jaeger, one of my former girlfriends who thought that Barbara would be perfect for me. She introduced us in the summer of 1960 and despite some comments like "...but Irving, she's so young," we married three months later in September at the Hotel Brewster in New York City. The photographer's camera broke and his car, with his spare camera inside, was parked on the other side of Central Park. By the time he returned, there was very little left to photograph! However, we did manage to take a photo with my small family. My sisters gave us as a wedding present a quilt made with the dunyha that we had brought from Europe. We established a real estate business, and raised two sons.

Our wedding photograph, September 18, 1960.
Standing in back from left.to right.: Eugene, Herman, Barbara, me, David, and Dorothy.
Front row from left to right: Diana, Freddie, Hermine, Marie, and Linda.

And this brings me to my story's conclusion. One day in 1972, we went to the Venezia Pizzeria, a local eatery. It had only been open for a short time and the owners were a young Italian couple. I was distracted by my children and did not realize that the husband was looking intently at me. My younger son, feeling very grown up, wanted to carry his own pizza from the counter to the table. Accidentally, he tilted the plate and the pizza fell to the floor. The owner rushed over and bent down to pick up the pizza, reassuring my son that he shouldn't worry about it, he'd bring him another. And then he looked up at me and proclaimed "I know you!" I smiled, quite sure that I didn't know him. Sensing my bewilderment, he quickly added, "You gave me candy!" smiling widely as though that were enough to jog my memory. Thinking through my day, I had been at only one account, my largest...Japan Airlines in the Cargo Terminal at JFK International Airport in Queens. I had many vending machines there, some of which were indeed filled with candy, but I couldn't recollect having given this particular man anything. "Were you a soldier in Italy?" he asked as he stood, taking my hand in his. I nodded that yes, I had been. "You gave me candy in Napoli," the man continued, "You were a soldier then, and I was just a boy." He gently stroked the hair on my son's head. "I remember you!" Still holding my hand, he guided me to our table and sat down next to us. In heavily accented English he explained. "The women and the children had been evacuated from Pignataro Interamna, our village near Monte Cassino. I was little, no more than six years old. Starving. Cold. Afraid. We had nothing. I was barefoot. And you, in your kindness, gave me chocolate. How could I forget your face? You looked like a god. From then on, every American soldier looked like you, and I called out and waved to them all. Because of the Germans, I was terrified of soldiers. Because of you, I loved Americans. I dreamed of America. I even became a soldier, like you, but I only worked at the Vatican and guarded three presidents of Italy. You gave us hope for something better. And here I am, in America." His wife came over to see what animated her husband so, and after introducing Josephine and giving her a short synapsis in Italian, Annibale "Joe" DiRaimo continued to tell us how the Germans ordered his father and the other men in the area to work for them. He told how, as a little child, he grabbed the German officer's leg and pleaded that they not take his father. They did anyway, right before his eyes. He told how his father, after being rounded up, jumped from the truck he was loaded onto and escaped. He concluded by explaining how, after the war, he came to America with his brother and sister, how he established his business, and how his mother and father remained behind in Italy. Imagine his surprise when he found out that, like he, I too was an immigrant. It never dawned on him that his American god was in fact a European Jew. He then asked politely about my family in Europe. What could I tell him?

Sitting with Joe DiRaimo in his pizzeria
Huntington, NY, 2014

Epilogue

Except for the occasional nightmare, from which I awaken with a scream, I tried to put my experience in the war out of my waking consciousness. I never spoke about it. Even people who thought they knew me, could only guess from my age that I was a veteran. When the Oyster Bay Jewish Center, the little synagogue that I helped establish on Long Island's north shore, gave me the honor of carrying a Torah from Czechoslovakia that had been saved by the Nazis for their so-called museum of the Jews, no one knew that the synagogue's mild mannered Torah reader had been a combat infantryman. They only knew that I was from Czechoslovakia and had lost family in the war. When the Cold Spring Harbor High School honored me for maintaining my vending machines in their teacher's lounge for 25 years, only then did they inquire about my history.

I finally spoke about my experiences during the war at the Syosset High School after I saw an advertisement in the local newspaper that they were looking for veterans who were willing to be interviewed for the Veterans History Project of the Library of Congress. The hour long interview took place at the high school with the encouragement of the school librarian, Ms. Lynn Ortleib. On the occasion of my 93rd birthday I was interviewed by Tony Pasqual on the Italian radio program, "Ciao Tony". One of my doctors commented that "without Jews like you, there wouldn't be Jews like me!" How true! Serving together with people of all races and religions shattered stereotypes and broke down many barriers.

Emil and I survived because we were each determined that we would not be the last of our families. The lessons we learned from our parents would be passed on to another generation and our determination to survive enabled us to do more than that. We each rebuilt our families and our lives.

Emil has two sons, six grandchildren, seven great-grandchildren with an eighth on the way. I have two sons and six grandchildren. Hermine gave birth to two daughters and had she lived longer, would have seen a granddaughter born. David's only son raised two boys. My hope and prayer is that each of them, through simple acts of kindness, can help mould the world into one that their grandparents and great-grandparents would be proud of; that they continue to live their lives as Jews with their heads held high, knowing their heritage and valuing the freedoms that we fought for and have bequeathed them.

I am now almost 95 years young and my wife and siblings live just as a memory in my mind. On my table sits an old black and white photo of my brother Lajos's children. I often cry when I look upon my nephews and nieces. They never had a chance to grow old. What advice can I give? More than anything, early education is essential. The priest in Polyán used to say, "Give me a child until the age of seven, and he is mine for life." How right! A child is like a sponge and can absorb anything. Rather than perpetuate the mistakes of the past, obsessing over imaginary borders and national pride, we should guide our children to understand that our similarities are far greater than our differences, and those differences should be cherished. They must learn that even a simple act of kindness, like giving a chocolate bar to a child, can create ever-expanding ripples in the world, edging us closer to Isaiah's prophecy: "and they shall beat their swords into plowshares, and their spears into pruning hooks; nation shall not lift up sword against nation, nor shall they learn war any more."

יזכור

Yizkor

"He will remember..."

EVEN THOUGH WE SUBMITTED TRACING REQUESTS after the war to the International Red Cross searching for information about our family, we didn't learn anything other than what we already knew. From the 23 immediate family members taken by the Nazis, just one person survived, our cousin Emil Schwartz. According to him, his baby brother, Shemaya (שמעיה), died in the stifling heat of the cattle car en route from Sátoraljaújhely to Auschwitz. Emil submitted pages of testimony in Yad V'Shem, the World Holocaust Remembrance Center in Israel, testifying that he witnessed our families being separated in Auschwitz and that those members of our family that didn't return home were murdered. From other archival sources it is known that three deportation trains from Sátoraljaújhely transited Kosice (Kassa) on May 18, May 21, and May 27, 1944. They carried 3439, 3290, and 3325 persons, respectively, to Auschwitz-Birkenau.

One of the distinctions that made the Holocaust unique among genocides was the German penchant for efficiency and record keeping. The Nazis used this to track the whereabouts and disposition of concentration camp inmates. It wasn't until 2010 that we received definitive documentation made by the Nazis themselves as to the fate of my family. The documents on the pages that follow are extraordinarily rare. They include confiscation records regarding property and money from Sátoraljaújhely and arrival logs, daily status reports, and death certificates from Mauthausen. Ironically, of the more than 200,000 meticulously created records of prisoners kept at Mauthausen and its sub camps, the Nazis, as they realized the war was lost, destroyed nearly all of them. However, approximately 10,000 of those records still exist. Miraculously, amongst these are records regarding my brother Lajos, my Uncle Márton, and my cousin Emil. To those that say this didn't happen, or that there weren't so many Jews murdered, let the evidence speak for itself.

MURDERED IN AUSCHWITZ

My father, Jeremias Gluck, age 68

ירמיהו בן מנחם אברהם

MURDERED IN AUSCHWITZ

Our grandmother, Chaia Moskovics Schwartz, 76

חיה בת יוסף שמעיה הלוי

M<small>URDERED IN</small> A<small>USCHWITZ</small>

Etelka
Klein
Gluck, 38

My sister-in-law, Etelka Klein Gluck (Lajos's wife)
and their children:

Emil, 13   Miklós, 8   Gyula, 6

Zoltan, 4

MURDERED IN AUSCHWITZ

My aunt Etelka Lefkovic Schwartz, אסתר
(Emil's mother and Uncle Márton's wife)
and their children:

Magda
העניטשע

Lilli
ליבה

Leib
אריה לייב

Samuel
שמואל

Siesel
זיסל

MURDERED IN AUSCHWITZ

Miksa
Schön

Mariska
Gluck
Schön
מרים

Mariska was my first cousin
(Uncle Lázár's daughter and Bertha's sister)
and their children:

Tibor, 13

Clara, 11

According to Manci Klein and Malvin Lefkovics, my niece Lenke Gluck, who was just 10 years old when taken, somehow survived the concentration camp, only to die after being liberated by the Allies.

Lenke, circa 1939

MURDERED IN MAUTHAUSEN

Lajos
Gluck

On May 28, 1944
my brother Lajos (חיים לייב) Gluck was transferred
from Auschwitz to
Mauthausen Ebensee Concentration Camp

He was assigned the #68247.

He was murdered on Oct 9, 1944.

On May 28, 1944
my Uncle Márton (מרדכי) Schwartz was
transferred from Auschwitz to
Mauthausen Gusen Concentration Camp

He was assigned the #67445.

He died on Dec 9, 1944.

Emil's brother, Herschel Tzvi (הרשל צבי)
(Hersu, Herman, or Bela, Nickname: Puju)
Schwartz remained with him for a time in
Mauthausen.

He was assigned the #67553.

Herschel Tzvi was taken back to Auschwitz in a
sick transport on August 20, 1944.

He was never seen again.

Sátoraljaújhely, Hungary to Auschwitz, Poland to Mauthausen, Austria

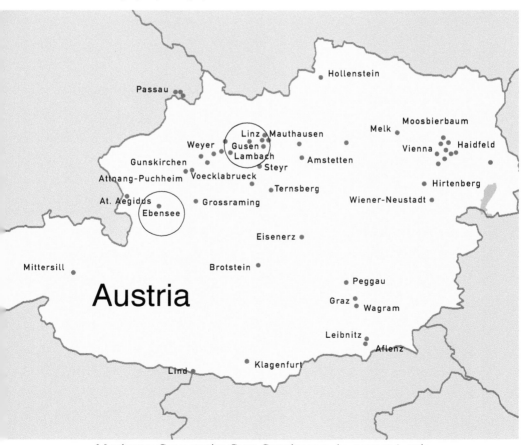

Mauthausen Concentration Camp Complex spread out across Austria.

THE CHILDREN'S LETTERS

Letters to: Dezső [Dave], Hersmendu [Herman], Ignác [Irving], Hencsu [Hermine], and Marcsa [Maria]

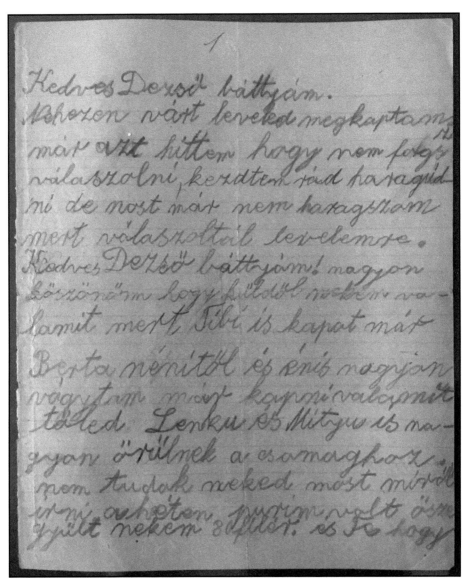

Dear Uncle Dezső,
I received the letter that I had been waiting for. I thought that you may not want to write to me. Before I received your reply to my letter I began to be angry, however, I'm not angry now because you answered my letter.

And my dear Uncle Dezső, I want to thank you very much for wanting to send me something. I'm really looking forward to receiving something from you. Tibi received something from his Aunt Bertha so I'm also waiting for something. Lenku and Mityu are happily looking forward to getting a package. I don't know what to write you this week. It was Purim and I got 80 filér.

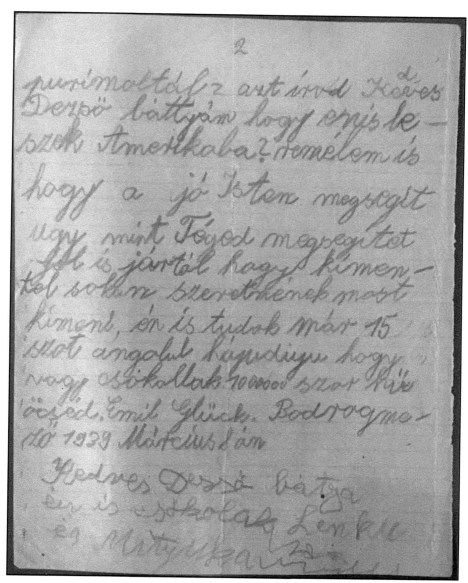

How did you spend your Purim? My dearest Uncle Dezső, I hope that I can be in America also! I hope that God will help us, like you have been helped in doing everything to get out from here. There are a lot of people that would love to get out from here, I already know 15 words in English. I'm kissing you 1,000,000 times, your nephew, Emil Glück, Bodrogmező,

1939 March 8.

Dear Uncle Dezső, we are also kissing you, Lenke and Mityukam.

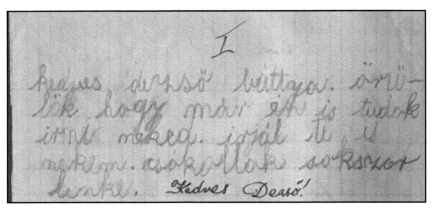

Dear Uncle Dezső,

I'm happy that I can also write to you already. Write to me, too.
I kiss you many times.
Lenke
[1939/12/19]

Dear Uncle Dezső,

The letter that you have written to me made me very happy. I would like to see you. How are you? Write to me always because I'm waiting impatiently, and when I receive your letter, I hurry to reply. I never thought that you would be in America. It's true, I may also be there one day. We kiss you all with love,
Emil, Lenke, and Mityu.
P.S. We also send our kisses to Jónász Bácsi.

Dear Aunt's and Uncles.

We are very happy that we have received official papers, and we hope that I too can go to America. At this time, I'm writing only a very little because I'm in a hurry to go to school. Grandpa bought a new suit for me for Passover for 14 pengős and a pair of shoes for 9 pengős and 50 filér. We are going to Lelesz to the temple. However, one side of the temple collapsed and we are going to Kalman Bácsi's home and using it as a temple. Kisses to all of you and to dear Jónás Bácsi and to the family and to dear Arthur Bácsi and his family.
Kisses to all, your nephew Emil.

Lenke and Mityu and Gyuszika.

PS. Mariska's clothing was used to make a dress for Passover

Dear Hencsu and Marcsa!
I kiss all of you also, Ignác, Hersmendel, Dezső, Uncle Jónász and his family.
Glück Lenke, Mityu, and Gyuszi

  Bodrogmező. 1940 II/19
  Dear Aunts and Uncles!
I don't know what to write now, because my mom (and others) already wrote
everything. I would have loved to be behind you when you were kissing Dezső
and Uncle Jónász. Send pictures about the first encounter with the relatives. Ignác,
you left the [wooden] gun here and my dad became a new recruit. I also would
like to be there with you. I'm sleeping with Grandpa [Zajdi] in your beds.
I kiss all of you. Dear Uncle Jónász and dear Aunt Helen, Uncle Arthur
(everybody with Arthur), and Uncle Dezső.

Glück Emil

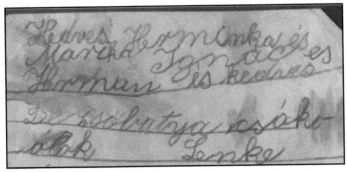

Dear Aunt Hencsu and Dear Aunt Marcsa,
Kisses to you all, Dezsőt, Ignácot, Hersmendut. Gluck Lenke.
Mityuka and Gyuszika also send kisses to all of you.

Dear Herminka and Mariska, Ignác, and Herman, and Uncle Dezső
I kiss you. Lenke

We too are sending our kisses to all of you, Lenke, Mityu, Gyuszi,
and Zoli. Mother has written everything. Great-grandfather is
sending his regards. Emil.

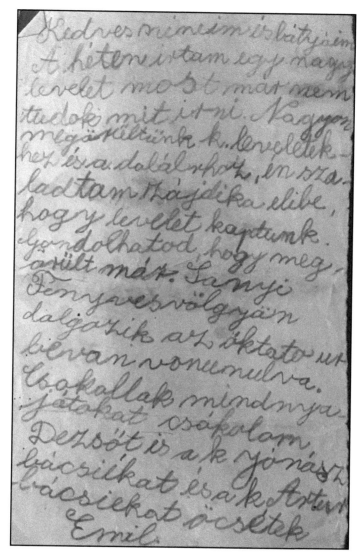

Dear Aunts and Uncles.
This week I've written a long letter so today I don't know what to
write. We were very happy to receive your dear letters and the
dollar. I ran to grandpa's to tell him that we have gotten a letter
from you. You can imagine how happy he was. Sanyi Klein is
working at Fenyves Valley. The instructor entered the Army.
Kisses to all of you, kisses to Dezső and dear Jónász bácsiekat and
dear Arthur bácsiekat. Your nephew Emil
[1940/2/22]

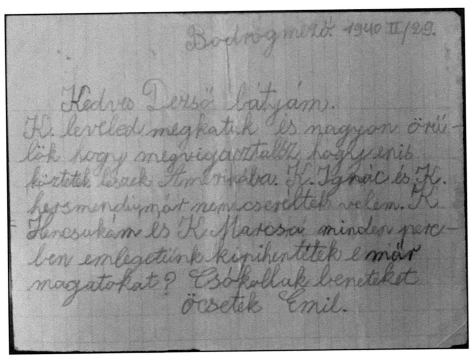

February 29, 1940
Bodrogmező

Dear Uncle Dezső
Received your dear letter and I'm happy that you have encouraged me that I could also be with you in America. Dear Ignác and Dear Hersmendu you would not switch with me. Dear Hencsukam and Dear Marcsa, we mention you every minute. Did you rest from your long journey? Kisses to all of you,
Your nephew Emil.

Dear Herminka and Mariska,

I'm very happy that you are well, and arrived luckily. I wish I could be where you are now. How do you spend your day? How are you? Me, thank God, I'm doing well. The doctor said in Pest, that I should have an operation on my leg after Passover. We did not decide yet. Write about everything exactly. What kind of nice things did you see? I'm sorry that I write so little, next time I will write you more. I wish a happy holiday to all of you. Write often and about everything.
I kiss you many times,
Magda
Smulkú and Libúka kiss all of you. Libúka is going to you in America.
[1940/3/20]

Drága Hencsuka és Mariska.
Nagyon megörültem a leveleknek és nagy
örömmel olvastam. Remélem, hogy továbbra
is fogtok irni. A jó Isten segitsen meg
benneteket. Hogy van Dezső? Őtüle is kaptunk
most egy levelet. Majd ha lesz időtök akkor
irjátok meg az Amerikaji (utat, hajóba mikor
utaztatok) utazásról mert reméljük,
hogy valamikor mink is fogunk utazni
ha a jó Isten megsegit. Ha aláirla fogtok lépni
irjátok meg mindegyikről külön, hogy milyen
aláirla lépet. Dezsőnek monggyatok meg hogy belyegeket
kulgon. Számtalanszor csókol benneteket
onoka testvéretek Pista és Herr Marán hogy van?
irjátok gyakran. A levelekre
étikes bélyeget ragzetek.

Királyhelmec   Herr...

1940. marc. 22.

Boldog Pürem és Husvétot
kivánok nektek minnyajótoknak

Herr...

Magda is csókoltat, leveleket leg
közelebb irni fog.

Dear Hencsuka and Mariska!

I was very happy to get your letters, and happy to hear you are well. Hope you will continue to write in the future. God should continue helping you. How is Dezső? We received a letter from him also. When you have time please write about your trip to America on the ship. We hope one day we will be able to go. Our God will help us. When you get a job, write us about it, all of you individually. What kind of work do you do? For Dezső also, tell him to send some stamps. Kisses many times, your nieces and nephews. How are Yitzhak (Ignác) and Hersmendu? Please write more often, we want to know.

Király Helmec   Hersu

1940 March 22

I'm wishing you all the best for Purim and Passover

Hersu

Magda also kisses all of you and will write next time

Bodrogmező: 1940 IV/3.

Kedves nénéim és bátyáim.
leveleteket örömmel olvastak és
nagyon örülök hogy a k. Artur
bácsi mirolunk se felejtkezett
meg az ithoni ujsag az hogy
nagy az árviz minden ob
dalrol a kazna is tele van
lehet csonokázni kivánok
nektek kellemes husveti unepeket
és gondoljatok ranis. Sietek be
fejezni a levelet mert iskolába
kel meni. Csokolom kezeit
Artur bácsiéknak Jenő bácsi
éknak és csokolom Dezsöt
minyájatokat üdzitek Emil.
csokol minannyájatokat és artur
bácsiékat és a kis lányát
irjatok meg hogy hivják
Glück Lenke.

Bodrogmező
1940 April 3

My dear Aunts and Uncles.
We read all your letters, and I am very happy to
know that dear Arthur bácsi did not forget us. The
news from home is that there is a great flood all
around us. The Kazna is full and you can use a boat.
I wish you all a pleasant Passover holiday and think
of me also. I'm in a hurry to complete this letter
since I have to go to school. I kiss your hands,
Arthur bácsinak and Jónás bácsinak and Dezső and
all of you.

Your nephew Emil.

Kisses to all of you and Arthur bácsit and his
daughter. Let me know in your letter her name.
Glück Lenke

Bodrogmező 1940 May 5

My dear Aunts and Uncles

Received your letters that I have been waiting impatiently for in which you write, dear Aunt Hencsu, that you have only received two letters from us. As of now we have mailed you nine letters. We have written to you all the news. At this time really, we have no news here. We thank you for the package that you have sent us in advance, and we are waiting for it with difficulty. Please write to us the name of Arthur bácsi's daughter and son. Please send us pictures so that at least we would know them and recognize them by their pictures. Dear Ignác and Hersmendu, Saturday's military exercises began and you are being missed from the group. Mityu and Gyuszi were looking for you and asking where are Ignác and Herman. Are they in the front or in the rear? Dear Ignác, Grandpa gave your [wooden] gun to Sanyi.

Give my regards to dear Jónász bácsi and dear Arthur bácsi. Kisses to Dezső, Hersmendu, Ignác, Marcsa and Hencsu, until we meet again in America.

Your nephew Emil Gluck

Dear Aunt Hencsu and Marcsa,

I will only write to you a little bit because I don't know too much yet. My kisses to Uncle Dezső, Jónász bácsi and his family, and Arthur bácsi and his family, and Ignác and Hersmendu, and Aunt Hencsu and Aunt Marcsa.

Lenke, Mityu, and Gyuszi

Dear Herminka and Dear Mariska,

Forgive me. I will write to you a few lines because I'm very tired and sleepy. If you have received my previous letter, this will add to it and next time, I will write more. As of now, there is no news. Kisses to you and Mariska and dear relations.

Etelka

Kedves néném is bátyám. [...]

Leveleteket minél nehezebben várjuk annál ritkábban jön. Például most az ajánlot leveletek öt hétig jöt gondolhatjátok, hogy ez a levél sokáig jöt már azt hitem, hogy mostanra a csomag is megjön márigen ránk férne de jó lesz ha pünkösdre jön is meg mit szóltok hat na rajvan egy leve- rünk most sönél van idáig a tanulas jól megy remélem, hogy ezután még jobban fogok haladni. Egy nagy ujságot irok nektek aKt, hogy Kocsis harzabodik veszi el Leca Ilonkát.

.

Dear Aunt's and Uncles,
The more we wait for your letters, the more difficult it becomes. Your letters come less frequently. The registered letter took five weeks. This letter took a long time. I believe that by now the package should have arrived too, and it would come in handy. We hope it comes in by the holiday Pünkös [Shavuot]. What would you say to that? Our teacher is at Shön's. We are learning and it is going quite well. Hope that it will be better in the future and I will progress. The big news is that Kocsis is going to marry Leco Ilonkat.

[Emil Gluck]
[1940/5/23]

Dear Aunt Hencsu and Aunt Marcsa

I received the one ribbon and one handkerchief. It is very nice and I thank
you. I am waiting for the rest. When I start going to school, I will write
nicer. Kisses to my Uncle Dezső, and Uncle Hersmendu, and Uncle Ignác,
and Aunt Hencsu and my aunt Marcsa. Lena. Dear Aunt Hencsu, I'm out of
breath and I can't wait for the red boots. Mityuka and Gyuszika.
[1941/8/4]

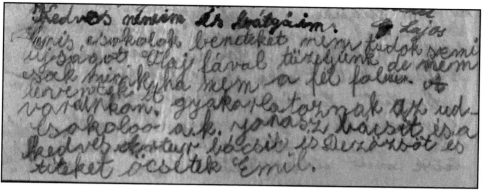

Dear Aunts and Uncles,
I kiss all of you also. I don't know any news. We use oil with wood to make the fire, not only us, but half of the town. The Levente practice here. Kisses to dear Uncle Jónász and dear uncle Arthur and Dezső also and you.
Your little nephew Emil

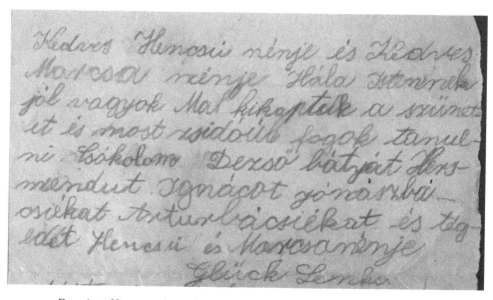

Dear Aunt Hencsu and dear Aunt Marcsa. Thank God we are well. Today we got a break and now I will learn Hebrew.
I kiss Uncle Dezső, Hersmendu, Ignác, Uncle Jónász, Uncle Arthur and you Hencsu and Aunt Marcsa,

Glück Lenke

Mityuka and Gyuszika kiss all of you and they are waiting for a little radio.

Dear Herminka and Mariska, we are happy in advance for the package, because we did not get any clothes for Passover. I kiss Dezső, Uncle Jónás and Ignác, Herman, Marcsa and Herminka

Gluck Lenke

Dear Aunts and Uncles,

I will try to write to you, so you can have something to read. I was very happy for your letter. I brought it home from the post office. I can write to you boys, that, if they whistle to the Leventes, then we always mention you. Sanyi was so happy for your letter, but he will not write now, because he is not at home.

Dear Ignác, even the teacher mentioned you this week. The Hegedus's son made a comment at the singing lesson, that we did not sing Ignác's "what do you see" [mitláte]

..and then the teacher said, that he should go to America and ask Ignác, what he can see. Yani Balint sends his greetings also and Kocsis too. Gerenyi (and others) send their greetings and Aunt Anna Pataki too. It is almost Passover. My mom is stuffing a goose also. We have eggs, thank God. We will give some to our Grandfather too for Passover and beet soup [ciberèt]. We just don't have milk, because the cow drinks it. We must eat the cow for Passover.

I kiss you dear Uncle Jónás and Uncle Arthur. Kisses for Dezső, Hencsu, Marcsa, Hersmendel and Ignác. Your little nephew [brother] Emil.

I will write one more piece of news: that they give sugar and blocks of fat.

Dear Uncles and Aunts,

Now I will respond to two letters, because two letters came in a week. We were very happy to get your pictures. I'm letting you know that I had my exam in school. Our report card is very good. Of course, there are better, but there are also worse. I got the worst grade from writing, because my writing is very sloppy. Father is at home now, because he was drafted, and he only comes back after Shavuot. We can hardly wait for the package. Now I'm having sewed a pair of dark blue pants from Zajdiak's [grandfather's] pants. Dear Hersmendel, if you eat good things in that hotel, then think about me also and, if you get a tip, then send me from it too. There is no special news. I kiss all of you and dear uncle Jónás and dear uncle Arthur, Dezső and all of you.
Your little nephew, Emil

Nazi
Record
Keeping

```
Zextrationslager Mauthausen              Mauthausen,den 29.Mai 1944
     Schutzhaftlager

         Liste der Zugänge vom 28.Mai 1944/ 1000 Ung.Juden
                                    vom K.L.Auschwitz
```

1.	Abrahamovits	Herman	12.6.23	Kuzmina	Landwirt	68001
2.	Abrahamovics	Lajos	25.11.24	Kuzmino	Landarbeiter	68002
3.	Abrahamovits	Naftali	16.7.99	Bardejev	Arbeiter	68003
4.	Ackerman	Izrael	19.8.00	Makorja	Landarbeiter	68004
5.	Ackerman	Jakob	15.3.96	Arussveg	Arbeiter	68005
6.	Ackermann	Samuel	27.6.23	Szplyva	Schuster	68006
7.	Adler	Jakob	10.7.25	Absa	Arbeiter	68007
8.	Adler	Jakob	16.7.27	Torockes	Lehrling	68008
9.	Adler	Mozes	8.5.92	Felsö Apsa	Arbeiter	68009
10.	Davidovics	Miron	21.9.26	Bilk	Gurbier	68010
11.	Adler	Salamon	23.11.14	Akna Sagatag	Fleischer	68011
12.	Adler	Volf	10.10.12	Ganits	Arbeiter	68012
13.	Alter	Abraham	15.8.26	Polena	Lehrling	68013
14.	Alter	Herman	22.1.28	Poleno	Schüler	68014
15.	Alter	Jozsef	1.6.24	Polena	Bäcker	68015
16.	Alter	Salamon	1.7.96	Poleno	Arbeite	68016
17.	Altman	Sandor	25.3.24	Debrezin	Angestellter	68017
18.	Altman	Sandor	18.8.29	Kolozvar	Schüler	68018
19.	Aniszfeld	Janos	18.2.03	Hodmezövasarhely	Arbeiter	68019
20.	Aron	Josef	5.7.99	Alsosuha	Maurer	68020
21.	Aron	Lövy	5.10.90	Kallosemjen	Kaufmann	68021
22.	Ausch	Mar	3.8.12	Szolva	Tischler	68022
23.	Auslander	Herman	30.7.90	Kunkscs	Anstreicher	68023
24.	Auspitz	Imre	6.10.27	Sarospatak	Lehrling	68024
25.	Bansel	Marton	21.1.01	Marosmezö	Arbeiter	68025
26.	Bansel	Mihaly	17.8.26	Korosmezö	Lehrling	68026
27.	Baneth	Tiber	6.5.29	Hatvan	Lehrling	68027
28.	Baran	Lajos	10.10.04	Hodmezövasarhely	El.Monteur	68028
29.	Bardoc	Imre	14.5.99	Vilmany	Tischler	68029
30.	Barta	Leszö	10.5.98	Budapest	Elektriker	68030
31.	Barch	Benat	7.5.99	Murmorusschiget	Tapezierer	68031
32.	Baum	David	26.10.98	Palota	Zimmermann	68032
33.	Baumon	Gjula	13.1.92	Hodoszcsepany	Maurer	68033
34.	Beck	Alexander	15.5.93	Budapest	Maurer	68034
35.	Beck	Bertalan	23.12.08	Coglid	Tischler	68035
36.	Benda	Volmos	25.1.00	Tibolet Barocz	Betonarbeit.	68036
37.	Benedikt	Ignac	14.10.99	Abaujszauto	Glaser	68037
38.	Berger	Adolf	5.2.05	Bosarfalva	Landwirt	68038
39.	Berger	Sandor	30.6.26	Bosarfolvo	Hilfsarbeiter	68039
40.	Berger	Aron	3.9.02	Bassarfalva	Landarbeiter	68040
41.	Berger	David	8.3.27	Nagyrakocs	Lehrling	68041
42.	Berger	David	22.4.97	Bosarfolva	Landwirt	68042
43.	Berger	Ilias	11.7.24	Szarmarnemeti	Holzarbeiter	68043
44.	Berger	Israil	28.11.24	Bosarfolva	Landarbeiter	68044
45.	Berger	Israel	2.9.23	Boho	Arbeiter	68045
46.	Berger	Kalman	6.7.09	Boho	Arbeiter	68046
47.	Berger	Lajos	30.4.96	Bmacsafalva	Landarbeiter	68047
48.	Berger	Majer	10.6.25	Zukov	Landarbeiter	68048
49.	Berger	Marton	4.4.23	Zsuko	Landarbeiter	68049
50.	Berger	Samuel	22.9.02	Bakarja	Landarbeite	68050

The first page of an **ORIGINAL TRANSPORT LIST** created by authorities on May 29, 1944 in Mauthausen noting prisoner arrivals from Auschwitz on May 28, 1944.
USHMM File 1319375_1

201.	Friedman	Henrich	12.11.26	Bilky	Landarbeiter	68201
202.	Friedman	Herman	25.8.26	Gvosnjfaln	Schuster	68202
203.	Friedman	Jena	5.4.28	Gvosnjfaln	Arbeiter	68203
204.	Friedman	Ignatz	28.12.11	Beregszasz	H.Arbeiter	68204
205.	Friedman	Jozsef	6.9.08	unkacs	Arbeiter	68205
206.	Friedman	Juda	29.1.29	Beregszasz	Landarb.	68206
207.	Friedman	Lajos	15.6.26	Szatmarnemeti	isler	68207
208.	Friedman	Mendel	2.9.23	Koho	Arbeiter	68208
209.	Friedman	or	2.3.11	Szatmar Udvari	Glasswar	68209
210.	Friedman	Samuel	13.6.05	Benedelci	Landarb.	68210
211.	Friedman	Samuel	8.3.27	Olvos	Lehrling	68211
212.	Friedman	Sandor	20.11.98	Kovacsvagasoh	Landarb.	68212
213.	Friedman	Vilhelm	24.12.03	Kassa	Schmetermaischtadt	68213
214.	Friedman	Volf	12.3.08	Beregszasz	Arbeiter	68214
215.	Friedman	Volf eb	28.10.96	Bartfolvo	Arbeiter	68215
216.	Friedman	Zoltan	2.8.18	Hernagymecdrny	Lehrling	68216
217.	Friedmann	rvin	15.3.25	Kassau	H.Arbeiter	68217
218.	Frischmann	Zoltan	13.3.27	Gady	Landarb.	68218
219.	Fromner	David	23.12.23	Kerec e	chneider	68219
220.	Fromer	Salamon	7.7.93	Alsoverecke	H.Arbeiter	68220
221.	Fund	Vilmos	4.10.23	inkacs	Landarb.	68221
222.	Furedi	iklos	21.5.28	Bagykanizsa	Lehrling	68222
23.	Fuchs	andor	15.7.95	U.Sen orfolvo	Zimmermann	68223
224.	Fuchs	alomon	19.1.25	Bolwe	Lehrling	68224
225.	Fuchss	Herman	11.7.28	Rano	Lehrling	68225
226.	Gasch	Ernst	12.2.25	aschau	rbeiter	68226
227.	Gedajlovits	oses	17.12.28	rhoss	enrling	68227
228.	Gedajlovics	amuel	13.12.07	Iso Anss	agearbeiter	68228
229.	Gedalavits	orol	21.12.24	Irhocs	chuster	68229
230.	Gedalawits	Samuel	20.8.88	Olschoapscha	Zimmermann	68230
231.	Geissler	Istran	25.11.03	Borkipolany	ischler	68231
232.	Gelb	David	2.4.24	Baregrakos	chneider	68232
233.	Gelb	aszlo	5.7.26	Koresc	Arbeiter	68233
34.	Gelb	iklos	29.9.02	Satoraljanjhely	aler	68234
35.	Gelb	or	27.3.27	Satoraljaujhely	Lehrling	68235
236.	Gelb	oric	14.3.12	Bereg Rakos	Schneider	68236
237.	Gelb	don	29.3.28	Koresa	Landarb.	68237
38.	Gelb	Zoltan	12.12.29	Karesa	Landarb.	68238
39.	Govurtz	Laszlo	26.6.28	Barkoszjlek	Schuler	68239
240.	Gluck	Abraham	11.11.99	Koho	H.Arbeiter	68240
2 1.	Gl.ck	Artur	21.2.28	Nagy Karoly	Lehrling	68241
242.	Gluck	Daniel	28.2.99	Felsovadasz	aurer	68242
243.	Gluck	Jakob	13.11.07	Raho	Landarb.	68243
244.	Gluck	Jenö	4.9.26	Folsova ass	Arbeiter	68244
245.	Gluck	Jeno	30.2.24	Nagkaref	H.Arbeiter	68245
246.	Gluck	Josef	15.3.26	etrova	Lehrling	68246
247.	Gluck	Lajosch	13.11.04	Bodrogmese	Arbeiter	68247
248.	Gluck	iklos	23.2.29	Szirvaralya	Schuler	68248
249.	Gluck	or	23.3.03	Nagy Bresna	Arbeiter	68249
250.	Godinger	Vilmus	7.12.24	Zarno	Fleischer	68250

My brother Lajosch Glück's name appears on line number 247 of this list.
USHMM File 1319379_1

```
K.L. M a u t h a u s e n                    O. U. den 10.
KR-Arbeitslager K.-Kalksteinbergwerk
```

V e r ä n d e r u n g s a n z e i g e :

Mit dem heutigen Tage werden dem San.-Lager des KLM nachstehende Häftlinge
überstellt:

	Name	Geburtsdatum	Geburtsort	Nr.	Nat./Rel.
1.	Ambartzumian Isaak	5.6.09	Chnsorek	50943	Krgf. SU
2.	Andronjuk Semen	-.-.02	Beresowow	56425	Ziv. Russe
3.	Andrulakis Theodoras	11.2.21	Volioness	58227	Sch. Gr.
4.	Antonini Alberto	31.3.02	Empoli	56898	Sch. It.
5.	Arrostiti Rolla	18.5.04	Montelupo	56906	Sch. It
6.	Bacchia Antonio	17.4.25	Cerso	50845	Sch. It-
7.	Bonanomi Pietro	28.4.21	Prato	56972	Sch. It
8.	Basz Wladyslaw	29.3.22	Oseredek	40199	Sch. Pole
9.	Bay Giovanni	29.4.91	Torino	56937	Sch. It
10.	Baumöhl Miksa	4.11.02	Bagamer	70159	Ung. Jude
11.	Beni Jzsak	23.6.24	Des	72208	Ung. Jude
12.	Bergmann Abraham	4.10.99	Piszakaresonfalva	68054	Ung. Jude
13.	Biesgin Nikolaj	9.5.13	Krutoje	54106	Ziv. Russe
14.	Blancher Jean	23.11.22	St.Junien	26971	Sch. Fr.
15.	Bojarkow Jefrem	18.5.12	Alexejewka	55944	Krgf. SU
	Bracci Gino	4.10.01	Livorno	56985	Sch. It
	Burkad Lipot	28.8.14	Szilagyszonlyo	69914	Ung. Jude
18.	di Caro Guiseppe	11.12.02	Palma	42625	Sch. It.
19.	Cerwenka Josef	20.4.94	Carnolice	42716	Sch. Tsch
20.	Chowietzkij Andrej	-.-.13.	Scheschtewitschi	15910	Ziv. Russe
21.	Chrustow Aleksej	15.9.21	Koschtschina	37869	Ziv. Russe
22.	Corbin Roger	1.11.03	Bihorel	27923	Sch. Fr.
23.	Corti Corrato	24.4.04	Capraia	57084	Sch. It
24.	Dainotti Francesco	10.1.08	Valgualnera	42062	Sch. It.
25.	Danziger Desider	21.8.96	Olaszliszka	68085	Ung. Jude
26.	David Sandor	7.7.99	Gassay	70178	Ung. Jude
27.	Drejew Petro	28.12.21	Komlykowka	57513	Ziv. Russe
28.	Duft Salamon	27.8.24	Polena	68121	Ung. Jude
29.	Einhorn Mayer	5.12.04	Alsaneresznice	69903	Ung. Jude
30.	Engel Jmre	24.6.99	Temesvar	69	Ung. Jude
31.	Erbszt Herman	25.4.25	Raho	68	Ung. Jude
32.	Errichetti Francesco	18.5.21	Ruoti	42	Sch. It.
33.	Fernetti Ricardo	21.4.25	Verteneglio	50	Sch. It
34.	Pilatov Piotr	30.7.97	Charkow	22256	Ziv. Russe
35.	Fleischmann David	16.1.13	Beregszasz	68150	Ung. Jude
36.	Fischmann Nandos	13.1.12	Alsovarko	69939	Ung. Jude
37.	Fogel Jzelor	6.10.93	Batyn	68185	Ung. Jude
38.	Freifeld Emil	5.5.25	Ristriz	72271	Ung. Jude
39.	Freyre Philipe	27.9.91	Pourtarlier	53782	Sch. Fr.
40.	Fried Alexander	20.12.96	Szalard	70194	Ung. Jude
41.	Friedmann David	12.5.85	Markaja	68198	Ung. Jude
42.	Friedmann Gabor	10.4.24	Matoszalka	69940	Ung. Jude
43.	Friedmann Armin	15.4.88	Nagyvarod	70198	Ung. Jude
44.	Galanti Cavaldo	25.7.22	Firenze	57121	Sch. It
45.	Glück Jenö	4.9.26	Felsövadasz	68244	Ung. Jude
46.	Glück Lajosch	13.11.04	Bodroguese	68247	Ung. Jude
47.	Goldberger Henrik	27.7.29	Magyrakoc	68251	Ung. Jude
48.	Gosalischwili Wassil	16.3.05	Tbilisv	38065	Krgf. SU
49.	Gottesman Josef	25.4.21	Harsvolva	68260	Ung. Jude
50.	Gottlieb Marton	27.7.03	Sotmac-Nemeti	68266	Ung. Jude
51.	Griwa Grigorij	12.3.14	Jelkamenka	36981	Sch. Russe
52.	Gross Lipot	20.7.07	Kisvardo	70214	Ung. Jude
53.	Grünberg Leiser	10.1.84	Voloc	68273	Ung. Jude
54.	Grünfeld Herman	27.7.04	Balszer	68284	Ung. Jude
55.	Gurkin Jwan	27.2.96	Bogdanowa	79607	Ziv. Russe
56.	Grasman Soloma	7.1.96	Miko	68268	Ung. Jude

56 Namen

DAILY STATUS REPORT created by authorities in Mauthausen on September 10, 1944 noting prisoners who were to be transferred to "Kalksteinsbergwerk." Lajosch Glück's name appears on line number 46 of this list. This list provides Lajosch Glück's name, date of birth, place of birth, Mauthausen prisoner number, 68247, nationality, and religion. USHMM File 1322274_1

KONZENTRATIONSLAGER MAUTHAUSEN
Schutzhaftlager   Mauthausen, den 13.September 1944

Veränderungsmeldung für den 12.September 1944

Vom Außenkommando Z e m e n t wurden rücküberstellt:

1.	Chorienskij	Andrej	1913	Scheschtschewitschi	15910	Ziv.Russe
2.	Browka	Thaddäus	9.12.04	Przemysl	20313	Pole Sch.
3.	Filator	Piotr	30.7.97	Charkow	22250	Ziv.Russe
4.	Jovanovic	Milorand	11.9.20	Braxina	24493	Jug.Sch.
5.	Latinin	Milan D.	14.3.14	Babina	24525	"
6.	Stavanovis	J van	17.3.06	Srbska T. nova	25469	"
7.	Simocher	Jean	23.11.22	St.Junica	26571	Franz.Sch.
8.	Corbin	Roger	1.11.05	Rihofel	27923	"
9.	Kolakovic	Stanimir	11.8.11	Bosoi	28980	Jug.Sch.
10.	Tschornyj	Iwan	7.12.23	Primirod	29293	Ziv.Russe
11.	Bielnikow	Fiodor	1918	Mohilew	31653	Ziv.Russe
12.	Trumbetza	Milan	19.9.12	Kovo	32998	Jug.Sch.
13.	Turko	Josef	11.11.19	Dublecko	33998	Pole Sch.
14.	Biengin	Mikolaj	9.5.13	Krutoje	34106	Ziv.Russe
15.	Matschenko	Leonid	25.2.22	Oleniowka	36125	"
16.	Kursenko	Wlas	10.2.04	Jereatowa	36469	"
17.	Palepenko	Danilo	15.5.08	Mogilew	36469	"
18.	Schmetzov	Andrej	17.10.97	Dnepropetrowsk	36859	"
19.	Grisa	Grigorij	12.5.14	Jelkawanka	36981	"
20.	Posnitnyj	Serge	24.9.06	Losowatka	37129	"
21.	Zalesnikow	Grigorij	25.1.04	Braschau	37258	Russe Sch.
22.	Wolczenko	Fiodor	2.2.04	Woronesch	37592	Ziv.Russe
23.	Chrustow	Aleksej	15.9.21	Kasontschina	37869	"
24.	Cchepkin	Aleksander	12.11.23	Kriwkowo	37893	"
25.	Gosalischwili	Wassil	16.3.05	Tbilisy	38055	Esf.Sch.
26.	Krutschenko	Aleksander	25.10.12	Kodymo	38085	"
27.	Sinko	Grigorij	15.11.20	Radjonowka	38140	"
28.	Bushnou	Aleksander	13.5.05	Zareutschyna	38163	"
29.	Andrulakis	Teodoros	11.2.21	Wolionaas	38227	Gr.Sch.
30.	Karupia	Joanis N.	12.2.03	Jerapetra	38272	"
31.	Nestakis	Emanuil E.	1909	Melissia	38376	"
32.	Turexakis	Emanuil M.	25.12.04	Kandia	38376	"
33.	Ristowic	Milorad	1.4.23	Zamcanje	38597	Jug.Sch.
34.	Kacilo	Alexander	4.8.07	Walka Tom.	38990	Pole Sch.
35.	Domk	Jan	5.2.12	Slawno	39068	"
36.	Jmzanski	Waclaw	31.1.12	Wilno	39355	"
37.	Mercier	Albert	17.6.04	Paris	39952	Franz.Sch.
38.	Radilo	Mirko	15.9.20	Korcula	39973	Jug.Sch.
39.	Bast	Wladyslaw	29.3.22	Oseredek	40199	Pole Sch.
40.	Truchanskij	Alexej	1918	P.Jaltuschki	40364	Ziv.Russe
41.	Santoro	Vittorio	2313.19	Sperandaso	40753	It.Sch.
42.	Kulinski	Anton	15.5.11	Hohenfried	40944	Pole Sch.
43.	Lobjedjew	Wasilij	13.4.19	Tacheplowki	41742	Esf.Sch.
44.	Schuduzow	Dsische	1917	Ciup	41830	"
45.	di Caro	Giuseppe	11.12.02	Palma	42025	It.Sch.

1089   1088

The first page of a **DAILY STATUS REPORT** created by authorities in Mauthausen noting prisoner transfers to the Mauthausen sub-camp, "Zement" on September 12, 1944.
Cont'd on following page.
USHMM File 1309369_1

DAILY STATUS REPORT created by authorities in Mauthausen noting prisoner transfers to the Mauthausen sub-camp, "Zement" on September 12, 1944. Lajosch Glück's name appears on line number 117 of this list. This list provides Lajosch Glück's name, date of birth, place of birth, Mauthausen prisoner number, 68247, nationality, and religion. USHMM File 1309371_1

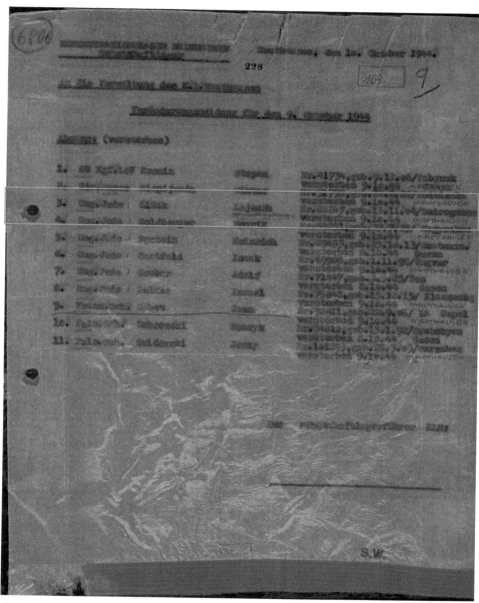

ORIGINAL DAILY STATUS REPORT created by authorities in Mauthausen on October 10, 1944 noting the names of those prisoners who died on October 9, 1944. Lajosch Glück's name appears on line number three of this report. This report provides Lajosch Glück's name, nationality, religion, Mauthausen prisoner number, 68247, date of birth, and place of birth. USHMM File 1286233_1

ORIGINAL REGISTER created by authorities in Mauthausen noting the names of those prisoners who died in Mauthausen. Lajosch Glück's name appears on line number 4202 of this list. According to this "death book," Lajosch Glück died on October 9, 1944 at 7:25 a.m. due to "Phlegmone," and "Sepsis."
ITS Archives, Bad Arolsen File 1289763_1

The continuation of the register that appears on the opposite page.
ITS Archives, Bad Arolsen File 1289763_2

Lajosch Glück's **ORIGINAL DEATH NOTICE** created by authorities in Mauthausen on October 9, 1944. This death notice provides personal information regarding Lajosch Glück including his arrival on May 28, 1944, his transfer to the health facilities (Sanitätslager - S.L.) on September 12, 1944, his date of death on October 9, 1944 at 7:25a.m. and original/ regular Block assignment 16 in Mauthausen.
USHMM File 1461366_1

KL. MAUTHAUSEN			T/D Nr.						

GLÜCK Lajosch
NAME · Vorname

13.11.1904 Bodrogmese 68247
Geb.-Dat. Geb.-Ort Häftl.-Nr

	Korrespondenz . . . . . ☐	
Häftl. Pers. Karte . . . . ☐	. . . . ☐	Dokumente: 1
Häftl. Pers. Bogen . . . . ☐	. . . . ☐	
Effektenkarte . . . . . . ☐	. . . . ☐	Inf. Karten:
Schreibst.-Karte . . . . . ☐	. . . . ☐	
Nummernkarte . . . . . ☐	. . . . ☐	Bemerkungen:
Blockkarte . . . . ☐	. . . . ☐	
Revierkarte . . . . . . ☐	. . . . ☐	
Krankenblätter . . . . . ☐	. . . . ☐	
Todesfallaufnahme . . . ☐	. . . . ☐	Umschlag-Nr.:
Todesmeldung . . . . . ☑	. . . . ☐	
Sterbeurkunde . . . . . ☐	. . . . ☐	

The envelope created in the postwar era by staff members at the International Tracing
Service which holds this death notice.
USHMM File 1461365_1

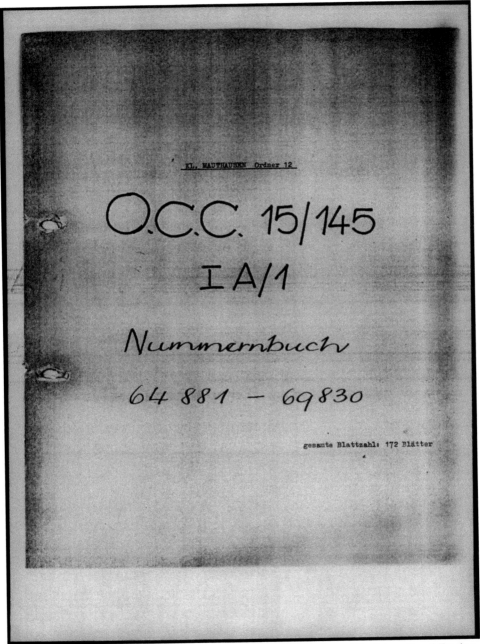

KL., MAUTHAUSEN Ordner 12

O.C.C. 15/145

I A/1

Nummernbuch

64 881 — 69 830

gesamte Blattzahl: 172 Blätter

Above: The cover page created in the postwar era by staff members at the International Tracing Service for the register that appears on the following page.
USHMM File 1278494_1

ORIGINAL PRISONER NUMBER REGISTER created by authorities in Mauthausen. Lajosch Glück's name appears on the line beside his prisoner number, 68247. This register provides his name religion, nationality, date of birth, place of birth, and notation of his date of death in Mauthausen, October 9, 1944.
USHMM File 1278613_1

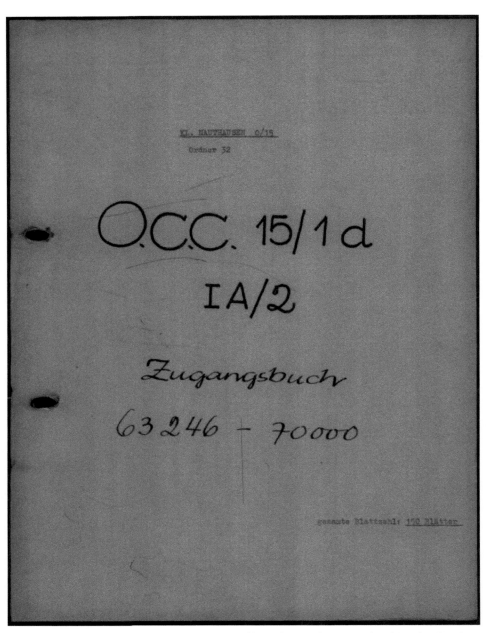

The cover page created in the postwar era by staff members at the International Tracing Service for the list that appears on the following page.
USHMM File 1282164_1

232	Ung.Jude	Gelb David	7.4.24	Schneider	-	Solvay 2.6.
233	"	Gelb Laszlo	6.7.26	Arbeiter	-	"
234	"	Gelb Miklos	29.9.02	Maler	-	6.6.44
235	"	Gelb Mor	27.3.27	Lehrling	-	Wels II No.1
236	"	Gelb Moric	14.3.12	Schneider	-	Solvay
237	"	+Gelb Odoen	28.3.28	Landarb.	G.	4.3.45
238	"	+Gelb Zoltan	12.12.29	"	G	17.12.44
239	"	Gewuertz Laszlo	26.6.23	Schueler	-	Wels II No.3
240	"	+Glueck Abraham	11.1.90	H.Arbeiter	G	7.3.44
241	"	Glueck Artur	21.9.28	Lehrling	-	Solvay 2.6.
242	"	Glueck N Daniel	28.2.99	Maurer	-	"
243	"	Glueck Jakob	13.11.07	Landarb.	-	"
244	"	Glueck Jenos	4.9.26	Arbeiter	-	Gusen 27.1.
245	"	Glueck Jeno		H.Arbeiter	-	Solvay
246	"	Gluk Josef	15.3.26	Lehrling	-	"
247	"	+Glueck Lajosch	13.11.04	Arbeiter	G	9.10.44
248	"	Glueck Miklos	23.2.29	Schueler	-	Floridsdorf
249	"	Glueck Mor		Arbeiter	-	Solvay
250	"	Godinger Vilmus	7.2.24	Fleischer	-	Wels II No.3.
251	"	+Goldberger Henrik	27.7.29	Landwirt	G	9.10.44
252	"	Goldberger Ignac	12.2.00	Angest.	-	Solvay
253	"	Goldenber Bernat	4.5.26	Schneider	-	Wels II No.3.
254	"	Goldenberg Mozes	15.10.12	Landarb.	U	24.8.44 Ausch.
255	"	+Goldenberg Samuel	29.7.15	"	G	13.3.45
256	"	Goldstein David Ners	5.2.96	Zimmerm.	-	Solvay 2.6.
257	"	Goldstein Mendel	11.12.26	Lehrling	-	"
258	"	Goldstein Isidor	1.10.28	Schueler	-	Zement 16.11
259	"	Goldstein Zoltan	23.9.97	Maurergeh.	-	Solvay 2.6.
260	"	Gottesman Josef	25.4.21	Schneider	7.3.	-
261	"	+ Gottesmann Farkas	2.9.02	H.Arbeiter	G	3.3.45
262	"	+ Gottesmann Sandor	4.9.05	Zimmerm.	G	16.1.45
263	"	+ Gottesman Martoj	15.5.23	Tischler	G	25.12.44
264	"	Gottesman Marton	24.5.27	Lehrling	-	Solvay 2.6.
265	"	Gottesman Moritz	12.12.24	Arbeiter	-	"
266	"	+Gottlieb Marton	27.7.03	"	G	30.3.45
267	"	+Gottseyen Deszo	20.6.83	Landwirt	G	12.4.44
268	"	+Graaman Salomon	7.1.96	Arbeiter	G	4.12.44
269	"	+ Gross Julius	12.5.01	"	G	23.6.44
270	"	+ Grosz Istvan	8.3.17	Monteur	G	31.3.45
271	"	Grosman Sandor	15.2.20	Maler	-	Wels II No.3.
272	"	+ Gruen Marton	1.11.03	Schuster	G	29.1.45
273	"	+Gruenberg Leiser	10.1.84	Arbeiter	G	14.9.44
274	"	Gruenzweig David	13.12.17	Tischlerl.	-	Solvay
275	"	+Grfoss Benjamin	18.5.98	Schuster	G	4.12.44
276	"	Grosz Lebi	30.1.01	Schuhm.	-	7.4.45
277	"	Gruen Zoltan	31.8.28	Schueler	-	Solvay
278	"	Gruenszweig Burech	2.7.10	Tischler	U	24.8.44 Aus.
279	"	+ Gruenbaum Marton	15.7.26	Landarb.	G	1.3.45
280	"	+Gruenberger Hes	6.1.27	Lehrling	G	11.12.44
281	"	Gruenberger Genioe	20.9.26	"	-	Solvay
282	"	+ Gruenhut Elemer	1.3.99	Elektroing	G	4.12.44
283	"	+ Gruenfeld Ernce	31.1.28	Schueler	-	Wels II No.3.
284	"	+Gruenfeld Herman	27.7.04	Bauer	G	14.9.44
285	"	Gruenfeld Sandor	12.6.08	Angest.	-	Solvay
286	"	+Gruenspan Mikas	1.5.92	H.Arbeiter	G	6.3.45
287	"	Gruenstein Isidor	3.12.26	Tischler	-	Solvay
288	"	Gruenszweig Zigmond	15.2.09	Friseur	-	"
289	"	Gubner Jeno	27.9.28	Lehrling	-	"
290	"	Gugik Moric	15.8.26	Tischler	-	"
291	"	+Guttman Iszak	12.8.08	Haendler	G	29.1.45 Sa
292	"	Guttman Mihaly	1.4.27	Lehrling	-	Solvay
293	"	+ Gutman Soemu	7.3.24	Landarb.	G	26.3.45
294	"	+Hana Elemer	22.9.06	Zimmerm.	G	9.12.44
295	"	+Hacker Ignatz	13.5.98	Istallat.	G	7.1.45
296	"	+Halem Samuel	9.4.02	Zimmerm.	G	6.3.45
297	"	Halm Bela	10.10.25	Waldarb.	-	Solvay 2.6.
298	"	Halm Daniel	12.9.24	Tischler	-	Solvay 2.6.

ORIGINAL LIST OF ARRIVALS IN MAUTHAUSEN. Lajosch Glueck's name appears beside his prisoner number, 68247. This list provides his name, date of birth, occupation, and date of death, October 9, 1944.
USHMM File 1282261_1

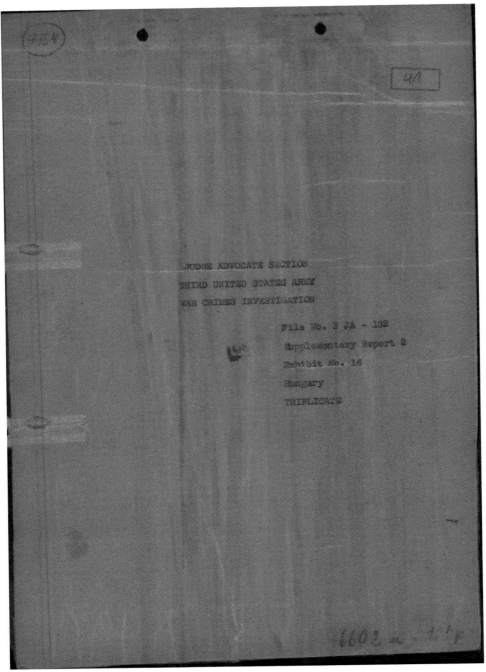

JUDGE ADVOCATE SECTION
THIRD UNITED STATES ARMY
WAR CRIMES INVESTIGATION

File No. 3 JA - 132

Supplementary Report 2

Exhibit No. 16

Hungary

TRIPLICATE

The original cover page of the list that appears on the following page prepared by the Third US Army War Crimes Investigation..
USHMM File 1302174_1

H U N G A R Y

7ν

Name	Place of Birth	Birth Date	Death Date
Gestetner Artur	Györ	28. 2.27	29. 1.45
Gestetner Benö	Györ	14. 2.93	4. 8.44
Gestetner Ernö	Györ	15. 12.22	3. 1.45
Geszterdi Laszlo	Genutecved	1. 4.97	6.11.44
Gevurtz Heinrich	Holmi	16. 3.03	10. 6.44
Gewürtz Marton	Tot	14. 9.12	25. 4.45
Gidali Abraham	Alör	18. 1.94	22.11.44
Gidali Jenö	Szegesvar	2. 12.02	19. 8.44
Gidali Jozsef	Becskeresztur	1. 6.95	14. 1.45
Gildner Adolf	Bukarest	16. 6.96	9. 7.44
Gitli Marton	Unterhomorod	19. 6.00	10. 9.44
Glancz Andor	Bylrj	14. 10.97	21.10.44
Glancz Bela	Kaschau	11. 12.25	19. 5.45
Glancz Endre	Stuhlweissenburg	5. 2.11	14. 4.45
Glancz Miklos	Dunaszentgyörgy	8. 4.02	10. 3.45
Glancz Zoltan	Kassa	7. 12.23	20. 4.45
Glanz Sandor			25. 5.45
Glanz Simon	Huszt	23. 5.32	7. 4.45
Glaser Jakob	Ujlak S.	24. 12.93	12. 8.44
Glaser Oszkar	Kürt	24. 5.91	12. 8.44
Glaser Rudolf	Kürt	14. 6.92	16.12.44
Glaser Wilhelm	Seeg	5. 6.03	7. 5.45
Glatter Mikea	Asvanyavaros	1. 5.26	5. 9.44
Glattstein Jakob	Tiszadorogno	17. 5.92	27. 6.44
Glaxer Mozes	Alahszentjerug	8. 1.26	12.12.44
Glöckner Jenö	Nagyarzef	11. 6.09	6. 2.45
Glück Abraham	Roho	11. 11.99	7. 2.45
Glück Aladar	Debreczen	9. 5.98	28. 3.45
Glück Andreas	Erminelyfolva	27. 10.22	10. 4.45
Glück Arthur	Satoszentpeter	11. 3.05	14. 1.45
Glück Bela	Munkacz	27. 6.22	23. 4.45
Glück Bernard	Varpalonka	19. 5.95	10. 5.45
Glück Dagoech	Bodrognese	12. 11.04	9.10.44
Glück David	Tiszaferegyhaza	13. 2.96	8. 3.45
Glück Danes	Nagyszalonta	20. 7.03	10. 5.45
Glück Dezsö	Hirod	24. 5.17	12.12.44
Glück Endre	Nagyarsad	11. 5.03	26. 4.45
Glück Ernö	Szatmarnemety	19. 7.25	1.10.44
Glück Ferenc	Georoda	17. 9.91	3. 1.45
Glück Heinrich	Nagykaroly	15. 5.32	1. 9.44
Glück Hermann	Mako	6. 8.01	5. 5.45
Glück Hermann	Georoda	20. 5.03	14.11.44
Glück Herman	Nagykaroly	5. 4.97	28.11.44
Glück Ignatz	Szilagy	29. 4.27	29. 4.45
Glück Istvan	Mezötelegad	6. 11.23	23. 4.45
Glück Jakob	Raho	12. 11.07	30. 4.45
Glück Josef	Tajta	6. 9.95	12. 5.44
Glück Jozsef	Holod	3. 1.15	26. 4.45
Glück Jozsef David	Petrova	3. 5.08	10.10.44
Glück Lajos	Bodrogmese	9. 10.44	15.11.04
Glück Sandor	Szancslippo	23. 5.18	5. 1.45
Glück Sandor	Kossa	8. 1.21	2. 3.45
Glück Sandor	Polejte	26. 7.02	30. 8.44
Glück Stefan	Satoraljanekely	29. 5.26	31.10.44
	Bascholmasch	4. 3.97	19. 3.45

—30—

A list of **HUNGARIAN NATIONALS WHO PERISHED IN MAUTHAUSEN.** This list was created in the postwar era. Lajos Glück's name appears sixth from the bottom of this list. This list provides his, place of birth, date of birth, and date of death in Mauthausen, October 9, 1944. However, the dates are reversed on the list. USHMM File 1302205_1

DEM SONDERSTANDESAMT VORGELEGT   Datum: ....

Name: ....*Glück, Lajos*........   Man: *68447*

geboren am *13.11.1904* in *Bodrogmese* Nat. *Ung. Jude*

gestorben am *9.10.1944, 7 25* in *Mauthausen*

Todesursache *Allg. Sepsis*

beerdigt am .... in ....

STERBEURKUNDE Nr. *3353 Abt. M* (Stempel)   Datum: *4.10.55*

ausgestellt aufgrund folgender Dokumenten

bitte wenden

Front and back, of Lajos Glück's official death certificate. This certificate was based on original material created by Mauthausen authorities. According to this death certificate Lajos Glück died on October 9, 1944 at 7:25 a.m. of Sepsis in Mauthausen.
USHMM File 22246500_1 and 22246500_2

	Ja	Nein	Initialen
1. Totenliste *44/4202*			
2. Zugangsbuch/Blockbuch		6 JA 1900	
3. Nummernbuch *Mau*			
4. Personalkarte			
5. Effektenkarte/Effektenzettel			
6. Postkontrollkarte/Schreibstubenkarte			
7. Personalbogen			
8. Revierkarte/Nummernkarte			
9. Arbeitseinsatzkarte			
10. Todesmeldung/Blockmeldung *Mau*			
11. Eidesstattliche Versicherung			

0KV15/44-eIB/4 Veränd.
Mldg.
0KV15/30 M A/1 Totenbuch

```
                              6.12.50
   Name:    G L U C K    Lajos _____ No.T 218998

   Nee: ___ Jeremias & Lina nee SCHWARTZ Nat; Czech Jew
   B. D.:   1905(?)                      X Ref:         MI
   B. P.:   Bodrogmezo(or Polany) CSR till 1938, later Hungary
   Address: as above
   Occupation: acc.to inf. from Foreign Service, State Depart-
   Last news: ment, U.S. Government, early 1946(Forcibly taken
   Date:          away by Hungarian Government, appr. April 1944.
   Enquirer's name: American National Red Cross, Washington,
   Address:         o/b G L U C K    Irving
   Relation:        50 Linwood Ave. Columbus 5, Ohio
        s  brother  (Enq. dd. 25.10.50)
```

Above: A record of an inquiry that I submitted 25 October 1950 to the International Tracing Service seeking additional information concerning my brother Lajos Glück. USHMM File 22246498_1

Below: A record of an inquiry that I submitted 15 February 1993 to the International Tracing Service seeking additional information concerning my brother Lajos Glück. USHMM File 53553204_1

```
   T/D           :                        218998
   Kartennummer  : 1019931111011   Kennummer: 000000
   Name          : GLÜCK                   Lajos
   Name2         :
   Name3         :
   Geb/Tarnname  :
   Ehefrau/-mann :
   Eltern        : Jeremias u. Linus, geb. Schwartz
   Geburtsdatum  : 1905       /        Ort: Bodrogmezö/HU-Polany/CSFR
   Religion      : jüd.       Nationalität: tsh
               Haft im KL Ujhely/Ungarn und Auschwitz?
   5.11.1945  letzte Nachricht aus Lelesz/CSFR


   Eingangsdatum : 15.02.93
   Antragsteller : Irving Glück, üb. AVM
   Straße        : One Laurel Lane
   Plz/Wohnort   : Syosset, NY 11791
   Land: USA
   Datum/Namensz.: 11.11.93 rh
```

My brother Lajos
Bodrogmező, Austria- Hungary, circa 1915

This is the only picture of my brother, Lajos. He is standing to the left.
Next to him is my mother, on her lap is Hermine, and on the right is David.
Standing is a maid.
Bodrogmező, Austria- Hungary, circa 1915.

FACING PAGE: The PROPERTY CONFISCATION RECORD dated 17 April 1944, of the 8th Gendarmerie district which included Királyhelmec, recording the expropriation of property from Márton Schvarc. It reads in part:

Listed: Márton Schvarc of Királyhelmec was detained with the following:
1 piece men's pocket watch, nickel, 37 cm long chain
281 pengo, that is two hundred eighty one pengo cash

USHMM File RG39.005 reel 1

Márton Schwarc. Notice the pocket watch hanging from his vest.
Királyhelmec, 1938

M.kir.kassai VIII.csendőrkerület.   Királyhelmeci Őrs.

Jegyzék.

Schvarc Márton királyhelmeci lakostól őrizetbe vett tárgyakról.

1 darab férfi zsebóra nikkel,37 cm hosszu lánccal.

281 P,azaz Kettőszáznyolcvanegy pengő készpénz.

Királyhelmec,1944.Aprilis 17.

119

átvételi elismervény
arról,hegy a fentebb irt értékeket a királyhelmeci csendőr őrsparancs-
nokságtol a mai napon hiánytalanul átvettem.

Királyhelmec,1944.Aprilis 26.

FACING PAGE: The PROPERTY CONFISCATION RECORD dated 18 April 1944, of the 8th Gendarmerie district which included Királyhelmec, recording the expropriation of property from Márton Schvarc. It reads in part:

Note: Márton Schvarc of Királyhelmec was detained with the following items:
1. 490 pengő, cash
2. a pair of gold earrings with jewels
3. 1 pc gold diamond ring
4. One pc silver graduation ring belonging to his daughter Magda
5. 1 pc nickel pocket watch, Alpina brand

USHMM File RG39.005 reel 1

Márton Schwarc's daughter, Magda. Notice the braces on her right leg that she needed after recovering from polio. Királyhelmec, 1938

I.

J e g y z e t.

Schwarc Márton királyhelmeci lakostól őrizetbe vett alábbi tárgyakról:
1/ 490 pengő azaz négyszázkilencven pengő, készpénz.
2. 1 azaz egy pár arany fülbe való, köves.
3. 1 drb azaz egy drb arany brilliáns gyürü.
4. 1 azaz egy drb ezüst, Magda felirásu gyürü.
5. 1 azaz egy drb nikkel zsebóra , Alpina feliréssal.

Királyhelmec 1944.április 18.

115

Átvételi elismervény

arrol, hogy a fentebb irt értékeket a királyhelmeci csendőr őrsre m ssnek-
ségtől a mai napon hiány nélkül átvettem.

Királyhelmec, 1944.április 26.

...ZENTRATIONSLAGER MAUTHAUSEN   Mauthausen, den 28. Mai 1944
Schutzhaftlager

Transportliste.

Am heutigen Tage werden nach dem Nebenlager GUSEN nachstehende 1000 Häftlinge (Zugänge vom 28.Mai 1944 vom K.L.Auschwitz, /Ungarische-Juden/) überstellt:

1.	Hecht	Emil	5.7.24	Biclyva	Student	67001
2.	Weiss	Israel	9.11.98	Olatschevtis	Schneider	67002
3.	Guttmann	Samuel	21.9.96	Satoralyaulyhely	Arbeiter	67003
4.	Ackerman	Solomon	25.8.95	Salyva	Schuster	67004
5.	Edelmann	Isydor	6.9.95	Med Zaplyn	Arbeiter	67005
6.	Streiter	Bernat	8.4.23	Tisabogdany	Holzarbeiter	67006
7.	Akerman	Bernath	7.4.24	Tökesfolu	Landarbeiter	67007
8.	Roth	Adolf	23.3.26	Hatmeg	Landarbeiter	67008
9.	Kleisst	Zsigmont	15.1.09	Munkacs	Schneider	67009
10.	Bikel	Hermann	21.7.93	Lelevestelep	Schneider	67010
11.	Schwartz	Ari	17.6.18	Buxad	Arbeiter	67011
12.	Majerowitz	Josef	9.6.97	Keselmöse	Ägerbeiter	67012
13.	Kremer	Michal	11.3.22	Averujfalu	Landarbeiter	67013
14.	Klein	Emil	13.5.97	Tokaj	Landarbeiter	67014
15.	Schvimmer	Somu	15.2.23	Cserlen5	Landarbeiter	67015
16.	Lust	Ignaz	5.7.96	ten	Schreiber	67016
17.	Zufern	Elias	11.6.01	Ikörmozu	Arbeiter	67017
18.	Weber	Alexander	22.5.22	Tied	Arbeiter	67018
19.	Roth	Deszo	5.1.94	Pele	Landarbeiter	67019
20.	Krausz	Henrich	5.12.26	Nagykavoly	Arbeiter	67020
21.	Rogner	Mikasa	2.7.04	Lillya	Arbeiter	67021
22.	Pollak	Lazar	25.3.97	Felsoviso	Bowater	67022
23.	Friedmann	Jenö	12.11.96	Kass	Glaser	67023
24.	Guttmann	Leopold	19.11.02	Tapoli	Kaufmann	67024
25.	Berkovits	Salomon	11.7.96	Apa	Landarbeiter	67025
26.	Farkas	Ludovit	18.6.99	Kisvarkany	Landwirt	67026
27.	Friedman	Pinkasz	2.12.24	Nagy Lakocz	Arbeiter	67027
28.	Pollak	Arsel	24.8.14	Borsa	Landarbeiter	67028
29.	Iczkowits	Izidor	19.3.12	Bembö	Landarbeiter	67029
30.	Friedman	Josef	26.6.03	Kiszakoo	Landarbeiter	67030
31.	Schenbrun	Gjula	15.12.24	Felsofolu	Gärtne.	67031
32.	Weiss	Abraham	192	unkacs	Arbeiter	67032
33.	Majormann	Isak	19.1.05	Köremeszt	Landarbeiter	67033
34.	Glattstein	Jakob	17.6.90	Tiszadorogma	Kaufmann	67034
35.	Rosenthal	Ferdinand	17.10.15	Koronezst	Landarbeiter	67035
36.	Rosenberg	Josef	24.11.05		Glaser	67036
37.	Lobi	Moses	13.9.97	Komorsan	Arbeiter	67037
38.	Grun	Vilmos	4.9.24	Mew terebes	Holzarbeiter	67038
39.	Zicherman	Movses	18.3.24	Stanvolvo	Landarbeiter	67039
40.	Meier	Salomon	? 10.05	Köremose	Waldarbeiter	67040
41.	Salamun	Risik	16.3.99	Körösmezö	Holzarbeiter	67041
42.	Wiisz	Alexander	1904	Beregrakos	Zahntechniker	67042
43.	Mazor	Denider	8.9.97	Kerusmesze	Arbeiter	67043
44.	Berkovics	Markusz	20.5.05	Terebs ferpatek	Bäcker	67044
45.	Lebi	Israel	4.1.28	Czataarneneti	Arbeiter	67045

426

The first page of an **ORIGINAL TRANSPORT LIST** created by authorities on May 28, 1944 in Mauthausen noting prisoner transfers from Auschwitz to the sub camp Gusen on May 28, 1944. USHMM File 1319353_0_1

401.	Weisz	Benjamin	26.9.02.	Viak	Fotograf	67401
402.	Hecht	Jakob	26.5.01.	Rahou	Schuster	67402
403.	Kahan	Mihaly	16.12.04.	Raho	H.arbeiter	67403
404.	Jakobovits	Mor	6.4.12.	Altina	Arbeiter	67404
405.	Zwinger	Miklos	12.11.26	Tokaj	Schneider	67405
406.	Fischer	Samuel	22.2.25	Roho	Fleischer	67406
407.	Gubner	Izsak	14.5.99.	Gereny	H.Arbeiter	67407
408.	Lebovic	Ignac	10.5.17.	Rokozmezo	Schuster	67408
409.	Reszavics	Lajos	14.6.26	Raho	H. rbeiter	67409
410.	Halm	Izso	3. .26.	Tiszabogdany	rb er	67410
411.	ckerman	Josef	.8.01	Munkacs	Arbeiter	67411
412.	nda	endel	15.3.00.	Uglya	rbeiter	67412
413.	Goldglahns	Hermann	15.5.83.	Vetes	Landarbeiter	67413
414.	eisz	Zoltan	15. 1.15.	Nagy Karoly	Landarbeiter	67414
415.	lein	Joszef	11.11.09.	Batiz	H. rbeiter	67415
416.	Herskov c	zar	10.6.96.	Torockez	rbeiter	67416
417.	El ck	oltan	3o. .26.	Nagykavol	rbeiter	67417
418.	Berkovics	Izrael Jakob	29.6.97.	Turja Remede	B ckwr	67418
419.	lein	Jozsef	15.3.18.	Buda est	Kürschner	67419
420.	Friedmann	Lajos	1o.1. 5	Asnyohaza	H. reiter	67420
421.	idliaz	ndor	13.1.25	Nagy-Kovesd	Landarbeiter	67421
422.	Reich	Bela	2o.6.25	zerenes	Arbeiter	67422
423.	chwarcz	lias	22.3.91	Tiszadob	Beamter	67423
424.	Bernath	Bela	5.1.25.	V mfolu	chuster	67424
425.	ckermann	dalbert	5.1.99.	Munkacs	rbeiter	67425
426.	Hübscher	Mikols	17.4.13.	ator ljujhel	chne der	674
427.	Fried	Mozes	17.1 .26.	Borsa	Lehrling	67427
428.	tern	Erno	16.1o.25	B rvolj	rbe er	67428
429.	Holpert	Herman	31.7.26	Nagyrakoc	rbeiter	674 o
430.	Friedman	Mor	26.1o.93	a ujhely	K ufmann	67430
431	eintraub	Antal	13.12.03	Zemplena rd	kaufmann	67431
432.	Lebovics	Jeno	24.1 .25.	Bogy rkd	lat arbeiter	67432
433.	bisch	Vilhelm	1o. .21.	Raho	Metzger	67433
434.	reizman	Herman	5. .26.	Majo mandty	rbe ter	67434
435.	Tischler	Herman	24. .oo.	Komorzan	Müller	67435
436.	Goldschlag	Moric	21.6.24	r mez	gefacharbeiter	
						67436
437.	Jakubovits	nhird	8.9.24	Bukowinko	L nd rbei er	67437
438.	Herm latein	Herman	16.9.91.	Brod	aufmann	67438
439.	eisz	lomon	18.12.oo	Fels Viznice	L. r eiter	67439
440.	Gottesmann	amuel	15.1o.93	F de esfalva	l ndarb iter	67440
441.	Grosz	lomon	6.2.13.	Munkacs	rbeiter	67441
442.	teg	arton	25.1.25	Munka s	rbeiter	67442
443.	e sz	Leopold	15.3.17.	Podhering	Zahntech er	67443
444.	Ladnier	Mozes	5.o.o7.	Luszko	chuster	674
445.	chwartz	Marton	20.6.95.	Kiralyhelmec	r eiter	67445
446.	erner	dolf	27. .o8	g nez	iget	67446
447.	Hollender	olf M jer	24.3.o1.	Bereg K vesd	chuster	67447
448.	Berkő	Jos	6.3.o4.	R fajnaujfalu	Ringm cher	67448
449.	illinger	braham	12.7.26	L damoc	rbeiter	67449
450.	Mozes	Ferenc	24.6.99.	Nagypeleske	l ndarbeiter	67450

My Uncle Márton Schwartz's name appears on line 445 of the same **TRANSPORT LIST**.
USHMM File 1319361_0_1

489.   Schwartz   Emil   15.8.29   Kiraly Helmeto   Landarb.   6748

My cousin Emil Schwartz's name appears on line 489 of the same **TRANSPORT LIST**.
The original digital image has been edited by adjusting brightness, contrast, and sharpness.
USHMM File 1319362_0_1

551.	Moskovits	Henryk	18.2.05	Szatmarnemeti	Hutmacher	67551
552.	Friedmann	Israel	18.10.91	Kekstarsko	Landwirt	67552
553.	Schwartz	Bela	15.5.26	Kiraly Helmets	Arbeiter	67553
554.	Gotteszman	Herman	79.94	Fedelesfolva	Landarbeiter	67554
555.	Mermelstein	Mendel	25.3.23	Trostanics	Landarbeiter	67555
556.	Halberstam	Abraham	10.5.07	t opkov	Arbeiter	67556
557.	Salamon	Miklos	27.8.25	Kaschan	Arbeiter	67557
558.	Salamon	Beni	15.4.98	Maromorsigget	Arbeiter	67558
559.	Weinberger	Tomas	28.10.28	Kassa	Lehrling	67559
560.	Halpert	Marton	8.12.26	Kassa	Arbeiter	67560
561.	Veisz	Jozsef	13.4.28	Harsfalva	Lehrling	67561
562.	Halpert	Zoltan	17.4.28	Kassa	Arbeiter	67562
563.	Bardos	Georg	7.2.29	Kassa	Arbeiter	67563
564.	Elyovics	Salamon	24.4.28	Munkacs	Schüler	67564
565.	Gottesman	zender	16.4.26	Volocz	Schüler	67565
566.	Dornstein	Sandor	13.12.28	Körösmezö	Lehrling	67566
567.	Heisler	Marton	20.7.26	Volocs	Lehrling	67567
568.	Weisman	Heinrich	22.1.26	Szatmarnemety	Arbeiter	67568
569.	Mermelstein	Jakob	30.4.30	Magayar Kani za	Schiler	67569
570.	Leuchter	Jenö	15.5.29	Garo	atok	Lehrling
						67570
571.	Ackerman	Albert	10.3.28	Islen	Landarbeiter	67571
572.	Egri	Miklos	22.2.28	Nagyszälös	Lehrling	67572
573.	Zisowic	Martin	8.6.28	Brod	Schusterlehrl.	67573
574.	eisz	Herman	12.3.28	Huklivor	Lehrling	67574
575.	Strickberger	Miklos	10.12.30	dcse	Schüler	67575
576.	Rosenbaum	Maier	22.7.26	Szatmarnemety	Arbeite	67576
577.	Mermelstein	Naftula	9.6.30	olva	Lehrling	67577
578.	Gutmann	Somu	29.10.26	Kisletsfalva	Lehrling	67578
579.	Wolf	Jenö	21.2.26	Kistoronya	Arbeiter	67579
580.	Friedman	Vilmos	20.4.29	Beregszasz	Lehrling	67580
581.	Steinberg	Josef	16.12.1	Huklivo	Schuster	67581
582.	Simonovics	Leopold	2.5.87	Köbles	Kaufmann	67582
583.	Labi	Izidor	24.4.27	Minkacs	Arbeiter	67583
584.	Breitbart	Desző	29.1.28	eloös	Arbeiter	67584
585.	Weiser	Abraham	10.3.28	szkatarszka	Arbeiter	67585
586.	Fuksz	Mozes	21.11.27	Also Verecke	Lehrling	67586
587.	Klein	Jozsef	9.8.26	Alsoverecke	Lehrling	67587
588.	Klein	Jenö	12.2.28	lsoverecke	Lehrling	67588
589.	Zegelstejn	Moze	1.5.26	Alsoverecke	Schüler	67589
590.	einer	Herm Ber	5.1.27	elsö Visö	Schüle	67590
591.	Salomon	Geza	27.3.28	Minkacs	Lehrling	67591
592.	Frisch	iber	27.7.28	Szephalom	Lehrling	67592
593.	Senderowitsch	Benö	23.10.26	Toroszkösz	Lehrling	67593
594.	Friedman	Mozes	17.1.29	Kisrakec	Schuler	67594
595.	Lefkovits	Bernat	20.3.30	Satoraljaujhely	Arbeiter	67595
596.	Klein	Izrael	25.7.27	Magyarkozian	Lehrling	67596
97.	Klein an	Vilmos	9.11.27	Arassvek	Lehrling	67597
598.	Fislovics	Mendel	18.9.28	Zarnya	Lehrling	67598
599.	Heiszler	Zoltan	1.9.27	Voloc	Lehrling	67599
600.	Herskovics	Bernard	28.9.28	Mesarfolvo	Schüler	67600

Emil's brother, using the name Bela, appears on line 553 of the same **TRANSPORT LIST**.
The original digital image has been edited by adjusting brightness, contrast, and sharpness.
USHMM File 1319364_0_1

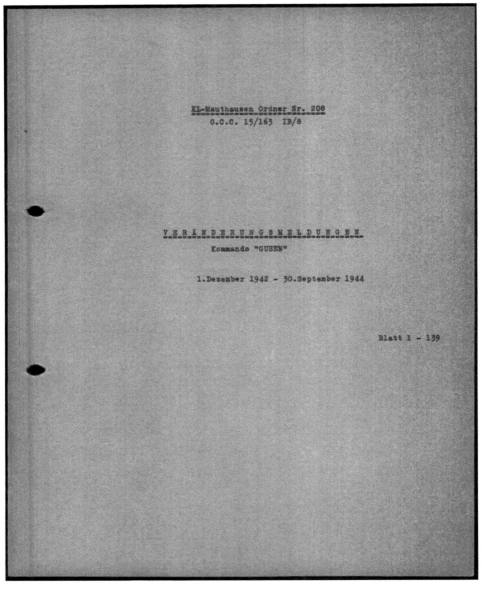

KL-Mauthausen Ordner Nr. 208
O.C.C. 15/163 IB/8

V E R Ä N D E R U N G S M E L D U N G E N

Kommando "GUSEN"

1.Dezember 1942 - 30.September 1944

Blatt 1 - 139

An **ORIGINAL FOLDER** containing messages regarding Mauthausen prisoner changes in Gusen between December 1, 1942 and September 30, 1944.
USHMM File 1310919_0_1

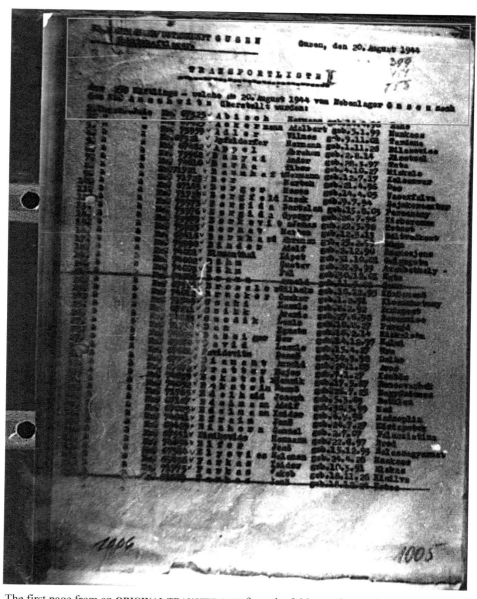

The first page from an **ORIGINAL TRANSFER LIST** from the folder on the previous page indicating on the top: 150 prisoners which on 20 August 1944 were transferred from sub-Camp Gusen to KZ (Konzentrationslager) Auschwitz. The original digital image has been edited by adjusting brightness, contrast, and sharpness.
USHMM File 1311004_0_1

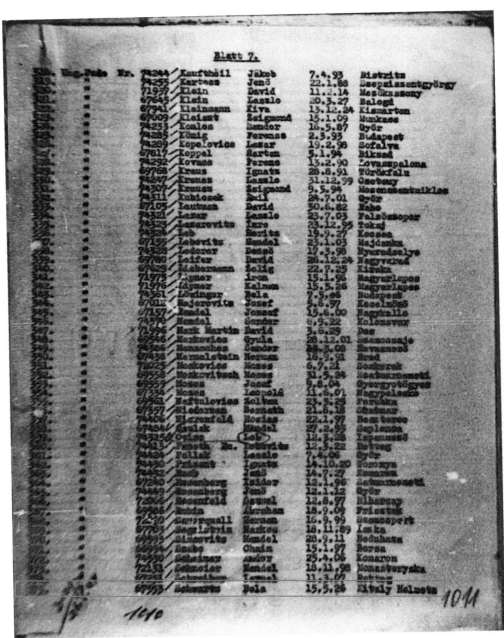

Page 7 from the same **ORIGINAL TRANSFER LIST** with Bela Schwartz on line 375 and his prisoner number 67553, confirming his transfer back to Auschwitz on August 20, 1944. The original digital image has been edited by adjusting brightness, contrast, and sharpness. USHMM File 1311013_0_1

Name: S C H W A R T Z , Bela   Mauth.Häftl.Nr. 67 553

geb.   Ung.Jude

am: 15.5.26   in: Kĭraly Helmete   Nat. -

Überstellt am 28.5.44 zum   Transportliste
Nebenlager Gusen   des KL-Mauthausen

(Zugang am 28.5.44 von Auschwitz)

                                      OCC 15/198

                                      Ordner Nr. 269

                                      Seite: 161

International Tracing Service file card for my cousin, Bela Schwartz. It reads
Transferred on 28.5.44 to the Gusen Sub-Camp. Entered on 28.5.44 from Auschwitz. It
indicates his birth day, birthplace as Királyhelmec, and his prisoner number 67553.
The information was compiled from Mauthausen Transport List OCC 15/198, folder #
269, page 161. Original digital image was low resolution. It was printed, rescanned,
and edited to reduce pixelation.
USHMM File 2228232_0_1

Sherwin Gluck

Entry for Márton Schvartz in the so called **MAUTHAUSEN GUSEN DEATH** book. His name
appears on the first line of the right hand page of the book.
USHMM File (SchwartzMártonBRG-17.002M.0001.00000228.jpg).

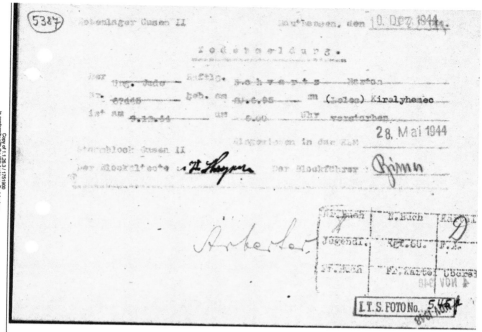

Above: **DEATH CERTIFICATE** (Todesmeldung) for Márton Schvartz, issued in Mauthausen.
The original digital image has been edited by adjusting brightness and contrast.
USHMM Files (SchwartzMártonA1751899_0_1.jpg

Below: The ITS envelope created in the postwar era which holds this death notice.
ITS Archives, Bad Arolsen. File # 1.1.26.3 / 1751900

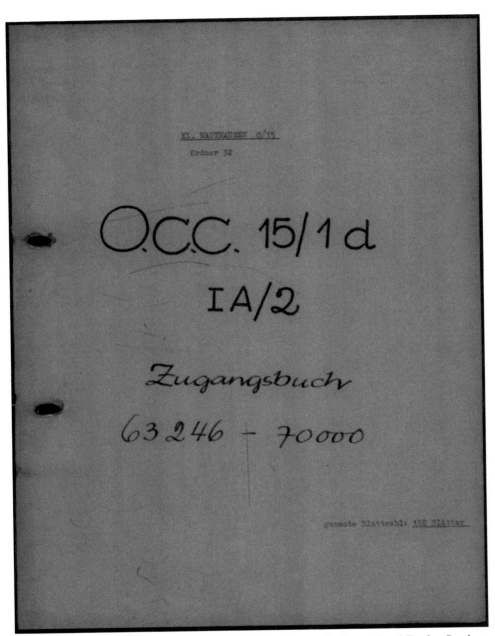

The cover page created in the postwar era by staff members at the International Tracing Service for the lists that appear on the following pages.
USHMM File 1282164_1

ORIGINAL LIST OF ARRIVALS IN MAUTHAUSEN. Márton Schwartz's name appears beside the last three digits of his prisoner number, 445. This list provides his name, date of birth, occupation, and date of death, December 9, 1944.
USHMM File 1282246_0_1

— 313 —

No.		Name	Date of birth	Occupation	Status
67430		Hirsch Wilhelm	5. 7. 9?	Arbeiter	gest. 25.11.44
481		Goldschlag Pinkas	7. 1. 96	Tischler	gest.26.12.44
482		Appel Abraham	2. 8. 14	Arbeiter	überst.24.8.44 KL-Auschwitz
				28.Mai 1944	
483	Ung.Jude	Weber Mozes	21.6.05	Schuster	gest.7.3.44
484		Chulak Mendel	27.2.99	Landarbeit.	überst.20.8.44 KL-Auschwitz
485		Handon Salomon	29.10.94	Weber	gest.21.12.44
486		Veiss Adolf	3. 1.09	Schneider	gest.22.1.45
487		Grünbaum Isidor	15.6.24	Arbeiter	gest.17.8.44
488		Schwartz Emil	15.8.99	kronbiter	gest.3.11.44
489				Arbeiter	überst.24.8.44 KL-Auschwitz
491		Brisch Imre	23.3.24	Schneider	1.12.
492		Goldglancz Rosen	25.8.06	Landarbeiter	gest.14.2.45
493		Markus Josef	15.7.12	Maurer	gest.29.12.44
494		Fried Adolf	12.10.23	Arbeiter	gest.1.10.44
495		Hermann Desso	9.7.80	Kaufmann	gest.8.6.44
496		Steinber Jakob	20.11.26	Landarbeiter	
497		Major Moritz	25.12.25	Arbeiter	gest.9.9.44
498		Steinberg Mozes	13.1.99	Landarbeiter	gest.18.11.44
499		Major Naten	19.10.99	Arbeiter	überst.20.8.44 KL-Auschwitz
500		Roth Salomon	17.3.27	Schneider	
501		Akermann Lajos	3.5.26	Feldarbeiter	
502		Gross Israel	5.2.01	Schuster	gest.8.8.44
503		Klein Adolf	8.12.26	Arbeiter	gest.9.2.45
504		Schön Hermann	29.3.90	Fleischer	gest.15.11.44
505		Mayeresik Salamon	5.2.03	Kaufmann	überst.20.8.44 KL-Auschwitz
506		Flegmann Mor	23.10.96	Landarbeiter	überst.20.8.44 KL-Auschwitz
507		Farkas Herman	5.10.24	Landarbeiter	gest.13.1.45
508		Grünfeld Herman	1.5.96	Kellner	gest.29.12.44
509		Kreismann Erno	8.10.24	Landarbeiter	gest.29.1.45
510		Vogа Israel	12.5.16	Kirstenmacher	gest.29.1.45
511		Heimlik Mozes	23.11.22	Arbeiter	
512		Glück Heinrich	15.5.22	Arbeiter	gest.1.9.44
513		Gottlemann Heinrich	21.3.98	Fleischer	überst.24.8.44 KL-Auschwitz
514		Issek Anton	25.5.06	Glasschneider	gest.4.1.45
515		Dub Jeno	26.11.24	Arbeiter	gest.30.11.44
516		Weisberger Herman	3.8.25	Arbeiter	gest.18.7.44
517		Burkowitz Ignatz	24.2.24	Fleischer	gest.8.11.44
518		Marcu Elias	15.12.96	Schuster	gest.5.1.45
519		Weinberger Hugo	17.4.99	Landarbeiter	gest.29.7.44
520		Frankfurter Moriz	2.3.00	Arbeiter	überst.24.8.44 KL-Auschwitz
521		Farkas Zoltan	13.6.97	Arbeiter	gest.20.12.44
522		Fischmann Moritz	2.1.25	Buchdrucker	gest.17.10.44
523		Safir Eugen	12.5.87	Schuster	gest.8.6.44
524		Schwarcz Jenö	25.7.87	Schneider	überst.20.8.44 KL-Auschwitz
525		Grossmann Vilmos	15.6.92	Gastwirt	gest.27.7.44
526		Roth Jenö	21.10.22	Student	
527		Jakubovics Aron	24.1.26	Arbeiter	
528		Svarc Abraham	11.4.23	Schuster	überst.20.8.44 KL-Auschwitz
529		Berger Mendel	13.9.24	Arbeiter	gest.12.2.45
530		Grosz Aron	3.4.84	Student	gest.31.1.45
531		Fruchter Juda	13.12.01	Landarbeiter	8.24.8.44 Auschw.
532		Rubinstein Samuel	21.3.26	Schneider	gest.13.11.44

ORIGINAL LIST OF ARRIVALS IN MAUTHAUSEN. Emil Schwartz's name appears beside the last three digits of his prisoner number, 489. This list provides his name, date of birth, and occupation. USHMM File 1282247_0_1

— 320 —

25. Mai 1944

No.	Name	Date of birth	Occupation	Notes
	Glück Arwin	12.2.14	Landarbeiter	
	Grossmann David	6.11.18	Arbeiter	gest.15.1.45
	Rosenberg Anton	3.8.01	Schuster	gest.9.6.44
537	Klein Samuel	9.7.05	Arbeiter	
538	Kohn Irma	11.3.19	Landarbeiter	
539	Steinberger Ignatz	31.7.98	Glaser	gest.19.10.44
540	Grossmann Niklos	9.3.26	Maser	gest.25.1.45
541	Weiss Hermann	14.5.23	Glaser	gest.31.3.45
542	Roth Geza	4.7.08		
543	Roth Simon	3.9.09	Malermanipulant	gest.18.2.45
544	Bündel Leopold	14.4.03	Angestellter	gest.22.1.45
545	Kuhn Josef	18.11.24	Landarbeiter	gest.13.6.44
546	Ferenci Jenő	13.11.07	Arbeiter	gest.21.11.44
547	Berger Lipolt	12.8.94	Schneider	24.8.
548	Fried Zoltan	22.3.00	Kaufmann	gest.15.1.45 überst.24.8.44 Kl.-Auschwitz
549	Weinberger Major	19.11.91	Landarbeiter	gest.10.7.44
550	Weber Marton	31.5.98	Schuster	gest.16.8.44
551	Moskovits Henryk	18.3.95	Hutmacher	gest.21.12.44
552				
553	Schwartz Bela	15.5.26	Arbeiter	überst.20.8.44 Kl.-Auschwitz
554	Rottmann Herman	7.9.94	Landarbeiter	gest.26.10.44
555	Mermelstein Kendel	25.9.25		
556	Halberstam Abraham	10.5.07	Arbeiter	gest.5.2.45
557	Salamon Miklos	27.9.23		gest.2.10.44
558	Salamon Deni	15.4.89		gest.10.10.44
559	Weinberger Tesza	26.10.25	Maler	gest.25.2.45
560	Halpert Marton	8.12.26	Tapezierer	gest.15.11.44
561	Vales Josef	13.6.28	Schneider	
562	Halpert Zoltan	17.4.28	Maler	gest.21.12.44
563	Dardos Georg	7.2.29	Tischler	gest.17.11.44
564	Ilyovics Salamon	24.4.28	Schüler	überst.24.8.44 Kl.-Auschwitz
565	Gottesman Sander	16.4.26	Schüler	gest.6.2.45
566	Bernstein Sander	13.12.28	Lehrling	
567	Adsler Marton	20.7.26	Schuhmacher	gest.4.3.45
568	Neisman Heinrich	22.1.26	Arbeiter	gest.21.6.44
569	Mermelstein Jakob	30.4.30	Tischler	gest.5.3.45
571	Lachter Jenő			
572	Beri Miklos	22.2.28	Landarbeiter	gest.23.12.44
573	Klawio Martin	8.6.28	Lehrling	gest.11.2.45
574	Weiss Herman	15.3.28	Schusterlehrling	6.3.m.
575	Strickberger Niklos	10.12.30	Lehrling	
576	Rosenbaum Roger	22.7.26	Schüler	gest.17.11.44
577	Mermelstein Bertula	9.6.30	Arbeiter	
578	Gutmann Geza	28.10.25	Lehrling	
579	Wolf Jenő	21.2.26	Lehrling	
580	Friedman Vilmos	20.4.29	Arbeiter	
581	Steinberg Josef	16.12.12	Lehrling	gest.17.7.44
582	Simonovics Leopold	25.5.07	Schuster	gest.25.7.44
583	Lebl Zsider	24.4.17	Kaufmann	gest.15.2.45
584	Weiser Abraham	10.3.28	Schneider	
585	Breittert Bernő	20.4.28	Schneider	gest.18.2.45
586	Lukas Roger	21.11.27	Tischler	gest.11.3.45
587	Klein Josef	22.6.86	Schneider	
588	Klein Jenő	12.2.26	Maker	
589	Zegelstein Moses	1.5.29	Maker	

ORIGINAL LIST OF ARRIVALS IN MAUTHAUSEN. Bela Schwartz's name appears beside the last three digits of his prisoner number, 553. This list provides his name, date of birth, occupation, and date of transfer to Auschwitz, August 20, 1944.
USHMM File 1282248_0_1

ID Prisoner Number Mauthausen Gusen Other Camps	Name (Other Surname(s))	Date ofBirth Place of Birth Nationality	Arrived Reason for Arrest Night and Fogdecree
13157 67445	SCHWARTZ, Marton	20Jun 1895 Kiralyhelm_ Ungarn	28-May-44 Jude FALSE
13531 68247	GLÜCK, Lajosch	13-Nov-04 Bodrogmese Ungarn	28-May-44 Jude FALSE

The information contained in the Mauthausen / Gusen Concentration Camp Death Record Book for Márton Schwartz and Lajos Gluck. These entries are based on original material created by Mauthausen authorities. Jewishgen.org

Occupation	Death Cause / Date / Place	Transfers	Comments	Source
	09-Dec-44 Gusen	Gusen		AMM Y/36;
Arbeiter	09-Oct-44	Solvay (Ebensee) Mauthausen		AMM Y/43;

```
Name:     S C H W A R T Z , Marton
geb.
am:    --         in:     --              Nat.: --
```

zur Zeit im KL Auschwitz (21.5.1944)	HPK des KL Mauthausen
siehe T/D - 391 210	
SCHWARTZ, Emil geboren am 15.8.1929 in Kiralyhelmec (Sohn)	

Above: International Tracing Service file card indicating Márton Schwartz's presence in Auschwitz and Mauthausen. The German reads: "Currently in Auschwitz (21.5.1944). See T/D 391 210 Schwartz, Emil. Born on 15.8.1929 in Királyhelmec (Son) USHMM Record

Below: ORIGINAL MAUTHAUSEN GUSEN PRISONER IDENTIFICATION CARD created by authorities in Mauthausen for my cousin, Emil Schwartz. It indicates his home address in Királyhelmec, his arrival to Auschwitz, and his prisoner number 67489.
Yad v'Shem Item #4083057

Häftlings-Personal-Karte — JUDE — Häftl.-Nr.: 67.489

Fam.-Name: Schwartz
Vorname: Emil
Geb. am: 15.8.29 in Kiralyhelmec
Stand: led.   Kinder: keine
Wohnort: Kiralyhelmec K.Zemplen
Strasse: Horthy M.G.18
Religion: isr.   Staatsang. ung.
Wohnort d. Angehörigen: Eltern &
Marton & Etel g.Lofkowits
K.L.Auschwitz
Eingewiesen am: 21.5.44
durch: RSHA
in KL.: Auschwitz
Grund:
Vorstrafen:

Überstellt am: 28 Mai 1944 an KL. GUSEN

Strafen im Lager:

Visiting Israel in 1968.
From Left to Right: Emil's sons: Misha, Dudi, Emil, me, and Emil's wife, Lilly.

FACING PAGE: The PROPERTY CONFISCATION RECORD dated 25
April 1944, of the 8th Gendarmerie district which included
Királyhelmec, recording the expropriation of property from Miksa
Schön, my cousin Mariska's husband. It reads in part -
List: Schön Miksa inhabitant of Bodrogmező was detained with
the following items:

1. 20 pengő, cash
2. a pc nickel pocket watch with inscription
3. 1 pc gold ring with a diamond
4. 1 pc gold ring 2 grams
5. 1 pc gold chain 37 cm long with a white pendant
6. 1 pc lady's gold ring with engraving

USHMM File RG39.005 reel 1

m.kir.kassai VIII.c csendőrkerület.

Királyhelmeci őrs.

Magyar Országos ...

Jegyzék.

Schön Miksa királyhelmeci lakostól őrizetbe vtt tárgyakról.

20 P,azaz Husz pengő készpénz.

1 darab nikkel férfi zsebóra Tissot felirattal.
1 darab női aranygyürü kék burnafejet ábrázoló kővel.
1 darab aryn karikagyürü 2 gramm.
1 darab aranylánc 37 cm hosszu végén csüngős medál fehérkővel.
1 darab női pecsétgyürü arany kcrcsu bevéséssel 1 gramm.

Királyhelmec,1944.aprilis 23.

FACING PAGE: The PROPERTY CONFISCATION RECORD dated 25
April 1944, of the 8th Gendarmerie district which included
Királyhelmec, recording the expropriation of property from Jozsef
Lefkovics, the father of the boys I studied with in Polyán. It reads
in part:

List: Lefkovics Jozsef inhabitant of Bodrogmező was detained
with the following items:
1. 1 pc gold ring 2 grams
2. a pc men's nickel pocket watch

USHMM File RG39.005 reel 1

m.kir.kassai VIII.csendőrkerület.

Jegyzék.

1944 JUN 19.

Lefkovics József bodroghozói lakostól őrizetbe vett értékekről.

1 darb arany karikai gyürü 2 gr
1 darab férfi nikkel zsebóra

királyhelmec,1944.április 23.

FACING PAGE: The PROPERTY CONFISCATION RECORD dated 22
April 1944, of the 8th Gendarmerie district which included
Királyhelmec, recording the expropriation of property from Lajos
Schwarc, Uncle Márton's brother. It reads in part -
List: Schwarc Lajos inhabitant of Lelesz was detained with the
following items:

1. 2 silver candlesticks with arms
2. 5 silver candlesticks
3. 1 pc men's nickel pocket watch "Kirnfe"
4. 168 Pengő cash
5. 50 Pengő travel expenses deducted*

USHMM File RG39.005 reel 1

*Author's Note: They had the chutzpa (Yiddish for audacity, nerve) to not only
steal 50 Pengő, but to mark it on the confiscation record as "travel expenses"
to transport them on cattle cars to Auschwitz.

M.kir.kassai VIII.csendőrkerület.   **Királyhelmeci örs.**

1944 JUN 15

Jegyzék   ''1944 JUN. 15

Schwarc Lujos Lelszi lakostól őrizetbe vett tárgyakról
2.drb ezüst gyertatartó karos.
5.drb ezüst gyergtyatartó egyes
1 drb.nikkel férfi zsebóra "Kirnfe" felirattal,
168 P.azaz Egyszázhatvannyolc pengő készpénz.
50 P.azaz Ötven pengő utiköltségre levonva.

Királyhelmec,1944.április 22.

224

MILITARY AWARDS AND HONORS

 The **Bronze Star Medal** is an individual military award of the U.S. Armed Forces. The Bronze Star Medal (without the "V" device) may be awarded to each member of the Armed Forces of the United States who, after 6 December 1941, was cited in orders or awarded a certificate for exemplary conduct in ground combat against an armed enemy after 7 December 1941. For this purpose, the U.S. Army's Combat Infantryman Badge (see below) is considered as a citation in orders. The medal is the fifth-highest combat decoration and the tenth highest U.S. military award. I was awarded the Bronze Star Medal in 2013.

 The **Combat Infantryman Badge** (CIB) is the U.S. Army combat service recognition decoration awarded to Infantry holding colonel rank or below, who personally fought in active ground combat while an assigned member of an infantry of brigade size or smaller, any time after 6 December 1941. The CIB was created during World War II to recognize the fact that out of all Army occupational specialties, infantrymen in combat face the greatest risk of being wounded or killed under fire.

 The **Good Conduct Medal** for the Army was established in 1941. It is awarded to any active-duty enlisted member of the United States military who completes three consecutive years of "honorable and faithful service". Such service implies that a standard enlistment was completed without any non-judicial punishment, disciplinary infractions, or court martial offenses.

The **World War II Victory Medal** is a  campaign medal that commemorates military service during World War II and is awarded to any member of the United States military who served on active duty, or as a reservist, between December 7, 1941 and December 31, 1946.

The **American Campaign Medal** is a  military award of the U.S. Armed Forces that recognizes those service members who served in the American Theater of Operations during World War II.

The **European-African-Middle Eastern** **Campaign Medal** (EAME) is a military award of the U.S. Armed Forces awarded for any service performed during World War II in the European, North African, or Middle Eastern theater. Colored bands representing Germany (on the ribbon's right side), Italy (on the ribbon's left side), and the United States (in the center of the ribbon) are on the ribbon. The brown and green areas of the ribbon represent the terrain of the area of conflict, which ranged from beaches and sand, to grass and woodlands, to mountains. For those service members who participated in one or more military campaigns, 'Service Stars' are authorized to be worn on the medal. The four bronze service stars awarded to me were for:

> **Naples-Foggia**: August 18, 1943 – January 21, 1944
> **Rome-Arno**: January 22, 1944 – September 9, 1944
> **Rhineland**: September 15, 1944 – March 21, 1945
> **Central Europe**: March 22, 1945 – May 11, 1945

A fifth bronze service star for **Anzio**: January 22, 1944 – May 24, 1944 mistakenly wasn't awarded until August 29, 2018. The additional service star entitled me to receive a new EAME campaign medal with one silver star.

The **Presidential Unit Citation** (PUC) was awarded to the 6th Armored Infantry, First Armored Division for combat at Monte Porchia from December 13, 1943 through January 12, 1944. It is awarded to units of the United States Armed Forces for extraordinary heroism in action against an armed enemy. The unit must display such gallantry, determination, and *esprit de corps* in accomplishing its mission under extremely difficult and hazardous conditions so as to set it apart from and above other units participating in the same campaign. The collective degree of valor (combat heroism) against an armed enemy by the unit nominated for the PUC is the same as that which would warrant award of the Distinguished Service Cross (the 2nd highest honor that can be given) to an individual. As with other Army unit citations, the PUC is in a larger frame than other ribbons, and is worn above the right pocket. All members of the unit may wear the decoration, whether or not they personally participated in the acts for which the unit was cited. Only those assigned to the unit at the time of the action cited may wear the decoration as a permanent award.

The **Meritorious Unit Commendation** (MUC) was awarded to the 67th Military Police Company for its service in France and Germany. The U.S. Army awards it to units for exceptionally meritorious conduct in performance of outstanding services for at least six continuous months during the period of military operations against an armed enemy occurring on or after 1 January 1944. Service in a combat zone is not required, but must be directly related to the combat effort. The unit must display such outstanding devotion and superior performance of exceptionally difficult tasks as to set it apart and above other units with similar missions. The degree of achievement required is the same as that which would warrant award of the Legion of Merit (the 6th highest honor that can be given) to an individual. The Laurel wreath is a traditional symbol of high merit and honor. The patch is worn on the right sleeve.

An **Overseas Service Bar** is a decoration of the U.S. Army which is displayed as an embroidered gold bar worn horizontally on the right sleeve of the U.S. Army dress uniform. Each bar signifies 6 months of overseas service. My five bars equalled two and a half years.

A **Service Stripe**, or hash mark, is a decoration of the United States military which is presented to enlisted members to denote length of service. The U.S. Army awards each stripe for three years service. I received one service stripe.

Private First Class is designated by a single chevron and is more common among soldiers who have served in the U.S. Army for one year or more.

Branch Insignia Collar Devices represent a service member's specific field of service and their particular skill set. The U.S. enlisted disk

is worn on the right collar and the branch insignia on the left. The crossed rifle insignia shown here is for Infantry personnel.

Honorable Discharge Patch and Pin, aka "The Ruptured Duck" was issued to discharged soldiers and was worn above the right breast pocket. The purpose of this patch was that it allowed the GI to travel home while wearing his uniform and not be ordered around by an officer. It got its nickname from the ugly eagle in the center.

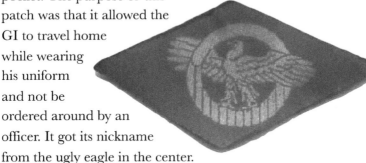

Sharpshooter   Marksman   Clasp (rifle)

A **Marksmanship Qualification Badge** is presented to US Army personnel upon successful completion of a weapons qualification course. They are issued for a variety of weapons and are awarded in three grades (highest to lowest): expert, sharpshooter, and marksman. Suspended from the badge are clasps that indicate the type of weapon the individual has qualified to use. The level at which one qualifies is dependent on the weapon, firing range, and the course of fire. The badges are not permanent awards. When a Soldier re-qualifies with their weapon at a different level, the Soldier replaces their qualification badge with a new badge that reflects their current level. I was awarded the Marksman Marksmanship Qualification Badge with Machine Gun Bar (.30 caliber) and the Sharpshooter Marksmanship Qualification Badge with Rifle Bar (M-1).

**7th Army
Shoulder Patch**

**1st Armored Division
Shoulder Patch**

NEWSPAPER ARTICLES

OYSTER BAY
Enterprise-Pilot

Also covering Bayville, Centre Island, Cove Neck, East Norwich, Luttingtown, Laurel Hollow, Locust Valley, Matinecock, Mill Neck, Muttontown, North Syosset, Oyster Bay Cove, The Brookvilles

Vol. 7 No. 39 Oyster Bay, N.Y. 11771   **Thursday, June 9, 1983**   © *Community Newspapers Inc. All Rights Reserved USPS 390230*   **Two Sections: 36 Pages 35ᶜ per copy**

Processional in which the holocaust Torah scroll is carried under the Chupah (canopy) with honor guards. Participating were (l. to r.) William Goebels, Larry Bard, Max Malkiel, Irving Gluck, Dr. Ronald Feldman, Ira Rubenstein, and Skip Ackerman.

Rabbi Harold Kamsler (left) and Irving Gluck hold Torah scroll.

Speakers and organizers of the ceremony included (l. to r.) Robert Mandel, center president and co-chairman of the program; Rabbi Harold Kamsler, co-chairman; Ambassador Naphtali Lavie, consul general of the state of Israel to New York; and Senator Alphonse D'Amato.

OB Jews dedicate holocaust Torah

Many handkerchiefs were in view on Sunday among the crowd of approximately 400 who attended a holocaust Torah scroll dedication at the Oyster Bay Jewish Center.

In a ceremony highlighted by a moving speech by Senator Alphonse D'Amato, the Torah scroll dedicated on Sunday "came home" to the Holy Ark at the Jewish center. It is one of 1,500 scrolls hidden in a disused Czechoslovakian synagogue since World War II, when Hitler destroyed synagogues in Bohemia and Moravia and gathered the scrolls, planning to use them as curiosities when all the Jews had been annihilated in the "final solution."

The Torahs are now memorials to the martyred Jewish communities from which they came. The scroll in Oyster Bay came from Eiberkostaletz, a small community near the German border.

The dedication was preceded by a reception. At the ceremony, D'Amato said in his speech that the holocaust was not only a Jewish experience, but one shared by all humanity. He talked about his feelings upon visiting Yad Vashem, a memorial museum in Jerusalem depicting the concentration camp experience.

He said that the voice of hate is returning and that people who love this nation must raise their voices. He said that Jews have "arrived" in America, but that Jews had also been in prominent positions in Germany when Hitler took over and destroyed more than 6-million of them. "When we want to look the other way...we betray our country...we do not have the right to be quiet," he said.

He said that the holocaust story must be told and retold so that it doesn't happen again. He praised the leaders of the Jewish center for conducting such a program.

Prior to D'Amato's speech, Robert Mandel, president of the Jewish center, spoke, quoting from "The Diary of Anne Frank."

Solomon Zynstein, president of the American Federation of Jewish Fighters, Camp Inmates, and Victims of Nazism, made an impassioned plea for remembrance of those lost.

State Senator Ralph Marino, obviously moved by Zynstein's comments, also talked about the importance of remembering and introduced D'Amato.

Following the speakers, the Torah processional took place.

The Torah was carried by Irving Gluck, a member of the Jewish center, and Torah reader at services. He left Czechoslovakia before the Nazi occupation. He was born in a small town not far from where the Torah originated.

The Torah was carried by honor guards under the Chupah (canopy). The Torah was received by long-time member David Bernstein, who is official Torah reader at the center. The dedication was conducted by Rabbi Harold Kamsler and the was followed by a memorial candle lighting.

Six candles were lit by survivors, including Tibor Rakos, Joe and Esther Abrams, Kurt and Amalie Seelig, Alfred and Lilia Kuhn, Nicole Pinsky, David and Nadzia Josefowicz, and Claude Caplin. They were in remembrance for the 6-million lost. Children and grandchildren of survivors lit the Menorah symbolizing a brighter future.

Following the dedication, Ambassador Naphtali Lavie, consul general of the State of Israel in New York, and a survivor, talked about being one of 22 youngsters who were sent by his father, a rabbi, to rescue 48 scrolls from a synagogue scheduled for destruction. The scrolls were rescued and buried, but all the youngsters subsequently were shipped out of the area and the scrolls were lost. "We have survived to write new scrolls. We keep them because they keep us," he said.

Preceding the processional, a cantata was performed by the center's chorale. That was arranged and written by Joyce and Joseph Kahn and narrated by Jack Bernstein and Sandra Mandel. The final song, "I believe with perfect faith," a slow chant, was sung as the Torah procession took place. It is the song that was sung often by holocaust victims on the march to the gas chambers.

Members of the chorale included Dr. Michael Falkove, Bert Hoffman, Sy Hoffman, Jill Kahn, Joseph Kahn, Joyce Kahn, Barbara Kroner, Beth Mandel, Robert Mandel, Tibor Rakoss, Ben Raymon and Shelly Schachter.

The ceremony lasted approximately two hours. It was followed by coffee and cake. The program was chaired by Sandra and Robert Mandel and Rabbi Kamsler. Working on the committee were Gattele Altabet, Bertha Hoffman, Sy Hoffman, Isa Kantor, Etta Kamsler, Dorothy Raymon, and Mirah Rubenstein.

Annual meeting

A colonial soldiers supper will precede the annual meeting of the Oyster Bay Historical Society on June 16 at 7 p.m. in the garden of Wightman House on Summit Street, Oyster Bay.

Annual reports will be given and the election of officers and trustees will take place at 8:30 p.m. following the dinner.

As part of the program there will be a Revolutionary soldier muster by members of John Grennel's Company, 3d New York Provincial Forces.

Gluck: A Man And His Machines

Jessica Berger & Randi Goetz

rving Gluck is a vendor who has
ed the Cold Spring Harbor Dis-
for twenty-eight years; however,
ot the mere fact of his longevity
has made him an exceptional
on who will be missed by the
ty. Although most of the faculty
r him as a generous vendor and
stimes "healer," it would surprise
y to learn that he is also a holo-
t survivor.

rving Gluck, a World War II vet-
 was born in Czechoslovakia.
eft his native country when he
eventeen and came to the United
es. He did not know then that his
r brother, father, and grandfa-
would become holocaust victims,
he would never see them again.
end of the Cold War has recently
'ed a glimmer of hope that he
someday find out where they are
ed.

He credits his uncle with saving
fe since he barely avoided man-
ry conscription for males over
ge of fifteen. Hungary under the
ag of Nazi Germany had seized
er in 1938 and were drafting men
he service. Irving, a brother and
sisters were sponsored by his
who lived in the United States
vas a professor at Ohio State.

*He was a hard working,
.est, and caring man who
wanted to serve"*

- Dr. Browne

When Irving landed in the United
s, he could not speak English,
e studied hard and mastered the
age.
n addition to English and Czech,

Mr. Gluck speaks German, Italian,
and Spanish.

In 1943 he volunteered for the
U.S. Army. From 1943 to 1945 he
served as a military policeman. He
survived four major battles and was
awarded four bronze stars. While
serving in Africa, he became a naturalized American citizen. After the
war he started his vending business
by selling goods to schools. He saw a
need to feed people, and he also enjoyed the engineering challenge of

Irving Gluck and Mr. Rowley with sodas from his vending machines.

maintaining and adapting machines.
Although there is never any bit-
terness in his recollections, Mr. Gluck
remembers with disappointment one
of his encounters with anti-semitism
after the war. He was delivering food
to a cafeteria when one of the patrons
commented, "Here he comes, just
another Jew grabbing every dollar he
can!" In his typical mild mannered
way, Irving Gluck reached into his
pocket and produced a copy of his
discharge papers and then asked the
patron to share with him what he had
done for his country?

In 1960 Irving married his wife
Barbara, who was an elementary
teacher in East Norwich. They had
two boys: Jarritt, who is now twenty-

eight, and Sherwin who is twenty-two
and an engineering student at the
University of Pennsylvania. Sherwin
has inherited his father's interest in
invention and has recently developed
a wheelchair that can ascend stairs.

Mr. Gluck is an avid reader who
has many diverse interests, one of
which is medicine. He has studied
Eastern and Western medicine and
has developed some unusual forms of
healing. One of his methods is "hand
healing" which does not involve any
form of actual physical contact. Although two reporters from the Harbor View were given a demonstration, they still remained skeptical.
However, Mr. Howard Nepo, art
teacher, overcame his initial cynicism
by having Mr. Gluck relieve him of
chronic pain that resulted from a broken foot.

As a vendor, he was perceived by
the faculty and students in a similar
way. According to Dr. Browne, "He
was a hardworking, honest, and caring man who wanted to serve."

Mr. Pryal commented, "People
were always more important than
profit. He always supplied free sodas
to anyone in the faculty room whenever he was in the building. If anyone
left a note claiming that he/she had

lost money in his machine, he would
never question the amount but leave
the money with another teacher."

His interest in people extended
to their personal lives. Eugene
Walker, a night custodian, recalls, " I
once contracted to haul debris for
him, and he insisted on tipping me
and my partner one hundred dollars
each. He then suggested that I begin
my own vending business. When I
said that I did not have any capital to
invest, he took me to his warehouse
and offered to give me twenty vending machines. He was a generous
man."

*When I said that I did not
have any capital to invest, he
took me to his warehouse and
offered to give me twenty
vending machines. He was a
generous man."*

Mr. Gluck left with many happy
memories. When asked what he enjoyed most, he said "Meeting people
and serving them." His one disappointment was the short impersonal
notice he was given to remove his
machines once the district solidified to
install their own "Vending today is a
big business run by corporations, it is
unfortunate that the personal element seems to have been eliminated."
On the day he removed his machines
he left cases of soda, but to the people
who knew him he left much more.

Behar...

continued from page 4

definitely. If you could sit here and
read the hundreds of letters I've received from victims ... this is what every journalist wants. If you could see
what this article has done, you would
understand."

When asked for his thoughts on
journalism as a profession, Behar
observed, "Journalism has a histori-
cally high amount of divorce and al-
cohol abuse. The hours are terrible.
You never know when the next all-
nighter will come. But there are a lot
of laughs and occasionally you really
help people. And you never stop
being a student. It is not a high paying
job. People are compelled to do it -
you have to love it. If it's something
you want, if you have the desire in
you, there's no one to help or stop you
but yourself. To succeed in journalism, you must be completely and to-
tally persistent." Mr. Pryal added, "It
doesn't hurt if you are a special person to begin with."

English Program Reviewed ...

Ir. Pryal feels that "There are
widely held misconceptions
t the differences between stu-
in honors classes and regular
es. In my experience at CSH,
you get beyond four or five stu-
s, there is not much difference in
evel of ability among the next
/-five or forty. Also, students in
e classes are not always there
use of a desire to be challenged
love for the subject. Some are
vated by peer pressure, elitism,
ntal expectation, or the pragmatic
n that it will look good on a
ge transcript. All honors students
ot always do the work in any

class.

There is no denying that CSH has
mature, gifted, and highly motivated
students who need to be challenged.
The area of disagreement is how we
can best provide for them. I cannot
accept the idea that the only way to
achieve academic excellence is
through homogeneously grouped
honors classes."

This year's program was an experiment with several benefits and
drawbacks. Next year could bring
some new changes as well since there
will be five rather than four sections
and more than one teacher in the
grade level. There will not be a single

honors section so students will be
able to retain some of the benefits of
flexibility in scheduling. Mr. Blake
would like to see the honors option
and the active learning approach continue in all eleventh grade classes, but
he admits that "another teacher might
not want to do it, and he/she certainly
shouldn't be forced to." No matter
what the other changes, however, Mr.
Pryal says "no one envisions a single
honors class in the near future." And
depending on where a person stands
on the subject of the successes or
failures of this year's class, that news
could either be a welcome relief or a
great disappointment.

The Harbor View, Monday, March 23, 1992

Cold Spring Harbor High School Achievement Award
June 23, 1992

Nella foto di Hanit, qui sotto, Irving Gluck (a sinistra) fu uno dei soldati americani nel dicembre del 1943 che sbarcarono a Nettuno, paese di Annibale Di Raimo che (allora di 6 anni) aveva incontrato il soldato Gluck spesse volte perchè distribuiva caramelle e cioccolatini ai bambini del paese. I due si sono rivisti a Syosset nel 1972 in una pizzeria dove Irving Gluck stava mangiando una pizza con il nipotino. Annibale (gli amici lo chiamano Joe) lo ha riconosciuto e gli ha chiesto se per caso fosse stato in servizio militare nel dicembre del 1943 a Nettuno. La risposta fu sì e da allora non si sono più lasciati. Irving Gluck in America svolse l'attività di economista, Joe invece ha lavorato in Vaticano e con 3 presidenti (Saragat, Segni e Gronchi) come carbiniere di scorta. In America, Joe ha una pizzeria. Di tanto in tanto nonno Irving porta tutta la famiglia a mangiare la pizza nella nuova pizzeria in Huntington di Annibale (o meglio Joe). Joe legge il giornale America Oggi tutti i giorni, ed i nipotini di Nonno Irving studiano l'italiano a Syosset.

In the photo taken by Hanit, Irving Gluck (left) was one of the American soldiers in December 1943 who landed in Nettuno, the town of Annibale Di Raimo who (then aged 6) had met Soldier Gluck often because he was distributing sweets and chocolates to the children of the village. The two met in Syosset in 1972 in a pizzeria where Irving Gluck was eating a pizza with his son. Annibale (friends call him Joe) recognized him and asked him if by chance he had been in service in December 1943 in Nettuno. The answer was yes and since then they have not left each other. Irving Gluck in America was an economist, while Joe worked in the Vatican with 3 presidents (Saragat, Segni and Gronchi) as a police escort. In America, Joe has a pizzeria. Occasionally grandpa Irving takes the whole family to eat pizza in Annibale's (or rather Joe's) new Huntington pizzeria. Joe reads the newspaper "America Today" every day. And Grandpa Irving's grandchildren study Italian in Syosset. *America Oggi, March 5, 2012, page 31*

Interview with Tony Pasqual of "Ciao, Tony" on November 14, 2014

OUR PROPERTY*

*An internet search of Slovakia's land records (http://
www.katasterportal.sk/kapor/) kept at the 'Geodetic and
Cartographic Institute' (GKÚ) in Bratislava show that the
government transferred ownership of much of our properties to
Ignac Klein and they are in his name, his sisters' names, and
others, as well as the State to this day. The search was run using the
following parameters:

> Region: Košický,
> District: Trebišov,
> Municipality: Pol'any,
> District: Pol'any

Our Property - The new Village Hall has the red roof.

The empty lot where our old house once stood.
Imagery Capture: May 2012 © 2019 Google.

The location of our new house at #35 that became the village hall.
Although rebuilt, #35 is still Polyán's Village Hall.
Imagery Capture: May 2012 © 2019 Google.

EXTRACT FROM PROPERTY RECORD NO. 39

Parcel #114/2
2273 m², Gardens

Land Use Code 5100 - Land, primarily in the urban zone, with planted
vegetables, fruit, ornamental greenery, and other agricultural crops.
The Land is located in an urban zone.

Parcel #115/2
801 m², Built up areas and courtyards
Land Use Code 13100 - Land with Residential buildings with a registration #
The Land is located in an urban zone.
The Landowner owns the building constructed on the land.
Registration #36 on plot #115/2
Construction Type 510 - House
The building is on the ground

Owners
1 Szuperák Mária r. Puškárová, Mgr., Ibrányiho 1242/15
Král'ovsky Chlmec. PSČ 077 01, SR
Date of Birth 06.07.1964
Title: Contract Signed Under V-582/06, č.z.43/06
Receipts 1/91 Signed Under Z-684/97

2 Szuperák Mária r. Puškárová., Ibrányiho 1242/15
Král'ovsky Chlmec. PSČ 077 01, SR
Date of Birth 06.07.1964
Title: Certificate of Inheritance Z-325/04, 7D/508/2003-č.-z. 12/04

3 Szuperák Imrich r. Szuperák., Ibrányiho 1242/15
Král'ovsky Chlmec. PSČ 077 01, SR
Date of Birth 23.10.1958
Title: Contract Signed Under V-582/06, č.z.43/06

Extract from Property Record No. 62

Parcel #82
804 m^2, Built-up areas and yard

Land Use Code 13100 - Land with Residential buildings with a registration #
The Land is located in an urban zone.
The Landowner owns the building constructed on the land.
Registration #20 on plot #82
Construction Type 510 - House
The building is on the ground

Owner
Brablecová Helena r. Kosztyuová, 076 84,
Pol'any, č.20, SR
Date of Birth 29.04.1949

Title
Deed Gifted under V-19/95

Extract from Property Record No. 539

Parcel #781
344 m^2, Water areas
The Land is located outside of the urban zone.

Owners
1 Kost'o, Ján. 076 84,
Bačka, č. 57, SR
Date of Birth 18.03.1952

Title
Certificate of Restitution Laws 323/92 N-311/99, Nz-311/99 under
Z-658/99
PKV 170

Extract from Property Record No. 787

Parcel #3744, 8281 m^2, Permanent Grassland
The Land is located outside of the urban zone

Owners
1 Republic of Slovakia

Title
č.d.11 zo dna 03.01.1955 pod'ia zápisnice zo dna 18.11.1954
Decision of OU in Trebisov, cat. Section C.1121/00 dated 13.09.2000
Z-1089/2000
PKV 780, 563, 733, 674, 687, 608, 608(3), 552, 514, 501, 512, 729, 521, 191, 362

2 Slovak Land Fund
Búdkova 36, Bratislava, PSČ 817 15, SR

EXTRACT FROM PROPERTY RECORD NO. 792

Parcel #772, 1230 m², Permanent Grassland, 1
Fields of meadows and pastures that have always been covered with grass

Parcel #358, 133 m², Built-up areas and Courtyard, 1
Parcel #773, 2103 m², Water areas, 2
Parcel # 1978, 263 m², Other areas Land, 2
Parcel # 2445, 2372 m², Permanent Grassland, 2
Parcel # 3380, 800 m², Other areas, 2
Parcel # 3381, 15760 m², Arable Land, 2
Parcel # 3394, 68537 m², Arable Land, 2
Parcel # 3395, 1123 m², Other areas, 2
Parcel # 3396, 49728 m², Arable Land, 2
Parcel # 3397, 5643 m², Water areas, 2
Parcel # 3398, 72457 m², Permanent Grassland, 2
Parcel # 3399, 3052 m², Arable Land, 2
Parcel # 3400, 30555 m², Water areas, 2
Parcel # 3401/1, 493 m², Permanent Grassland, 2

1 - The Land is located outside the built-up area of the village.
2 - The Land is located in a built-up area of the village.

Owner
1 Klein Ignác, SR (SPF)

Title
PKV 1
Decision of OU in Trebisov, cat. Section C.1121/00 dated 13.09.2000
Z-1089/2000
č.d. 601 dated 24.06.1949 on the basis of actual possession;
č.d. 601 dated 24.06.1949 according to the minutes of 23.06.1949

Owner's share: 29799926/9999999999

EXTRACT FROM PROPERTY RECORD No. 882

Parcel #1323, 6272 m², Arable Land
Parcel #1324, 643 m², Water areas
Parcel #3693, 13045 m², Permanent Grassland
The Land is located outside of the urban zone.

Owners
1 Klein Ignác, SR (SPF)
2 Kleinová Margita, SR (SPF)
3 Kleinová Ružena, SR (SPF)

Title
Decision of OU in Trebisov, cat. Section C.1121/00 dated 13.09.2000
Z-1089/2000
č.d. 601 dated 24.06.1949 according to the minutes of 23.06.1949
PKV 573

Administrator
Slovak Land Fund Bratislava
Búdkova 36, 817 47 Bratislava 11, SR

Note
Owner Numbers 1, 2, 3 are the managers of all the real estate

Extract from Property Record No. 903

Parcel #1458/1, 5131 m², Water areas
Parcel #1459/1, 1174 m², Permanent Grassland
Parcel #1460/1, 39608 m², Arable Land
The Land is located outside of the urban zone.

Owners
1 Klein Ignác, SR (SPF)
2 Kleinová Margita, SR (SPF)
3 Kleinová Ružena, SR (SPF)

Title
Decision of OU in Trebisov, cat. Section C.1121/00 dated 13.09.2000
Z-1089/2000
č.d. 601 dated 24.06.1949 according to the minutes of 23.06.1949

4 Republic of Slovakia

Title
č.d.835 zo dna 14.09.1956 podi'a rozhodnutia zo dna 12.08.1956 č.379/56
Rozhodnutie OU v Trebisove, kat. odboru c.1121/00 zo dna 12.09.2000
Z-1089/2000
PKV 522

Administrators
5 Slovak Land Fund Bratislava
Búdkova 36, 817 47 Bratislava 11, SR

6 Slovak Land Fund
Búdkova 36, Bratislava, PSČ 817 15, SR

Note
Owner Numbers 1, 2, 3, 4 are the managers of all the real estate

EXTRACT FROM PROPERTY RECORD NO. 952

Parcel #3921, 72588 m^2, Forest Land
Parcel #3924, 11943 m^2, Forest Land
Parcel #3933, 19864 m^2, Forest Land
Parcel # 3934, 34154 m^2, Water areas
Parcel # 3936, 13810 m^2, Water areas
Parcel # 3937, 31303 m^2, Water areas
Parcel # 3938, 3603 m^2, Water areas
Parcel # 3939, 6792 m^2, Water areas
Parcel # 3944, 44701 m^2, Water areas
Parcel # 3948, 49716 m^2, Forest Land
Parcel # 3954, 18469 m^2, Water areas

The Land is located outside the built-up area of the village..

Owners
289 Klein Ignác, SR (SPF)
290 Kleinová Margita, SR (SPF)
291 Kleinová Ružena, SR (SPF)

Each owner's share: 27007911 / 9999999999

Title
č.d. 601 dated 24.06.1949 on the basis of actual possession;
č.d. 601 dated 24.06.1949 according to the minutes of 23.06.1949
Decision of OU in Trebisov, cat. Section C.1121/00 dated 13.09.2000
PKV 2

(A Soldier Died Today) by A. Lawrence Vaincourt
JUST A COMMON SOLDIER

He was getting old and paunchy and his hair was falling fast,
And he sat around the Legion, telling stories of the past.
Of a war that he had fought in and the deeds that he had done,
In his exploits with his buddies; they were heroes, every one.

And tho' sometimes, to his neighbors, his tales became a joke,
All his Legion buddies listened, for they knew whereof he spoke.
But we'll hear his tales no longer for old Bill has passed away,
And the world's a little poorer, for a soldier died today.

He will not be mourned by many, just his children and his wife,
For he lived an ordinary and quite uneventful life.
Held a job and raised a family, quietly going his own way,
And the world won't note his passing, though a soldier died today.

When politicians leave this earth, their bodies lie in state,
While thousands note their passing and proclaim that they were great.
Papers tell their whole life stories, from the time that they were young,
But the passing of a soldier goes unnoticed and unsung.

Is the greatest contribution to the welfare of our land
A guy who breaks his promises and cons his fellow man?
Or the ordinary fellow who, in times of war and strife,
Goes off to serve his Country and offers up his life?

A politician's stipend and the style in which he lives
Are sometimes disproportionate to the service that he gives.
While the ordinary soldier, who offered up his all,
Is paid off with a medal and perhaps, a pension small.

It's so easy to forget them for it was so long ago,
That the old Bills of our Country went to battle, but we know
It was not the politicians, with their compromise and ploys,
Who won for us the freedom that our Country now enjoys.

Should you find yourself in danger, with your enemies at hand,
Would you want a politician with his ever-shifting stand?
Or would you prefer a soldier, who has sworn to defend
His home, his kin and Country and would fight until the end?

He was just a common soldier and his ranks are growing thin,
But his presence should remind us we may need his like again.
For when countries are in conflict, then we find the soldier's part
Is to clean up all the troubles that the politicians start.

If we cannot do him honor while he's here to hear the praise,
Then at least let's give him homage at the ending of his days.
Perhaps just a simple headline in a paper that would say,
Our Country is in mourning, for a soldier died today.

In Memory of My Father, Irving Gluck
November 14, 1921 - October 20, 2016

Afterword

"Signs and Serendipities"

SERENDIPITIES: the occurrence and development of events by chance in a happy or beneficial way. I can't think of a better word to describe the events in my father's life, and some of the things that happened in the moments immediately following his death, and shortly thereafter. I relate them because I have always prided myself in being quite rational. That would explain my degree in engineering. I consider myself to be religious, but I have always tried to find the rational explanation for biblical events. These serendipities have challenged my strictly rational outlook. I can't explain them. They continuously astound, and assuage, me. I share them with you, the reader, as a bookend to my father's incredible story.

My father died peacefully just shy of his 95th birthday. I sat alone, next to him, as he lay in a small room in the emergency department. It was extraordinarily crowded that day, and there were many patients lying in beds in the corridor outside his room. When the undertaker arrived from the funeral home, he wasn't sure how we would be able to move my father's body out of the room without creating a scene. On her own, the attending nurse asked if I was willing to pretend that my father was sleeping, as we wheeled him through the crowd of patients, to be transferred to the undertaker's vehicle. This was eerily similar to my grandfather's decision to do the same with my grandmother's body on their journey across the Hungarian-Czechoslovakian border 84 years earlier. A sign...

When the undertaker contacted the military cemetery in Calverton asking for an honor guard for a Bronze Star

Recipient, there was no record that my Dad had received the Bronze Star. I rushed home to find the receipt for the medal, and then became determined to correct my Dad's service record. As I compiled documents, I discovered that my Dad's unit, the 6th Armored Infantry Regiment, had earned the Presidential Unit Citation for the battle at Monte Porchia, and that his MP unit, the 67th MP Division, had earned the Meritorious Unit Citation for its work in France and Germany. Neither citation, nor his service at Anzio, were listed on his discharge papers. I filed the necessary paperwork to make the corrections, and waited. If everything had been filed correctly when my Dad received the Bronze Star in the first place, I wouldn't have done any research. A sign…

While going through my Dad's papers, I noticed a photograph of him sitting on a lion somewhere in Italy, and I became obsessed with finding the location of this lion as we began to ponder taking a family trip there. I searched photographs online of lions in Italy without success. Who knew that many cities in Italy had statues of lions, and every lion would have a different shape?

About nine months after my Dad died, we landed in Italy to retrace, as much as we could, my Dad's journey as a combat soldier. We toured Anzio and Nettuno with a registered tour guide. We stood at the edge of the "Pine Woods" where my Dad had dug in, and had his glasses shattered. It was a very powerful experience. I asked the tour guide if she recognized the statue of the lion in the picture. She grew up in the region and was familiar with every aspect of the Italian campaign, but she didn't recognize the statue.

We drove south from Rome, heading towards Cassino, with the hope of finding Monte Porchia and ascending to its summit. As we neared Cassino, we weren't sure when exactly we would see the mountain with the abbey on its peak. We searched the beautiful blue horizon for any sign of the white structure. In the distance, I saw what I thought might be something, and my wife insisted that it had to be Monte Cassino. Neither of us were sure, but she argued that it was. Suddenly, the blue sky turned dark and cloudy, and it began to drizzle. The sky opened and it poured for thirty seconds and then, just as suddenly as it came, the storm passed and the skies were bright blue again. Monte Cassino was directly to our right, with Monte Porchia clearly visible in the distance. Another sign...

The night before we left Rome, for whatever reason I checked the reviews of the bed and breakfast in which we had reservations to stay in Naples. Someone posted that although it was beautiful, the road to reach it was small, treacherous, and very difficult to navigate at night, even with a small car. We had rented a large minivan. Then and there we decided to change our reservations, and I searched on my phone for an alternative. It was the height of the summer tourist season, and there weren't many rooms available within our budget. Finally, I found a bed and breakfast in Capua, a town located between Naples and Cassino. I had never heard of Capua, but it looked nice, and it was on our way. I booked it without paying attention to the listing details: cash only.

When we arrived to the bed and breakfast, Masseria della Casa, it was already late in the afternoon. We had driven from Rome, stopped to climb Monte Porchia, and were looking forward to getting some rest. After showing us our rooms, the owner informed us that he did not take credit cards, and that we could get cash from the cash machine down the road. Of course, I didn't have a card for a cash machine, and I brought only the cash we expected to need. Panicking, we tried unsuccessfully to pay with PayPal. "Don't worry," said the owner's husband and his wife. "Sleep tonight, and we'll resolve it tomorrow." Well, tomorrow came and the owner's wife (who was the de facto owner!) arranged for us to pay by credit card at a nearby restaurant, and the restauranteur would pay her in cash. Great! Except the restaurant wouldn't open until the afternoon. In the meantime, they recommended that we should enjoy the sights: a beautiful coliseum that rivaled the one in Rome, a museum of the gladiators that fought there, and the Mitrea (a Greek temple for the cult of Mithras). Off we went. After seeing the sights, there was one more sight listed on the back of our ticket to the museum: a metallurgical workshop. After visiting the Mitrea, I insisted that we find the metal workshop, despite everyone's protestations: it was hot, they were hungry, thirsty, and tired. We walked down a narrow street, just wide enough for a small car to pass through. On one side were shops, and on the other the stone wall of a building with niches for us to stand in when the inevitable car passed. The street exited to a large piazza. At its center was a monument made up of stone lions. Unwittingly, we had stumbled upon the place that my Dad had had his photograph taken 73 years earlier. A sign...

The author in Piazza Mazzini, Santa Maria Capua Vetere
North of Naples, Italy. July 2017